PRAISE FOR *GROI*

"You need not have grown up in the Puget Sound region to identify with much of what Rebecca Wallick has so poignantly related for posterity in this highly personal and nearly poetic account. But if you were fortunate enough to have done so, you will embrace this labor of love and honor, and see yourself mirrored in so many of its scenes. Historians have labored to record the evolution of the company we all know as Boeing, but have, for the most part, produced nuts-and-bolts, enthusiast-style publications that do little for the soul or for the unique community that has nurtured and enabled the beautiful aircraft which have resulted. This artfully narrated account breathes life into the extremely personal and human experiences that have, in some magical way, been shared at some level by so many, and provides more than a hint of what has made this aircraft manufacturer legendary. Lew Wallick would be so proud."

—Dan Hagedorn, Senior Curator, Museum of Flight

"This is an extraordinary book for aviation buffs and historians written by one of the few people that could write it. It is a fascinating story about the pioneers of jet transport flight testing—a story of the major contributions made by teams of pilots, engineers, and maintenance personnel while dealing with a large area of new aviation knowledge. It is also the story of the families that supported them and gave them some semblance of normalcy despite the exciting and sometimes dangerous aspects of their jobs. They were all an extraordinary group of individuals whose ground-breaking work is still used today, several generations later."

—John Cashman, Chief Test Pilot (Retired), Boeing Commercial Airplanes

"Becky Wallick has written a compelling narrative about her father, legendary Boeing test pilot S. L. 'Lew' Wallick, and his compatriots in a heady profession usually shrouded in mystique, even among aviation experts. Lew and his 'band of brothers' come to life under Becky's pen. The camaraderie, the straightforward acceptance of risk and flying adventure, the daily routine mixing flying and family, are all captured. So are the tragedies inherent in the profession, and their impact on lives of survivors. Aviation history also comes alive in this well-researched book, smoothly integrated into the story line. There are hair-raising moments as Becky matter-of-factly describes the hazards, the incidents, near accidents, and tragic events inherent in exploring the limits of aeronautical technology and new airplane designs. The contributions to design by the test pilots become clear; once a deficiency or product improvement opportunity surfaces through testing, then engineers have data to change the airplanes for the benefit of airlines, pilots, and passengers. Becky titles her book *Growing Up Boeing*. Some of us whose entire professional life occurred at Boeing are still growing up Boeing, more so now because this book reveals much that went on behind the scenes: little secrets, big secrets, closing the loop around stories previously only partially told. Literally, this is a 'can't put down' book that will capture the aviation and lay reader alike. It is a 'must read' for engineers and pilots, especially the young people who are inspired by the stories of Lew and his comrades and see themselves in a test pilot career."

—Peter Morton, Boeing engineer and Vice President of Human Resources (retired)

"Rebecca Wallick's delightful story of the lives of the test pilots who served Boeing during that company's golden years of military and commercial jets will more than excite aviation buffs. She tells her own story in parallel with that of her father, Lew Wallick, one of the truly great test pilots. There are periods of intense pressure on the flight test community of pilots and engineers, many humorous anecdotes, and some downright dangerous moments. From the B-47 to the 767, a well-written sweep of Flight Test history."

—Brien Wygle, Boeing test pilot and VP of Flight Operations (retired)

GROWING UP BOEING

The Early Jet Age Through the Eyes of a Test Pilot's Daughter

REBECCA WALLICK

Printed in the United States of America
First Printing, February 2014

ISBN (print): 0991364805
ISBN-13 (print): 978-0-9913648-0-0
ISBN (ebook): 0991364813
ISBN-13 (ebook): 978-0-9913648-1-7

Maian Meadows Publishing
3322-164th St. SW
Lynnwood, WA 98087

www.growingupboeing.com

Cover art: Sherri Shaftic
www.sherribydesign.com

Editing: Dana Delamar at By Your Side Self-Publishing
www.byyoursideselfpub.com

Photos: Cover (background): Sherri Shaftic; photos not part of the author's personal collection are courtesy of Boeing Archives (unless otherwise noted)

DEDICATION

To my father.

CONTENTS

MAP OF WASHINGTON STATE

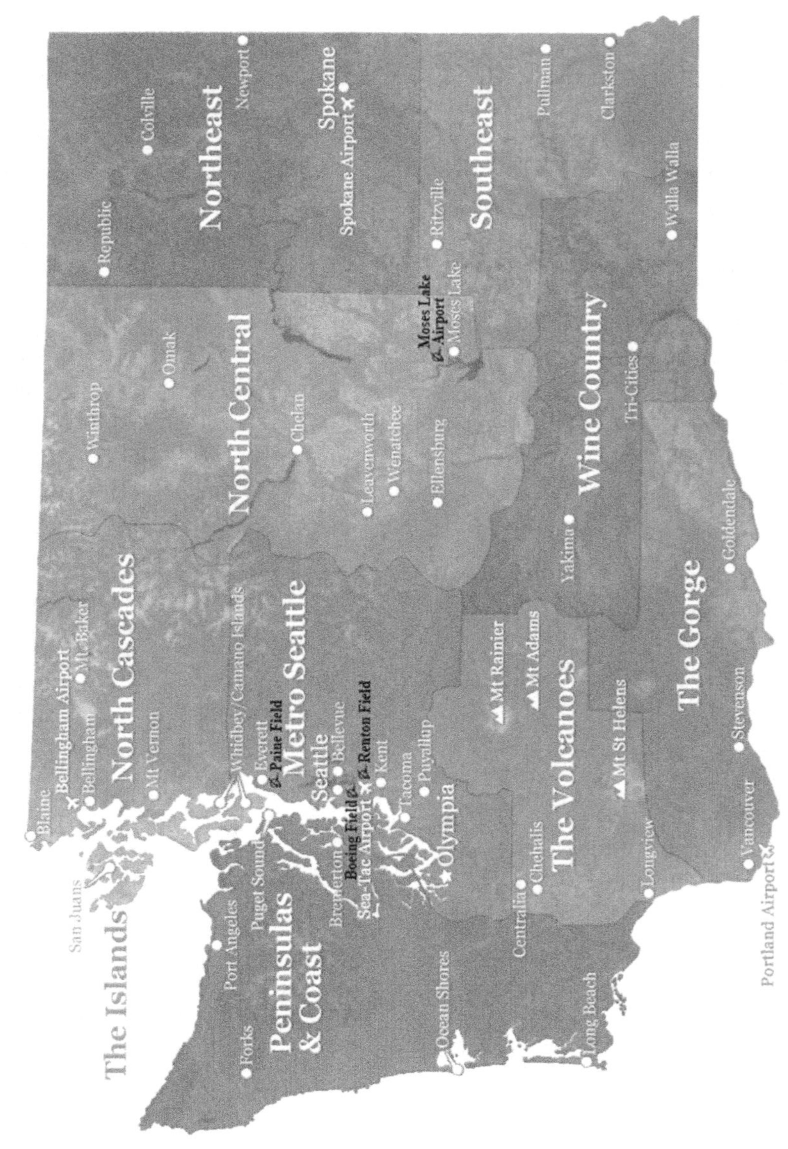

1 Map of Washington state, with airports marked.

DIAGRAM: FLIGHT-CONTROL SURFACES

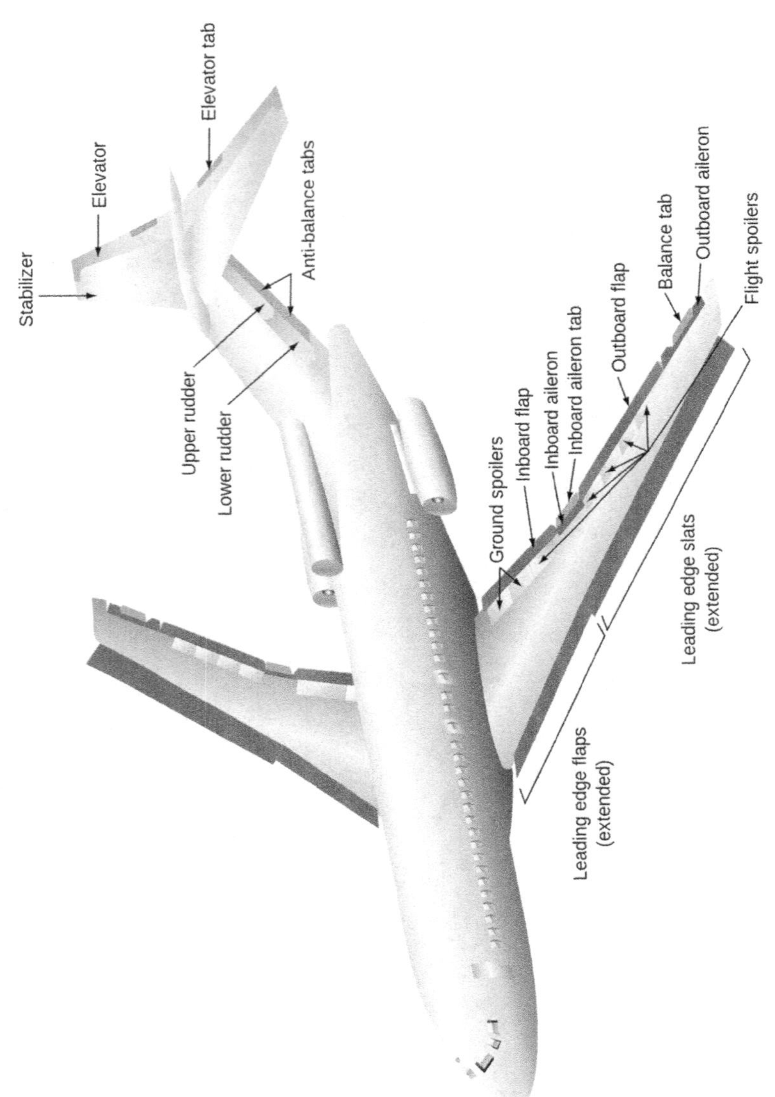

2 Boeing 727 flight-control surfaces. Federal Aviation Administration (2008)

INTRODUCTION: THE RETIREMENT PARTY

I walked into the hotel banquet room, a cavernous space with lots of big round tables covered in white linen cloths, eight place settings and chairs to a table. Dimmed chandeliers high overhead created an intimate mood. People dressed in evening finery moved about or stood in small groups, drinks in hand, chatting happily. Nondescript carpet dampened the loud buzzing of their voices and laughter. Everyone was happy, celebrating and toasting the guest of honor.

It was April Fool's Day, 1986. After thirty-five years as a Boeing test pilot, Lew Wallick—my father—was retiring.

There were many familiar faces—my father's colleagues and friends, many I had known my entire life. Two of my three brothers and their wives, and my Uncle Jesse and Aunt Annette were also there. I was twenty-nine years old, and I had travelled from eastern Washington, where I had begun my career as a small-town attorney, to attend the soiree. We'd all been invited for an evening of food and drink, stories, jokes, and a slide show highlighting my father's life and career milestones.

Eventually the crowd was asked to find their tables for dinner. My family's table was in the center of the room, and I took a chair next to my father. Amid the laughter and high spirits, meals were served. Soon, the lights dimmed to near total darkness, signaling the start of the slide show presentation.

Dennis Mahan, a flight test engineer who had worked closely with my father for many years, had created the slide show. I'd known Dennis since I was a kid. He was one of the younger guys in Flight Test working with my father, often showing up at social functions. He sported the look of the stereotypical Boeing engineer: thick-rimmed glasses; hair slightly long, but not *too* long, and neatly combed off his face; trim mustache; and just a touch of the nerd in his conservative yet casual dress. Dennis always wore a big smile, displaying a great sense of humor with a gleam in his eye. He was a bit of a prankster, very much like my father. To create the slide show, Dennis had acquired photos from my family, the Boeing Archives, and whatever sources he could hunt down.

Standing between my father and the projector, Dennis narrated with his usual teasing and dry wit. The first several slides covered my father's childhood on a Kansas farm. Dennis next described several highlights from my father's time as a Navy aviation cadet during World War II and his early career at Boeing, including the types of airplanes he'd flown, such as the B-47, the Dash 80, and the 707.

Then Dennis paused. Without narration, he slowly advanced through a series of eight slides, screen shots captured from an old, grainy film. They seemed to show a 707 *rolling*. The only background is sky. A few isolated guffaws erupted from the audience, but otherwise the room was silent. Like most, I was unsure what the slides represented, but I had a pretty good idea: here was the truth that Dad had always danced around whenever I'd asked him if he'd rolled a jet like Boeing test pilot Tex Johnston had over the Seafair crowd in 1955.

I looked at my father for his reaction. He remained silent and still, his face barely illuminated by the beam of the projector, looking straight ahead. He seemed a little embarrassed, caught off guard, but not displeased. Then very quietly, so that no one else could hear, he whispered to Dennis, "You've got them in the wrong order."

Dennis completed the slide show. Several of my father's colleagues—Brien Wygle, Phil Condit, Don Archer, Jim Lincoln, and Alan Mulally—finished the presentation by speaking about Dad and his career, offering toasts and giving him mementos commemorating his time at Boeing.

That night, I learned a lot about my father and his amazing career; many events he had been too modest to mention, despite my lifelong interest. But he remained tight-lipped throughout the evening whenever the topic of the roll came up. Watching him, I kept thinking he seemed embarrassed to have been publicly outed, but I didn't understand why. It had happened many years earlier. He was retiring; he couldn't possibly get into any trouble over it now.

✈

After Dad's retirement party—with the revelation of that secret roll—I reflected on all the flying stories I'd heard my father and others tell as I'd listened in awe throughout my life. I realized that there were many, many private test flying stories behind the formal press releases and the first flight news articles. I wanted to gather them. I needed to know, to understand, this man, my father. It took another fifteen years and my father's declining health before I began in earnest to ask questions and record the answers. I obtained many extraordinary stories, not only from my father, but also from some of the other Boeing test pilots and engineers who had been his colleagues. They all had been key players in the dawning of the commercial jet age. As Boeing test pilot Tex Johnston once said, the commercial jets they had tested and certified in the 1950s and 1960s "shrank the world by a factor of two." We, the traveling public, owe them an incredible debt for shrinking it then and even more since.

Even today, the commonly held belief inside and outside Boeing is that Tex Johnston was the only pilot to roll a commercial jet, and that he did it only that one time over Seafair. I now had photographic proof of at least one other roll, done by my father in a 707. I suspected there were more. After lots of figurative arm-twisting, I persuaded my father and some of the other test pilots to admit to me that they rolled Boeing's jets, some of them performing the maneuver several times and in several models over the years, long after it was strictly forbidden—on pain of losing one's job—by Tex Johnston himself and those who followed Tex as Director of Flight Test. No wonder it was such a well-kept secret.

Some things are so much fun you just can't stop doing them, even at the risk of losing your job. Certainly my father couldn't resist the urge to roll those big, beautiful jets he played such a key part in designing, testing, and certifying. He knew it wasn't reckless. But he was very careful whom he let in on the secret.

CHAPTER ONE: LAYING THE FOUNDATION

To most people, the sky is the limit. To those who love aviation, the sky is home.
—*Anonymous*

Escape Velocity

As a young boy growing up in the 1920s and 1930s, my father loved watching airplanes fly over his family's farm near Independence, Kansas. Newspapers and radio programs detailed the incredible exploits of Charles Lindbergh and the derring-do of the intrepid barnstormers of the time, the stuff that fueled the escape fantasies of many Depression-era farm boys. The roar of biplane engines enticed farmers and townspeople alike to come out to the local hayfield that doubled as an airfield to watch, perhaps to buy a short ride. Dad's younger brothers shared his fascination, and sometimes it seemed it was all they could talk about: flying. They all longed to be pilots.

One summer Saturday when Dad was twelve, he and his ten-year-old brother John were returning home with their father from the town market when they drove by a pasture with an airplane hangar and a house. This was where the local barnstormer lived. It was also where the Wallick boys loved to hang out, watching the airplanes take off and land, imagining what it would be like to see the world from a bird's-eye perspective.

They passed the field every Saturday, but on this particular day, their father agreed to stop and talk to the pilot. He negotiated the fee for a ten-minute ride: two dollars per boy. It was 1936, and such an expense wasn't taken lightly.

The pilot prepared his Travel Air biplane, putting the boys in the front open cockpit and fastening them both in with the single seat belt. He then climbed into the rear cockpit and fired up the engine. Dad and John quivered with excitement: their first airplane ride! Taxiing into position at the end of the field, the pilot revved the engine and released the brake. The biplane bobbed down the rough grass runway, wings bouncing as if imitating a giant bird. Finally reaching 35 to 40 miles per hour (mph), they lifted off, briefly leaving the bonds of Kansas. As the ground dropped away below them, the wind swirled through the boys' hair, the noise from the engine deafening but like sweet music to them. Grinning ear to ear, the brothers nestled together on the seat. They were flying! As the airplane climbed and leveled off, Dad realized they were too short to see the ground over the edge of the deep cockpit, so he unbuckled their seat belt. Both boys stood up to take in the view of sun-dappled fields of wheat and corn. The pilot immediately throttled back the engine to cut the noise and shouted at them to sit down and fasten themselves back in. They obeyed, still enjoying every minute of the experience, right through the rough landing back on the hayfield.

Though brief, that flight fanned the spark of my father's ambition to be a pilot. That ride was the biggest thrill of his young life, whetting his appetite for more. His fearlessness in standing up in the open cockpit during his first flight was an early clue that he would eventually gravitate toward one of the world's most dangerous yet thrilling occupations: experimental test pilot. Even learning a year later that the Travel Air pilot had died in a crash at that same field—the airplane had caught fire because of a fuel leak during a flight—didn't dampen my father's desire to fly.

In 1939, when Dad was fifteen, several Wallicks purchased a short ride in a Ford Tri-Motor airplane at the Coffeyville, Kansas, airport. Dad, his brothers John and Ed, and their father, as well as their uncle Frank and Frank's two sons, went up together in "The Tin Goose," which could carry twelve passengers.

Two more years would pass before my father got the chance to fly again, this time with an older cousin, who in 1941 was enrolled in the Civil Pilot Training Program. The cousin took Dad up in a Piper Cub—Dad being his first passenger—for a flight over the Kansas landscape. They circled over the Wallick farm. That early spark to fly was becoming a fire, a steadily burning desire to become a pilot.

By age seventeen, Dad's dream of flying obsessed him. But how could he achieve it? And where? Now that there was a war on, it occurred to him that he could learn to fly at the government's expense. In 1942, after Pearl Harbor and the official entry of the United States into World War II, the minimum age requirement for the V5 Aviation Cadet Program was dropped to eighteen, but parental permission was still required. Opportunity was knocking. Dad *ran* through the now-open door marked AVIATOR.

Dad turned eighteen in May of 1942, and that fall wanted to enlist. His father agreed to sign the permission form, but his mother was dead set against it. Eventually she realized that her eldest son's dream to fly took precedence over her motherly concerns, so she signed the consent the day Dad set out to enlist. Dad entered the cadet training program and continued working on gaining the two-year associate's degree required to start flight training. Entering active duty as a US Navy pilot in July 1943, Dad achieved escape velocity, leaving the Kansas homestead behind him for good.

The Desire to Fly

Throughout my life, surrounded by test pilots and familiar with the world of aviation, I have noticed this: one is either passionate about flying, or not. There seems no middle ground.

To fly like the birds is one of humankind's oldest and most persistent desires. Plato wrote in 370 BC, "The natural function of the wing is to soar upwards and carry that which is heavy up to the place where dwells the race of gods. More than any other thing that pertains to the body, it partakes of the nature of the divine." My father and the other Boeing test pilots I've known fell into the passionate-about-flying end of the spectrum. For virtually all of them, from that first moment they saw an airplane fly overhead during their childhood, the idea and desire to become a pilot burrowed into their consciousness and drove their life choices.

3 Navy air cadet Lew Wallick. Photo: Author's collection.

The test pilots I grew up around shared additional formative experiences beyond their early desire to fly: most were raised on farms, many in the Midwest, learning early to work hard; all saw World War II as an opportunity to learn to fly and start on their chosen career path; whether religious or not (and most weren't) they lived by a personal code best described as The Golden Rule—treat others as you would like others to treat you. They were humble, and they were gentlemen.

Along with that passion for flying, succeeding as a test pilot takes a blend of intelligence, persistence, mechanical know-how, common sense, resilience, love of adventure, calculated risk-taking, courage, and true grit—an ability to remain calm under extreme pressure.

While I don't count myself among those passionate about flying—I never felt compelled to become a pilot, and I don't enter that zone of perfect happiness true aviators do when I am aloft—I do have a passion for history and the stories aviators tell, their stories of adventure and daring.

A Test Pilot's Daughter

On the day I was born in December 1956, my father was doing what he did for a living, what he loved best: testing airplanes for The Boeing Company. I admit I find it very cool that my birth certificate lists my father's "Usual Occupation" as *Test Pilot*.[1]

3. CHILD'S NAME (Type or print) — a. (First) Rebecca — b. (Middle) Marie — c. (Last) Wallick

4. SEX F — 5a. THIS BIRTH Single [X] Twin [ ] Triplet [ ] — 5b. IF TWIN OR TRIPLET (This child born) 1st [ ] 2nd [ ] 3rd [ ] — 6 DATE OF BIRTH (Month) (Day) (Year) 12-18-1956

FATHER OF CHILD

7. FULL NAME — a. (First) Samuel — b. (Middle) Lewis — c. (Last) Wallick, Jr. — 8. COLOR OR RACE W

9. AGE (At time of this birth) 32 YEARS — 10. BIRTHPLACE (State or foreign country) Kansas — 11a. USUAL OCCUPATION Test Pilot — 11b. KIND OF BUSINESS OR INDUSTRY Boeing Airplane Co.

4 A portion of the author's birth certificate.

On that day, Dad was copilot with pilot Ray McPherson on

[1] My father was named after his father, who went by Samuel or Sam. In most Boeing press releases, my father was referred to as S. L. "Lew" Wallick, Jr. To everyone who knew him, he was simply Lew. My oldest brother is Samuel Lewis Wallick III, and goes by Sam; he has a son to whom he passed the family name and he goes by Sam IV.

the first flight of the number two KC-135, the military version of the 707. Dad had already gained lots of hours and experience flying Boeing's military jets—B-47s, B-52s—since hiring on with Boeing in 1951. By the time I came along, my father saw that his future lay in commercial aviation and concentrated on test flying the Dash 80 and the 707 while still flying Boeing's military airplanes.

5 Ray McPherson and Lew Wallick, XB-47D first flight, 1955. (Note McPherson's tartan helmet.) Photo: Boeing Archives.

From the Dash 80 and the 707 through the 767—the 1950s through the 1980s—my father was one of several test pilots intimately involved in designing, testing, certifying, and selling Boeing's commercial airplanes, helping put Seattle on the map as the Jet City. His colleagues told me—and I'm certain they would tell you, as well—that he was one of the best pilots Boeing had at that time.

All I knew is that he was a wonderful father who was also a pilot. He never bragged about himself. He didn't have to.[2]

---

[2] I'm conscious of the irony here: I'm bragging about my father, which he wouldn't want, or like. It goes against everything he taught me. But the frequent and consistent comments made by a broad range of his colleagues simply can't be ignored. He was *good*.

Boeing played a huge role in the economy of Seattle, Washington, where I was born and my brothers and I were raised. Decades before Microsoft, Starbucks, and Amazon, Boeing was the region's largest and most stable employer. For kids growing up in Seattle in the 1950s and 1960s, if you didn't have a parent or relative who worked at Boeing, one of your friends did. Residents grew used to the sound of airplanes both large and small flying overhead; airplane engines were the sound of jobs and prosperity. Everyone knew about Tex Johnston rolling the Dash 80 over the Seafair hydroplane races in the summer of 1955; it's a local legend still remarked upon to this day. Looking skyward when hearing the rumble of jet engines, locals learned to identify each new Boeing jet model as it flew by. Kids made and flew paper airplanes or model airplanes from kits, many dreaming of becoming pilots some day.

My father's extraordinary career as a test pilot shaped me in ways I didn't fully understand or appreciate until I was well into adulthood. In fact, I didn't realize he *was* a test pilot until I was in high school, and even then—in our family and among our friends—it was no big deal and not remarked upon. I mean, I knew he was a pilot. He regularly took us flying in many types of airplanes, which was always fun and in my world, pretty normal. But I had no clue that he was an *experimental test pilot*, or that such an occupation was dangerous or considered glamorous. My father suggested that if teachers or anyone else asked me what he did for a living, I should say he was a Boeing engineer. Which he was. He was a very skilled, very modest engineer who—I eventually learned—just happened to also be a highly skilled test pilot.

My father was also a funny guy. Test pilot humor was a bit geeky. They were, after all, engineers. Their humor was big on gentle teasing and practical jokes. Though they poked fun and tried to best each other in a friendly competitive way, they were never show-offs. They could take as good as they gave. They were friends at the office, in the cockpit, and outside of Boeing. Of course, when the opportunity arose, they didn't hesitate to tweak the noses of their manufacturing competitors or those whose outsized egos they felt might benefit from being brought down a notch. Some of their favorite stories came from those situations.

My father brought his sense of humor home with him. Or maybe it started at home; raising four rambunctious kids requires a keen sense of humor. The calm demeanor that made him an excellent test pilot served him well as a parent. There was always lots of laughter and gentle teasing in our house. And winks. I felt so special when Dad would pull someone's leg a bit, then look at me and wink, including me in the joke. He also gave me private winks to say "I love you, and appreciate you." He excelled at that.

When it came to raising kids, Dad's style was to be hands-on and directly involved—playing with, teaching, encouraging, and trusting us while helping us to become independent and responsible for ourselves. He gave us his full attention when he was home, but he never micromanaged. He helped us with our homework if we asked. He encouraged us to do our chores, while leaving the details of enforcement to Mom. We also had an amazing amount of freedom to explore and learn on our own. We were encouraged to go outside and play, to be kids, to be with other kids. Times were different then—kids could safely roam their neighborhoods without the constant watchful eye of one or more parents. Still, the amount of freedom my brothers and I had to entertain ourselves was remarkable even among our friends.

Shortly before I was born, my family moved into a brand-new house in a small Bellevue neighborhood called Spring Hills II, just north of the original and much larger Spring Hills development in the town of Clyde Hill. Bellevue lies east of Seattle, across Lake Washington, the two cities originally connected by ferry, then by a floating bridge in the 1950s. Back then, the commute wasn't too awful. Seattle's notorious traffic woes were a few decades off.

There were about thirty homes in Spring Hills II, which was shaped like a lollipop. The entrance was just south of where Highway 520 would eventually separate north Bellevue from south Kirkland.[3]

6 Wallick family posing in front of Spring Hills II house, late 1950s. Photo: Author's collection.

Fully contained and just off Bellevue Way (which was then a lightly travelled two-lane road), Spring Hills II was a great place for kids to ride bikes, play hide-and-seek and kick-the-can on the street, or head to a neighbor's house to play. There were few fences, most front yards were grass lawns where kids were invited to play, and family dogs roamed freely and played along with us. Most families were of the traditional sort—father working outside the home, mother working inside it. Everyone knew everyone else. We kids also knew that all the parents were sort of watching us when we played outside, and that they had implicit permission to tell us to knock it off if we got out of line. It was that sort of middle-class neighborhood. Bellevue was, at that time, a safe, suburban "bedroom" community of about 13,000 people with a single stoplight. Downtown was

[3] Before 520 went in, we kids would play in the wetlands of Yarrow Bay, searching for eels and frogs. After 520's opening, Mom wisely decreed we couldn't cross the highway, so we found a large culvert installed underneath the road for drainage that allowed us continued access to the wetlands.

dominated by Bellevue Square, with a Frederick & Nelson's department store, the Bel-Vue Theatre, and the Crabapple Restaurant. Nearby was a tiny ice-cream shop—Scandia Freeze—where we often went to get soft-serve ice-cream cones dipped in chocolate, especially after Little League baseball games. We were allowed to ride our bikes the half mile to Brown's Drug Store in the tiny North Town shopping mall, where we spent our allowances on comic books and candy. Bellevue felt small town.

Our house was the second one in, on the left side of the Spring Hills II lollipop stick. Behind the houses on our side of the street, a big steep gully thick with mature evergreens, ferns, and other undergrowth with a gently flowing creek (or "crick," as my Kansas-bred father pronounced it) at the bottom beckoned to us kids. At that time, there were no houses on the other side of the gully. It was a wonderful, safe, natural playground where kids could explore the woods for snakes and frogs, build forts, hitch up rope swings, and get dirty for hours on end.

Our rec room housed most of our toys, and we had space to set up an electric model train and slot car tracks, and any number of other games on the linoleum floor. For a while, one corner of the rec room hosted two old mattresses—one atop the other—a space where my brothers and I could wrestle (a game we called Murder) without getting hurt. There was also an old couch. My father sometimes set up our eight-millimeter film projector and screen, showing us scary (and very cheesy) sci-fi movies he'd bought. I'd curl up next to him on the couch and cover my eyes during the scariest parts, trying to ignore my brothers as they spooked me from behind. While we all preferred to play outside, our rec room was a pretty good alternative on bad weather days.

In his basement shop, Dad worked on projects, fixed things, and made toys for us—wooden hydroplane models to tow behind our bikes, a pair of stilts, and eventually small motorboats. He had learned to work with wood and make furniture while in high school.

A young, sturdy maple tree remained in the front yard as our house was being constructed. The tree grew as my brothers and I did, and by the time I was about five, it had limbs low enough to grasp yet strong enough to easily support our weight. By watching and imitating my brothers, I learned to scramble up the limbs and through the maple's leafy branches. As time went on, I got better and braver, and climbed higher. I was a bit of a pest, always tagging along with my brothers, doing what they did, or trying. I became quite a tomboy, gaining agility and strength.

One summer evening, a neighbor knocked on our front door. When Dad answered, he was greeted with a question. "Do you realize your daughter is up in that tree?" the neighbor asked, pointing at the maple.

Dad stepped out into the yard and looked up to see me sitting casually on a branch high up in the tree. I probably waved and smiled at him. Dad acknowledged to the neighbor that yes, indeed, there I was.

"Aren't you going to do anything?" the man asked, concerned and apparently a bit scandalized.

Dad shrugged. "No. She'll come down when she gets hungry or it gets dark," he replied, unperturbed. The neighbor left, shaking his head.

Dad knew I was fine in the tree. No frilly dresses and dolls for me. Dad encouraged my brothers and me to play in ways that built physical and mental skills and confidence, to test our limits in reasonable ways. I was treated like a fourth son and did the same things as my brothers, despite my mother's best efforts to get me interested in more feminine pursuits. There were lots of scraped knees and elbows along the way. I think Dad was more than a bit proud that his daughter was such a tomboy, that this trait had caused such consternation in a neighbor who thought little girls shouldn't be doing such things.

That story is one my father enjoyed telling. I think it appealed to his test pilot sensibilities—I was a risk-taking chip off the ol' block—as well as his sense of humor. For me, it's a perfect example of his approach to parenting, and the pride he took when his children exhibited the same sense of adventure and confidence that he did. It also shows how he used calm and humor to defuse confrontations.

Years later, I asked my mother about that tree, which was right in line with the windows of the family room. Did it ever bother her to see us climbing it? "I just closed the curtains; if you were going to fall, I didn't want to see it," Mom replied.

My parents' desire to maintain a family-oriented lifestyle continued when sometime around 1960 they bought an old summer cabin on Lake Sammamish, a few miles east of our Spring Hills II home. "The Cabin," as we referred to it, was located midway along the west shore of the lake in an area that would eventually become part of Bellevue. To me, it seemed very rural and far away. For several years, we'd pack up and spend the summer living in that cabin, swimming, water skiing, and playing with the neighborhood kids. It was small—a kitchen along one wall, an open living-dining room with an ugly green Naugahyde couch at the far end that converted to a bed where Mom and Dad slept; a tiny bedroom where Sam and Rick slept on air mattresses on the floor, and an alcove where Tim and I slept on bunk beds that left space for nothing else. It had one miniscule bathroom. It was heaven as far as my brothers and I were concerned.

We enjoyed being there so much, eventually my parents decided to build a house and live there full-time.

We moved into that house in 1967, when I was ten. That ugly green couch went into the new house, in a space below a stairwell near all the bedrooms. As teens, my brothers and I had a dedicated telephone for our lengthy dating conversations. (Me: "Tim, get off the phone!" Tim: "In a minute." Twenty minutes later, Me: "Mom, make Tim get off the phone!" In those days, the only home option was a single land line, the source of many sibling arguments.) My parents wisely put that phone right outside the door to their bedroom, so that those conversations couldn't go on endlessly into the night.

The Wygles—another Boeing test pilot family—also had a summer cabin on the lake, a bit north of ours. Next door to us were the Tates; the father was a Boeing engineer and one of his sons, Brian, would grow up to become a Boeing engineer on the 777 program. Nearby were the Campbells, another Boeing family. A quarter mile south along the lake lived the Nortons; he was a Boeing engineer, she was my Girl Scout troop leader. The tentacles of Boeing reached far and wide into the communities surrounding Seattle.

7 House, boathouse, and dock on Lake Sammamish, in a rare blanket of snow, 1971. Author's collection.

A unique feature of our life on Lake Sammamish was Butch, a harbor seal that somehow ended up in the lake with a red cord collar around his neck. He was already there when we acquired the cabin. According to local lore, a nearby family had fed and tamed him before they moved away. Butch spent most of his time within a one-mile length of shoreline, with our dock in the middle—gliding effortlessly under the water's surface like a shadowy torpedo, occasionally breaking the surface with his head, blowing air out his big nostrils and taking us in with his enormous, soulful black eyes. On the few occasions that I saw Butch snoozing out of the water, it was on a bit of sand next to a dock about 400 feet south of us, where ownership had changed hands, lending credence to the story of his history. I'll say more about Butch later. For now, I'll simply point out that as bizarre as it was to have a harbor seal cruising under our dock on a regular basis, my parents took it in stride and never even hinted that the seal could be dangerous to us while swimming. Indeed, Butch was wary of humans and never threatened anyone. As it turned out, he had good reason to be wary.

Though my parents weren't over-protective, they certainly didn't ignore us. Until we were trustworthy and safe—for example, around and in the water—we were supervised. We learned how to swim and safely handle boats of all kinds. Once we reached a level of competence, though, we were allowed to be on our own. Within the confines of our neighborhood (which we took to include all of Lake Sammamish after moving there, a lake that is seven miles long, one-and-a-half miles wide and shaped a bit like the mark of Zorro), we were free to explore and play for hours on end without adult supervision, especially during the summer months. We soon had a collection of small, kid-friendly boats at our disposal: a row boat, an aluminum boat with a small outboard motor, and a Styrofoam sailboat with a rudder and keel. Almost all of the neighborhood children had stay-at-home moms, but they were usually inside. Outside, we enjoyed a world ruled by kids.

When it was dinnertime, Dad would go outside and whistle for us to come home. Making an "O" by touching middle finger to thumb and then wrapping his lips around their tips, he could let loose a distinctive, three-toned whistle loud enough to be heard throughout the neighborhood. Usually, one blast was enough to elicit our standard response, "Coming!" from wherever we were. Unless we were inside someone's house—and we rarely were—this was a foolproof way to get us quickly home for dinner. Dad took some flak from neighbors for this practice. One father said to him, "You whistle for dogs, not for children." Dad's response was that it worked, and in his view was a lot better than yelling each child's name and disturbing the entire neighborhood.

I vividly remember watching the Apollo 11 moon landing in July 1969, when I was twelve. I came home to watch because Dad whistled for me and it wasn't dinnertime, which was odd. It was a summer Sunday. I was playing outside with friends and wasn't pleased about having to go home early. When I came inside, Dad said he thought we should all watch the moon landing, that it was an important and historic event. I was happy to be watching it with Dad, but it did seem rather slow and tedious, especially on a fine summer day when I'd rather be outside playing.

We Wallick kids were very lucky. We had access to opportunities and experiences many children did not, even in affluent, upper-middle-class Bellevue, and we knew it. Both of my parents were born and raised in rural Kansas, and while neither of their families struggled terribly during the Depression, the contrast between their own childhoods and what they provided my brothers and me was stark. It felt like we were living a *Leave It to Beaver* life. My father insisted, however, that we should never brag, and we should share with our friends what we had. Our house was always open to our friends and the neighborhood kids. My father stressed that just because we were so fortunate, we weren't any better than anyone else. He really made a point of this, and continued to do so throughout his life. He never put on airs and didn't appreciate anyone else doing so.

My brothers and I grew to be physically fit, active, and healthy. We had lots of friends who regularly came to our house to hang out, or who accompanied us on fishing and snow-skiing vacations. We all seemed to have inherited my parents' calm demeanors. We learned to rely on ourselves, which gave us confidence, including the capacity to say no when others tried to get us to do things we knew we shouldn't, or were dangerous. We were raised to assess a situation and our own abilities, then to take calculated risks and learn from our experiences, which is what test pilots do day in, day out. We made some mistakes, like all kids do; we learned to analyze and take lessons away from them so as to not repeat them.

Perhaps unusual for the early 1960s, I was allowed to be the tomboy I enjoyed being. Because I liked hanging out with my father in his shop or when he worked on our cars, I learned about tools and machines at an early age. When I took standardized tests in the first or second grade, I scored highest in mechanical aptitude. I clearly remember my father always encouraging me to dream of becoming anything I wanted—architect, doctor, teacher, lawyer, test or airline pilot. It didn't matter that women constituted a small minority in some of those occupations, especially his own. My dreams were never harnessed by gender.

This background is a glimpse into the world in which I was raised, a childhood influenced in every way by my father's career choice and his outlook on life and family.

Which brings me back to my father and his colleagues. Who were these guys, these test pilots? On one level or another, I've been trying to answer that question my entire adult life. Their reserved engineer personalities, coupled with their genuine modesty and humility, make it hard to see below their polished and accomplished surfaces. I think the best clues to what made them tick are found in their joy of flying airplanes and in the relationships they forged throughout their lives within the aviation community and beyond.

From the 1950s to the 1980s, Dad and his colleagues in Boeing Flight Test played a critical role in the dawning of the commercial jet transport age. They put their lives on the line almost daily, so that today, you and I can get on to a commercial airliner and sit back and relax, knowing we'll arrive safely at our destination. (Dad always reminded me that air travel is much safer than traveling by automobile.) They *loved* their jobs. I never once heard my father complain about having to go to work. I think they were aware that they were making history along the way, mindful that their actions and public personas would someday be judged as the history of aviation was written. Still, they never took themselves too seriously and they made work fun.

But it wasn't all fun. Some of the test pilots and flight engineers based in Seattle died on the job. There were two separate crashes in 1959 that resulted in fatalities. Those deaths touched my life; I grew up knowing some of the wives and children left behind, saw them frequently over the years. Those accidents and deaths forged tighter bonds among the surviving pilots and their families, as they circled round and supported the widows and children. The lessons learned from those tragedies became part of the life advice I was given growing up. Since those accidents, the rest of the test crews I grew up around have survived—sometimes just barely—through decades of test flying to retirement and beyond, all the while raising families and balancing work with lives well lived. They were in the right place with the right skills at the right time to work at jobs they loved while having a significant impact on aviation history and the way we all travel today.

8 Test pilots' meeting, 1959. Front row from left: Brien Wygle, Don Knutson, Ray McPherson (standing), Jim Gannett, Tex Johnston. Lew Wallick, hip on desk corner in middle of middle row. Photo: Boeing Archives.

This band of brothers (for it was virtually all men until the 1980s) in Flight Test had a *joie de vivre*, an approach to living life fully that made growing up with them an exciting adventure. As a child, I never found it odd that most of the people my family socialized with were also Boeing families: test pilots and engineers and their wives and children. Much later, as I started researching this book and talking to these men, who were then all well into their seventies and eighties, it became apparent that very much like the NASA astronauts of the same era, they were most comfortable around those who understood what they did for a living and didn't ask a lot of naïve questions. They truly relaxed only among their own kind. Their humbleness about what they did and their role in aviation history is almost as legendary as their skill at testing airplanes.

Because I am a test pilot's daughter, because I lived through those times with them—watching, listening, and participating when I could—they trusted me with their stories, knowing I would tell them honestly, with sensitivity and integrity. I've done my best to never betray that trust. Any errors in the retelling are strictly my own.

So sit down, buckle your seat belt, put your tray table up, and prepare to take off on a nostalgic flight back in time to the dawn of the jet age, when the best test pilots flew by the seat of their pants, putting new commercial jets through tests that stressed and pushed the edge of performance envelopes, discovering their limits and tolerances. Fly along on demonstration and proving flights as the test pilots help Boeing sell the airplanes to airlines around the world, meeting a few celebrities along the way. See how their adventurous spirits and need for speed infused their leisure activities and home lives.

Hearing these men tell their favorite stories, I could clearly see that working at Boeing had given my father and his fellow test pilots and flight test engineers the rides of their lives, no regrets. How lucky they were.

CHAPTER TWO: THE FORTIES AND FIFTIES

You only live once, but if you do it right, once is enough.
—Mae West, actress

The Navy and College Years

My father's training in the Navy took him all over the country, by train and truck. Often he and his fellow recruits lived and trained at small colleges in Iowa, New Mexico (where they had quarters in a college stadium and Dad did his first flying at West Mesa airport), and California. Dad soloed in a Taylorcraft on October 15, 1943, in California. While there, he met Robert Taylor, a well-known actor who contributed to the war effort by working as a flight instructor in the Naval Air Corps. Then it was off to Corpus Christi, Texas, a four-day train ride. Here the training got serious: learning to fly by instruments; navigating by radio; flying in formation; practicing gunnery, strafing, and dive-bombing runs; firing guns at targets towed by other airplanes. "Lots of fun flying," my father said of this time in his training.

Dad graduated from advanced training in January 1945, getting his commission. Everyone in his class was asked what sort of training they'd like next: multi-engine land aircraft, multi-engine water aircraft, or carrier aircraft. "Most wanted multi-engine because they thought the survival rate was better," Dad said. He wanted to be a fighter pilot and land on carriers. "There were twenty-five guys in my group. We all wanted to be fighter pilots. One guy wanted to fly torpedo bombers. To help him, I got a bottle of booze and befriended a yeoman. We all got what we wanted!"

9 Lew Wallick, Navy aviator, standing next to a Corsair. Photo: Author's collection.

After a quick visit home after getting his commission, Dad

went to Florida for operational and carrier training. This is where he got to do the flying he'd always wanted: Corsairs, with night flying, formation flying, combat tactics, and bombing runs. Carrier training came next, the most dangerous flying requiring the most skill. A Landing Signal Officer (LSO) guided the pilots through hours of touch-and-go's on a rectangle painted on an air field, simulating a carrier deck. Eventually, a week after my father celebrated his twenty-first birthday, it was time for him to do the real thing: land on a carrier.

Dad and two other pilots met at the airport in the early morning and climbed in to their Corsairs, taking off at sunrise. "We went out over the ocean about 100 miles to the carrier, the Guadalcanal, a small escort carrier. I was the lead. We were coming in with the sunlight from behind. The ship was a small speck, only 600 feet long.[4] I circled the ship, got permission to land, flew the pattern, set up the landing. The LSO says cut power; I drop, snag the line, and taxi to the front of the ship. I shut down the engine and got out on the deck. It was the first time I'd set foot on a ship deck!"

The next day, Dad and the other pilots started qualifying for carrier-based operations, doing twelve takeoffs and landings each over the course of three days. Dad qualified. Then, remaining on ship, they returned to port. Finished with training by early July 1945, he was sent to Grosse Ile, Michigan, into a holding pool for several weeks, waiting for assignment. In early August, he got orders to go to Norfolk, Virginia, to join the USS Lake Champlain, a brand new ship that was slated to participate in the invasion of Japan. The United States had just dropped the first atomic bomb on Japan. As he traveled by train to Virginia, Dad learned that Japan had surrendered. After reporting to his ship, Dad participated in a celebratory "good will" tour of the East Coast, flying over big, happy crowds in New York City, Philadelphia, and Boston. I can only imagine his joy at seeing so much of the country—often from the cockpit of a fighter—at such a young age. So different from the farm back in Kansas! Eventually my father's squadron was

---

[4] A regular carrier was 900 feet long.

disbanded. He could have left the Navy then, but elected to remain another six months, through June 1, 1946.

It was during those last six months of active duty that my father learned a valuable lesson: sometimes airplanes can bite. He had been assigned to Elizabeth City, North Carolina. He was flying a Grumman TBM Avenger (a torpedo bomber) when it had engine problems. "It was barely running," Dad said. "I was trying for a runway a half mile away. There was an open field between me and the airport, but it had stumps everywhere. The Pasquotank River looked better because my wheels were up. The river had a steep sheer bank, nearly vertical. I cut power and put the left wing down to turn, to avoid the bank. I hit the water with the wing and cart-wheeled, nose into the water, then settled on the belly. I got an adrenaline rush and quickly got out with my parachute. It was cold—December—but the airplane wasn't sinking. It was sitting on the bottom, with the top of the wing out of the water. I stayed on the wing." The tower, aware of his having ditched, sent a motorboat to get him. He stepped off the wing into the boat, never getting his feet wet. "Only my back got wet," he added. "I had taken the canopy off prior to hitting. There was a geyser of water when I hit and it went down the back of my jacket." The TBM sat there a couple of weeks until it was finally retrieved.

In June of 1946, Dad was discharged from the Navy and returned to Kansas. Using the GI bill, he enrolled at Kansas State University. It was there that he met my mother, Ruth, and they soon married. Dad also went into the Navy Air Reserve in Olathe, Kansas, as an active reservist in a Corsair squadron, which allowed him to continue flying. Dad graduated with a degree in mechanical engineering in January 1949. In February, accepting one of two job offers he'd received, he started working at Beech Aircraft in Wichita. Beech's Bonanza airplane was new and very popular then. Continental made its engines, but Beech was testing Franklin engines and asked for unpaid volunteers. Dad volunteered, flying during lunch hours and occasional Saturdays. Eventually he got assigned to test fly the C model of the Bonanza, which had an increased tail area and changed "V" angle over earlier models; he did most of the spin testing. He received $2 per hour for flight hours in addition to his $220 per month engineer's pay. It was at Beech that Dad met and befriended fellow pilot Joseph "Joe" Quentin Keller.

10 Lew Wallick standing on wing of his ditched TBM Avenger, 1946. Photo: Author's collection.

Getting to Boeing

By 1951, my father was eager to do more flying; he wanted to be a full-time test pilot, not just part-time. He talked to Beech's vice president, who said he'd think about it. My father had friends from Kansas State University who were working as engineers at Boeing, earning $75 per month more than he was. "Three weeks went by and I didn't hear anything, so I put my resignation in and went to Boeing," Dad told me. "I was not very patient back then." The extra money would come in handy, because by now my parents were living in government housing with one child, a second on the way. Dad started at Boeing's Wichita facility in May 1951. Joe Keller had the same idea and also left Beech, following Dad to Boeing with his young family.

Dad was transferred to Seattle in May 1955. Mom and my three older brothers followed three weeks later, accompanied by Mom's parents in a caravan of two cars loaded with belongings. Family photos and home movies from that period include many of those new Boeing families. There were group camping trips with young kids everywhere, and birthday parties attended by lots of other Boeing kids. The families sometimes drove up to Snoqualmie Pass to play in the snow. You get the sense that they all loved their new environment, so different from the plains of Kansas, even if it did rain a lot.

By the time I was born in 1956, the last of four kids, Dad had been a Boeing test pilot for five years, first flying B-47s, then the T-28 and T-33, and a B-25, then eventually the B-52, the XB-47D (which he hated, although he kept a large photo of one on his office wall, maybe to remind him how lucky he was to not have to fly it anymore), and the KC-135, with occasional time flying the F-86 chase plane (which he loved). In October 1955, Dad started getting time in the Dash 80, which convinced him he wanted to focus on the commercial side of Boeing test flying. On the day I was born, he was testing a KC-135. By the late 1950s and early 1960s, when I was old enough to start paying attention, Dad and the other Boeing test pilots and many of the flight test engineers were spending a lot of time at Edwards Air Force Base (AFB) as they tested all the jets—military and commercial.

It was normal for Dad's work to regularly take him out of town for a few or even several days at a time, sometimes as long as a month. So normal, in fact, that I never questioned it, worried about it, or thought it was different for other families.

If I noticed Dad wasn't home for dinner some night, I might ask Mom where he was. Invariably, the answer was either a simple "Out of town," which was shorthand for "he's traveling for work," or sometimes she gave a more particular answer, like "Edwards" or perhaps the name of another state or country. Mom usually just offered the quickest, shortest answer and that was that. I learned that if I asked, "When will Dad be home?"

the answer would be squishy—maybe Thursday, say, but he might also be delayed a day or two. None of us worried; he'd be back eventually. And when he was home, the focus was the family; he rarely talked about work around us. Instead, he was teaching us how to ride bicycles, taking us water skiing and snow skiing, helping with school work, or catching up on house projects.

Little did we children of test pilots and flight test engineers know just what was going on when our fathers were "out of town" or "at Edwards." Lots of it was dangerous, involving testing of airplanes. Some of it was straightforward, such as demonstrating airplanes to military and airline VIPs. Equal amounts of their time, especially at Edwards AFB and other off-site testing locations, might be termed "waiting" for perfect test conditions and "letting off steam."

Edwards Air Force Base

Edwards AFB was the scene of a lot of experimental test flying for Boeing after World War II, and still is today. Why Edwards AFB? The main factors are year-round good flying weather and long runways, beyond which lie miles of dried-up desert lake beds in case the runway isn't long enough. Additionally, Edwards AFB is so remote that the scream of jet engines doesn't bother anyone, nor will any civilian homes or buildings be endangered if something goes awry—like an access door blowing off during a flight, or an airplane crashing during takeoff or landing. The military facilities and personnel there are used to seeing new, advanced-design aircraft. They are adept at handling routine test flights as well as the occasional dropped part, accident, fire, or other disaster. At Edwards, Boeing crews can conduct various tests in relative safety, and also away from the media.

Edwards AFB is about 100 miles northeast of Los Angeles, California, in the high desert at 2,300 feet in elevation. In the 1950s, in was truly in the middle of nowhere, surrounded by miles of scrub brush and a few stunted Joshua trees. The Rogers and Rosamond lake beds were first used for military purposes in the 1930s, when the Army Air Corps did bombing and gunnery practice there. During World War II, the military built a facility next to what was then called Muroc Dry Lake—a salt pan in the Mojave Desert—and used it to train bomber and fighter crews before they were sent overseas. The training facility was called Muroc Army Airfield, but it really wasn't much more than a couple of Quonset huts used as hangars, some fuel pumps, a concrete runway, and some outbuildings and tents.

In the early 1940s, the nation's first jet aircraft—the Bell XP-59A Airacomet—was tested there. Most Army Air Corps test flying prior to and early in World War II was done at Wright Field in Ohio. But the military quickly realized the need for more space, where testing of top-secret new designs could occur away from prying eyes. The testing of the Bell XP-59A showed that Muroc was perfect for experimental flight testing—isolated, with a huge landing field and more reliable weather than Wright Field—so more facilities were added six miles away, on the north side of 44-square-mile Rogers Dry Lake. In the coming years, many a test pilot would be very thankful for the sheer size of the lake bed at the end of the runway.

Both the Army Air Corps and the Navy began testing all of their new jet aircraft at Muroc. By late 1946, a new sort of testing began: research tests to prove or disprove theoretical aeronautical concepts. It was an exciting time for those involved. Much of it was motivated by the Cold War and kept very secret. The rocket-powered Bell X-1 was the first in a series of experimental supersonic craft flown and tested at Muroc. In September 1947, the US Air Force was created as part of the National Security Act of 1947. One month later, Air Force Capt. Charles E. "Chuck" Yeager went into the history books as the first man to break the speed of sound in the X-1, high over Muroc and the desert lake beds. Muroc was the place to be if you were a test pilot.

The experimental test flights undertaken by Yeager and other military pilots to answer research questions were crude by today's standards. There were no formal safety standards and little feedback via instrumentation during each flight. Radar tracking was new, and the use of telemetry[5] was just starting. The *feel* of the airplane to the pilot—flying by the seat of his pants—provided the most critical feedback, sometimes by live-radio transmission from the cockpit to the ground crew. Reacting instantly and correctly to any unexpected event occurring during a test kept the airplane from crashing and the pilot alive to fly again another day. For the X-1, Yeager and his project engineer, Capt. Jack Ridley, were pretty much on their own; prior to each flight, they'd discuss what they had learned from earlier flights, creating a plan for how far and how fast to go. Then Yeager would take her up. It was that simple. And that hazardous.

Many experimental aircraft were lost during this period of pushing against the known parameters of flight, seeing how fast man could go as he punched holes in the sky. Any pilot who lost control of an airplane and was unable to eject and parachute to safety died instantly upon impact. Pilots referred to such mishaps as boring holes in the earth. Humor, even macabre humor, is one of the ways test pilots deal with the dangers inherent in their chosen occupation. Those pilots who did survive the dangers gained an almost god-like status.

By the time Yeager broke the sound barrier, two distinct types of test flying were occurring at Muroc: flight research—like the X-1—and the more "routine" testing and proving of new aircraft and systems within the military.

In 1949, the name of the base was changed from Muroc to Edwards Air Force Base in honor of Air Force Capt. Glen Walter Edwards, who died in the 1948 crash of the XB-49 flying wing. His death, at age thirty, was one of thirteen pilot deaths at the base that year. The new name given the base, where the Boeing test pilots conducted so many of their more dangerous and critical tests, was a grim reminder of the risks inherent in their jobs.

By June 1951, in recognition of what had become reality on the ground, Edwards AFB was officially designated the US Air

---

[5] Telemetry is an automated communications process by which measurements and data collected at a remote point—e.g., an airplane—are transmitted to receiving equipment on the ground for monitoring.

Force Flight Test Center, and the Air Force Test Pilot School was moved there from Wright Field. Test pilots would have 330,000 acres over which to learn flying skills and conduct their experimental flights.

Test Pilot School is just what it sounds like: a place to teach pilots how to test the capabilities and performance of new aircraft, including those rockets disguised as aircraft that Yeager and others flew. After World War II and into the 1950s, the dramatic increase in the power and speed of rocket engines and the new turbojets, coupled with the increasing complexity of the aircraft, made it critical that only the best test pilots be trusted with these expensive airplanes and test programs. Test pilots not only must quickly learn how to fly new types of aircraft and be highly skilled at it—and remarkably courageous—but they also must have the technical backgrounds that allow them to understand all the systems they're testing and evaluating. Then, they need to be able to tell the engineers what they experienced during test flights, using precise engineering lingo. The pilot's ability to articulate the experience of flying each aircraft is critical to helping the engineers design improvements and new models. As aviation moved into the jet age, these skills and knowledge were increasingly important to the success of any new program, military or commercial. Millions of dollars were invested in each aircraft and program. Not just any yahoo could be trusted with these aircraft.

The 1950s witnessed remarkably fast-paced progress in aviation. Speed and altitude records were being set, only to be bested a few weeks or months later. Scott Crossfield, a National Advisory Committee for Aeronautics (NACA, later the National Aeronautics and Space Administration, or NASA) test pilot, arrived at Edwards AFB in 1950. Crossfield became best known for his own test flying of the X-1 class of experimental airplanes. He once described the vibe at Edwards AFB at that time as one where the pilots "lived with the feeling that everything we were doing was something that probably had never been attempted or even thought of before." When the decade began, the edge of the speed envelope was Mach 1.45

(957 mph)[6] and man had flown as high as 72,902 feet in a first generation X-1. Those envelope edges would be consistently pushed outward over the course of the decade: in 1953, Crossfield was the first to reach Mach 2 (Mach 2.005 or 1,291 mph) in the Skyrocket, but within a month, Yeager took the next generation Bell X-1A to Mach 2.44 (1,650 mph), and in mid-1954, Maj. Arthur "Kit" Murray flew an X-1A up to 90,440 feet. By 1956, in an X-2, the altitude record was pushed to 126,200 feet by Capt. Iven Kincheloe, and weeks later in the same airplane, Capt. Milburn "Mel" Apt became the first to break Mach 3, flying Mach 3.2 (2,094 mph) before losing control of the airplane and crashing to his death (at age thirty-two) in the desert below, sadly boring yet another hole in the earth.

As all the rocket-propelled aircraft testing was going on, the military was also making huge strides in the design and testing of fighter aircraft at Edwards AFB, thanks to the advent of the turbojet. The Century Series of aircraft—the F-100 Super Sabre, F-102 Delta Dagger, F-105 Thunderchief, and F-106 Delta Dart—were making supersonic flight seem common. Given the huge advances in capability and performance these aircraft brought, flying, testing, and evaluating them required more skill than ever before. As the aircraft got more complex, so did the instruments used to record the data obtained, and the skills required of the engineers who evaluated the data. Oscillographs and strip charts became more common; the number of parameters recorded and interpreted increased exponentially. Telemetry systems were coming into more frequent use. Even magnetic tape and mainframe computers were starting to make the scene. More equipment and more parameters examined meant more people with high levels of education and expertise were required as part of any development and test program.

---

[6] Mach number refers to a ratio: object speed/speed of sound = Mach number. Any speed at Mach number less than 1.0 is subsonic, at 1.0 is transonic, and at greater than 1.0 is supersonic. The speed of sound is approximately 760 mph. The boom heard when an airplane breaks the sound barrier (exceeds the speed of sound) is the result of the aircraft's changing the density of the air around it, causing a disturbance, a shock wave.

Boeing's growth and success in the 1940s was based primarily on the military's need for war aircraft. Boeing had launched the B-17 in 1935 in response to the military's desire for a large, multi-engine bomber. That airplane became known as the Flying Fortress. Using the same general design, Boeing brought out the Model 307 Stratoliner in 1938, the first pressurized-cabin commercial transport, able to fly to 20,000 feet, above the weather. When the United States entered the war in late 1941, Boeing was tasked with providing the military with huge numbers of B-17 and B-29 bombers. Because of the urgent need for these aircraft, Boeing and its competitors cooperated in their manufacture: Lockheed and Douglas assembled many of the B-17s; Bell Aircraft and Glenn L. Martin Co. helped assemble B-29s. Boeing ramped up its factories in Seattle to meet demand. To have enough workers to produce as many as 350 airplanes per month by 1944, Boeing hired women to work the assembly lines alongside the men who weren't in the military, a trend seen across the country. Rosie the Riveter became a cultural icon, a symbol of all the women who helped the war effort by working in factories and assembly plants.

When the war ended in 1945, the demand for huge numbers of bombers also ended. Some 70,000 people lost their Boeing jobs. In an effort to recover from the loss of military contracts, Boeing created the 377 Stratocruiser, a luxurious four-engine airliner based on the B-29 bomber, but it wasn't very successful. Boeing also sold military derivatives of the Stratocruiser—the C-97 troop transport and the KC-97 tanker that would be used in aerial refueling.

Post World War II and into the Cold War era, Boeing focused on developing jet aircraft for the military—the B-47 Stratojet and the B-52 Stratofortress bombers. The B-47 prototype—the XB-47—first flew on December 17, 1947, with Boeing pilots Robby Robbins and Scott Osler at the controls. They flew from Boeing Field in Seattle to Moses Lake, Washington, which at that time was a World War II Air Corps training facility with a good runway. The B-47 was the first swept-wing multi-engine jet aircraft, with engines hanging in pods under the wings, a radical new design that was later carried forward to most of Boeing's commercial jets. In September 1949, the Air Force awarded Boeing the contract for the B-47, and the decision was made to produce them in the company's factory in Wichita because of heavy production demands for the KC-97 tanker in Seattle.

During this time of extensive development of new military aircraft—the B-47, B-52, and KC-97—Boeing was adding test pilots and engineers to its Wichita operation. My father hired on in January 1951 as a flight test engineer. He was promised a position as test pilot as soon as there was an opening, something Beech had failed to offer him. Brien Wygle was hired by Boeing in May 1951, starting in Seattle as a test pilot, based on his experience flying Vampire fighter jets in the Royal Canadian Air Force (RCAF) reserves. Born in Seattle in 1924, Brien moved to Canada with his family in 1927 and grew up on a farm near Calgary, Alberta. He joined the RCAF in 1942 and served as a pilot in Europe, India, and Burma. After the war, he attended the University of British Columbia, graduating with a degree in mechanical engineering shortly before hiring on at Boeing. He was soon sent to Wichita to work on the B-47 program. "I'm sure Lew looked at me with jaundiced eyes when I show up and start right in as a pilot because we were the same age," says Brien. In fact, Dad was just three months older than Brien.

Because so much of Boeing's work involved military aircraft, Boeing test pilots and crews were spending lots of time with their military counterparts, both in Wichita and Seattle, and at Wright Field and Edwards AFB. Everyone worked closely together, testing and demonstrating each aircraft's capabilities, or working to design improvements demanded by the military.

The knowledge gained from flight testing the B-47 formed the foundation for the design and development of the B-52 and all of the Boeing jet transports that followed, so to say it was a critical program is hardly an overstatement. Test flying B-47s was also a great way for young test pilots to gain skill and experience.

11 A B-47 in flight. Photo: Boeing Archives.

In the middle of the ongoing B-47 testing program, a tragedy occurred. On the first Saturday in September 1951, Boeing lost four test pilots in a midair collision of two B-47s in Wichita. The number of Boeing test pilots instantly went from thirteen to nine at a time when the demands for test flying were increasing. "That was a terrible tragedy," Brien remembers. "It was four careers lost; it was devastating." In fact, the only reason Brien wasn't flying one of those B-47s that day was because his wife and children were arriving from Canada, and he was waiting to welcome them. Because of the sudden loss of four pilots, Brien was quickly promoted to first pilot and given a project in experimental flight test. "It might have happened anyway," Brien says, "but it was precipitated by the accident. Lew was hired on as well, first of that group of engineers who were waiting to become test pilots. Lew quickly established a name for himself. He was just, in my opinion, one of the best test pilots we ever had."

My father started flying copilot on B-47s in October 1951, quickly gaining time and experience in multi-engine jets. He credited Dix Loesch and Ed Hartz with being his mentors in the business of test piloting. Dad also flew Boeing's F-86 chase plane as observer and photographer, enjoying the quick responsiveness of a fighter jet and flying in formation with the bigger jets.

12 Lew Wallick on an F-86. Photo: Boeing Archives.

By the spring of 1952, Dad was checked out and flying in the pilot's seat of the B-47 much of his flight time. (When a pilot is "checked out," it means he has qualified to fly without supervision.)

"We were both highly thought of at that time," says Brien. "We were younger than hell, so we rose up fairly quickly." In fact, they were both twenty-seven years old, married, and starting their families, two kids each at that time. Their careers, as well as their home lives, took parallel and complimentary paths, forging a strong friendship that would last throughout their careers at Boeing and beyond into retirement, allowing their wives and children to become close as well.

Flying the B-47 is where Dad and Brien learned the ropes and honed their skills as test pilots. "When I got to Wichita, the B-47 was huge," recalls Brien. "I had flown a lot of twin-engine airplanes, but I was coming off little single-engine fighter airplanes, and the B-47 was really big. At that point in my career, I could do anything, in my opinion. It was just exciting, this massive, big airplane—holy cow!"

Brien remembers an early experience testing B-47s in Wichita, one that was pretty dicey. The military was experimenting with adding propulsion at takeoff, so that the already heavy airplane could carry more weight. They were testing something called JATO—Jet Assisted Take Off, a U-shaped fitting on the back of the B-47 with eighteen rocket bottles attached. It was designed so that when the rocket bottles finished firing, the whole thing would fall off the airplane because otherwise it would be dead weight. In certain conditions, though, the apparatus got hung up, creating a very aft center of gravity (CG), which resulted in difficult handling conditions in flight because the nose would tend to go up, increasing the angle of attack and reducing the lift of the wings—in other words, creating a stall condition.

The test Brien was asked to fly involved taking off with normal CG, but in flight the CG would be transferred aft by manipulating how the fuel burned. "I found myself—all of twenty-seven years old, and just eight months a test pilot—doing stall tests!" remembers Brien. Stall tests are risky flying. "I'd stalled the airplane quite a bit, but of course the most difficult stall tests are when you have an aft CG, so even I was smart enough to go at this pretty carefully." The airplane flew miserably with such an aft CG—way outside normal limits—and was very unstable. "I got in the stall, and I couldn't get the nose down," Brien continues. "I didn't have enough elevator power to get the nose down and get my speed up. I'm sitting there, mushing along and I can't get the nose down. My instincts told me 'roll the airplane' so I rolled, and the nose dropped in the turn. I recovered airspeed, and I didn't do any more stalls."

Sometime around 1951 or 1952, my father was flying copilot with Boeing test pilot Dick Taylor on B-47 high-gross-weight takeoff tests in Wichita. It was during one of these takeoffs that Dad's inherent skill as a test pilot became evident. Dick credits Dad with saving both their lives that day. The B-47 had 10,000 pounds of concrete ballast in the bomb bay, the fuel tanks were full, and the airplane was fitted with JATO rockets to assist on takeoff because otherwise it was too heavy to get off the ground.

Right after takeoff rotation and gear up, Dick said "flaps up," and Dad started retracting flaps. Unbeknownst to either pilot, however, one of the flaps got hung up and didn't retract. Dad saw his control wheel turning sharply to the right and noticed Dick putting in more and more right wheel to keep the wings level. Dick wasn't sure why the airplane wanted to turn left, but thought maybe there was engine failure.

Dad immediately and instinctively stopped retracting the flaps and started moving them back down. As both control wheels came back to neutral and the airplane quit trying to roll to the left, Dad set the flaps and Dick flew the beast. They were only 100 to 200 feet above the ground and so heavily weighted as this played out, there was no room for error.

Not a word was said between them; they both simply reacted to the reality confronting them, true seat-of-the-pants flying. Dad instantly realized Dick's struggle with the wheel wasn't normal and made the connection between that and the most recent thing he'd done—retract flaps—so he moved them back down. That instinctual reaction allowed Dick to keep the airplane level and flying, avoiding a roll right into the ground.

The reactions and instincts that my father and Brien displayed while flying B-47s are what make certain test pilots extraordinarily good ones. No time to think; just *react.*

13 Dick Taylor and Lew Wallick with a B-47, Wichita. Photo: Boeing Archives.

Test Pilot School

One can forgive my father and Brien for having the sense, at the ripe old age of twenty-nine, that they were pretty good at what they did. Their instincts were spot-on, saving not only themselves but their crews, the airplanes, and perhaps even the Boeing programs that allowed them to have their dream jobs.

Still, the flying was dangerous, and the military's work with Boeing was extensive enough that all concerned had incentives to make sure key pilots were as skilled as possible.

In 1953, the military agreed to send some of Boeing's pilots through the Air Force Test Pilot School at Edwards AFB, at the military's expense. Brien went first, enrolling in the six-month course in early 1953; Dad followed three months later, overlapping Brien's class of students for three of his six months. Sometime later, Tom Edmonds would be the last Boeing test pilot to go through the school on the military's dime.[7]

14 Lew Wallick, center, and colleagues in the desert at Edwards AFB, Joshua tree in background. Photo: Boeing Archives.

Because each session of Test Pilot School was a significant time commitment, away from home, the Boeing pilots took their families along. They lived in military housing just west of

[7] Boeing would later send some of its pilots through Test Pilot School at company expense, including Paul Bennett. Eventually the cost to Boeing was $1 million or more per pilot, so not everyone got to go.

the main base for the entire six months, with access to the officers' club and amenities such as the swimming pool. Brien's wife Norma and his two oldest children were there with him; my mother and my two oldest brothers joined my father while he was there. The Wygles and Wallicks hung out together; the Boeing kids played with the children of military officers. Both of my brothers celebrated birthdays while at Edwards AFB, and Mom invited the kids of their military acquaintances to their birthday parties. Among my parents' military friends were Andy and Brooke Hontz.[8] Mom remembers being invited to tea with the base commander's wife. "I wasn't going to go," Mom told me, "until Brooke said I had to, and told me what to wear." Life at Edwards AFB was regimented, for the families as well as the aviators.

Every picture and home movie of my family from that time shows my brothers Sam and Rick (who turned four and two in September 1953) with crew cuts bleached blonde by the desert sun, their skin darkly tanned, wearing shorts or often just their underwear as they play with water hoses in a kiddie pool or ride tricycles in front of single-level homes with yards of sunburnt grass on streets devoid of trees or shade of any kind. Welcome to the desert. The kids seemed to thrive.

Brien has fond memories of those days. "I enjoyed it completely," he says. "Life was good. I was so excited I had a career like I did. I couldn't believe I was actually an experimental test pilot. It was the culmination of my career desires, and here I was, at Edwards Air Force Base, and going to Test Pilot School." He remembers their living quarters as newly constructed, comfortable apartments in the desert. He also remembers being at the pool at the Officer's Club one day. It had a high and a low diving board. "Lew was there. He got on the high board and did a half gainer. Just one. Perfect. I thought to myself, 'This guy is pretty cool.'"

My father was excited to go to Test Pilot School. Boeing paid expenses—salary plus a per diem—and like the Wygles, the Wallick family lived in military housing for those six months. While in Test Pilot School, Dad flew a T-28 (a trainer),

[8] Andy Hontz later died in a B-57 crash.

F-84 (fighter jet), B-25 (twin-engine bomber, the sort that Lt. Col. Doolittle flew in a secret raid over Tokyo in 1942, the first retaliatory air raid over Japan), and a T-33 (jet trainer, a two-seat version of the F-80 fighter). Students flew in the morning and had classroom work in the afternoon. They were taught basic testing techniques, progressing through each airplane model, doing certain tests during flight, writing reports, and getting graded. Dad was the only Boeing pilot in his class of fifteen; there was one other civilian, and the rest were military. "It was an intense and fun period of time," Dad remembered. He finished first in his class, as did Brien in his. Both credit this to the fact that they already had engineering degrees, whereas most of the military pilots did not.

15 Lew Wallick does a half gainer at The Desert Inn pool, near Edwards AFB, 1950s. Photo: Author's collection.

The wives kept life as normal as possible for their husbands and children, maintaining the home and finances, providing meals, and keeping an eye on their children. There were places to wine and dine nearby, including the infamous Pancho's, a tavern—more of a shack, really—which became a beloved destination for most of the test pilots and military personnel working at Muroc/Edwards AFB in the 1940s and early 1950s. It was an unpretentious place to wind down with others who understood what you did for a living, who spoke your language. The establishment was owned and bartended by a woman named Pancho Barnes and had a... reputation. "You didn't take your wife to Pancho's," says Brien, smiling at the memory of the place, although my mother remembers going there "to check it out." By the time Brien and Norma arrived, rumors were circulating about what really went on at Pancho's. "I never saw it as a brothel, but they did have bachelor girls who were not with other men, and of course Pancho Barnes who ran it was in a class by herself. She was a famous pilot once, set a lot of records. She was not the most attractive woman I ever met. She was a character. She was likable."

Indeed, Pancho Barnes was a character. Photos of her show a stout woman dressed in jodhpurs and boots, a white sweater under a dark leather flight jacket, a white scarf around her neck, a leather flight helmet and goggles on her head, and a cigarette in her hand. Her face and body bore a striking resemblance to that of comedian Jonathan Winters. Born Florence Leontine Lowe in 1901 in Pasadena, California, Pancho lived up to her middle name's translation: lion. She was strong, adventurous, and a leader who didn't let social conventions slow her down.

Florence Lowe's grandfather—Thaddeus S. C. Lowe—was an aviation pioneer who commanded the US Army's Aeronautic (balloon) Corps during the Civil War. At age eighteen, Florence married a clergyman named Barnes, and a few years later they had a son. When her mother died in 1924, Florence inherited half a million dollars, an incredible sum in those days. She was just twenty-three years old.

With her newfound wealth, Barnes became a globe-trotter and hostess extraordinaire, throwing parties that lasted days, even weeks. Eventually, while on hiatus from her life as wife, mother, and social patron, she travelled on a freighter to Mexico. During her months-long stay there, she became accustomed to wearing men's trousers and—while allegedly running guns for the Mexican revolutionaries—acquired the nickname "Pancho." Upon returning to California, Barnes bought a biplane and took flying lessons. She was a natural pilot, soloing after just six hours of instruction, a chip who didn't fall far from her grandfather's aeronautic block.

In 1930, Barnes set a women's world record for average speed (196.19 mph) in the second Women's Transcontinental Air Derby, a cross-country air race from Santa Monica, California, to Cleveland, Ohio, that was dubbed "The Powder Puff Derby" by humorist Will Rogers. That same year, Barnes became the first woman to fly from Los Angeles to Mexico City, wresting the women's speed record from Amelia Earhart.

Barnes also became a stunt pilot, and was the first woman stunt pilot in motion pictures. She performed in Howard Hughes' movie *Hell's Angels* and other films. She created a company that placed other stunt pilots in Hollywood productions, and in 1929 helped create the Association of Motion Picture Stunt Pilots. Pilots of all stripes respected her.

More relevant to my story in general and to Edwards AFB in particular, in 1933, Barnes and her son Bill purchased a ranch in the Mojave Desert, very near to the base. Later, she turned it into a resort called The Rancho Oro Verde Fly-In Dude Ranch. It included a private airfield and a tavern for the Army Air Corps men stationed at Muroc. Because of her Hollywood connections, many movie stars became regulars.

Perhaps Barnes's most famous friendship was with Chuck Yeager, a bond that was immortalized in the book *The Right Stuff* by Tom Wolfe, written in 1979 and made into a movie in 1983. There's a scene in the movie where Yeager and his wife rent horses at Pancho's and take a wild ride through the desert the day before he is to take the Bell X-1 up to attempt to break the sound barrier. When his horse stumbles, Yeager is thrown and breaks a rib. He hides the injury the next day so that he's not disqualified from the history-making flight. Such is the stuff of legend.

Pancho was an outspoken, cigar-smoking, trousers-wearing presence at the place, serving drinks and swearing up a storm. She was beloved by the pilots. The common refrain among those who frequented her establishment was, "If it wasn't for Pancho's, we'd have all gone crazy." When, in 1949, the Air Force Test Pilot School was moved from Wright Field to Muroc, Pancho's business boomed. When gorgeous young single women—who had heard about the abundance of sexy test pilots at Edwards AFB—started showing up at Pancho's, the entire resort became known as the Happy Bottom Riding Club. It was a place for the pilots to socialize and drink and swap stories; a release valve for the stress and danger of their work on base, and a way to relieve the boredom of life in the desert, far from the nearest city.

This was the world Brien and Dad stepped into when they went through the Air Force Test Pilot School at Edwards AFB in early 1953. Good timing, at least with regard to sampling the atmosphere at Pancho's tavern, because in 1952 a new commander at Edwards AFB started complaining about the civilian flights at Barnes's nearby airport, claiming they interfered with the base. Mostly, the government wanted Barnes's land for expansion. When Barnes refused to sell, rumors were spread that the Happy Bottom Riding Club was really a brothel. The Air Force forbid access to its men, depriving Barnes of a large number of her patrons. Lawsuits ensued, and while pending, on November 13, 1953, the Happy Bottom Riding Club went up in flames, the result of a suspicious fire. An era went up in smoke with it. During its heyday, the Club had over 9,000 members worldwide. Even though Barnes eventually won her lawsuits, after the fire she was forced to relocate to the nearby town of Cantil. Despite intentions of re-establishing the Club there, she never did. The government eventually got Barnes's original ranch land.

Barnes's legacy lives on, however. On the site of the former Happy Bottom Riding Club, service members at Edwards AFB hold an annual barbecue, where the remains of the pool, the tavern's foundation and chimney, and the barn can still be seen.

When Brien completed his course at Test Pilot School, Tex Johnston, Boeing's chief test pilot, had him transferred to Seattle to work on the B-52 program.

After Dad finished Test Pilot School at Edwards AFB, he returned to Wichita and continued flying the B-47. He got many hours of valuable flying time in, gaining skill and experience. He vividly remembered one series of tests he did for the military—not so much because they were dangerous (although they were) but because of the uniqueness of the flying experience.

In January 1954, Dad was assigned the task of piloting a B-47B to test ejection seats in flight, making sure the seats cleared the airplane's tail when ejected at high speed. An anthropomorphic dummy was strapped into the copilot's seat behind Dad in the two-person cockpit; the real copilot was riding below in the navigator's seat, in the nose of the airplane, primarily to extend the landing gear in case of an emergency.

To conduct the tests, Dad flew the airplane without its usual canopy—during a Kansas winter. "Doing the checklist, starting engines and taxiing to the runway with a typical 15-knot wind blowing was cold work!" he recalled. The B-47 had a good-size windshield, but that offered nowhere to hide from the cold breeze while on the ground. "Interestingly," Dad continued, "once exceeding about 250 knots[9] indicated airspeed, it seemed to feel warmer in the cockpit than at lower speeds, and better than being on the ground."

These tests were flown from the Boeing test facility at McConnell Air Force Base outside Wichita; the seats were fired over the Smoky Hill bombing range. A chase plane accompanied the flights to photograph the seat trajectory—and maybe the loss of the B-47's tail fin if things didn't go as planned. (This is a great example of my father's typical test pilot understatement in telling a story. If the seat had hit and destroyed the airplane's fin, he would almost certainly have lost control of the airplane—especially if the fin was lost while in a steep bank turn at high speed—and both men would have had to eject if they had hoped to survive.)[10]

During the first test, the seat and dummy were ejected, but

---

[9] One knot, or nautical mile, is equal to 1.15 statute miles per hour. In this case, 250 knots is roughly 288 miles per hour.

[10] The test conditions were 13,000 feet/295 knots, 13,000 feet/368 knots, and 13,000 feet/427 knots, all in level flight. After the level-flight firings, test conditions were 13,000 feet/310 knots/1.35 *g*, 13,000 feet/310 knots/1.65 *g*, and 13,000 feet/310 knots/2.0 *g*, with the airplane put into a 45- or 60-degree bank turn, or maybe a dive or straight-ahead pull-up to obtain the required *g* level. "These flights resulted in the fastest open cockpit flights of my career," said Dad.

the parachute didn't deploy. Dad could hear the explosion behind him—a small artillery shell was used to eject the seat—so he knew it had fired. He could only hope it cleared the airplane's tail. It did, but when the dummy was later found on the ground, it was a bit mangled, earning the nickname "Man of Steel." They placed that dummy in the hangar with the others awaiting future test flights. On the second test, there was a misfire; the seat and dummy stayed in the cockpit. The copilot suggested later that maybe the new dummy saw the mangled Man of Steel in the hangar and didn't want to end up in similar condition.

Everyone involved in these tests knew that in May 1949, before the military awarded a contract to Boeing for the bomber, Boeing test pilot Scott Osler (who flew the first flight of the B-47 in 1947) was killed when the canopy of the XB-47 he was testing at Moses Lake came off at high speed; the copilot, seated behind him, was able to land the airplane. And in the early years of military use, there were several serious injuries when personnel ejected from B-47s. In fact, the Air Force eliminated the ejection seats in intermediate derivatives until reinstating them in the B-47E because crews demanded them. Clearly, high-speed tests involving ejection seats were dangerous.

As it produced B-47s and B-52s, Boeing kept a keen eye on the growing demand for commercial airplanes and invested $16 million of its own funds in the development of the 367-80, a commercial jet for which it had no orders. A prototype, only one 367-80 was ever manufactured. Extensive testing of the Dash 80, as it became known, through the 1950s led to development of the military KC-135 Stratotanker and the iconic 707 commercial jetliner, the jet that would shrink the world for commercial travelers.

The test pilots and flight test engineers lucky enough to be hired for the B-47 program became the experience and knowledge base for the testing and development of the B-52, KC-135, 707, 727, 737, and 747 transports. The B-47 pilots in Wichita who were transferred to Seattle for the B-52 test program included Tex Johnston, Dix Loesch, Brien Wygle,

Ray McPherson, Don Knutson, Ed Hartz, Jim Goodell, Lew Moore, and my father.

The Dash 80: The 707 Prototype and the Start of It All

On July 15, 1954, the thirty-eighth anniversary of The Boeing Company, its new Model 367-80—the Dash 80—took its maiden flight over Seattle. Chief Test Pilot, Alvin "Tex" Johnston, was in the pilot's seat, with Dix Loesch his copilot. Tex said, "She flew like a bird, only faster." A prototype for the 707 and KC-135 tanker, the Dash 80 was a test bed, first to convince the military to go ahead with the KC-135, then as a way for Boeing to test all sorts of configurations of the wings, tail, and landing gear—whatever improvements the Boeing engineers dreamed up for the 707 or that the military demanded for the KC-135. Because it was a test airplane, it had only a few "passenger" windows in the cabin, and its interior was mostly instrumentation with some passenger seats for test crews. From the outside, though, it looked like the early 707s that soon followed it into the skies.

Most everyone who has lived in Seattle or worked at Boeing, as well as anyone interested in aviation history, has heard about Tex rolling Boeing's new Dash 80 over the Seafair festivities on Lake Washington during the summer of 1955. It was unexpected, dramatic, daring, and caught on film. The media went wild with it. The stunt was a *very* big deal in the new world of commercial jet aviation.

Bill Allen was Boeing's president at the time. Boeing had much riding on the 707 prototype, its first commercial jet airliner. Seattle was hosting two conventions of aviation industry players at the same time as the week-long Seafair festivities: the International Air Transport Association and the Aircraft Industries Association. Seafair was (and still is) a multi-day summer festival with parades, Highland games, pirates staging a mock-invasion of the city, the crowning of fair royalty, and numerous small events. The culmination of Seafair's festivities is the Gold Cup unlimited hydroplane races on Lake Washington on Sunday afternoon. In more recent years, the Blue Angels have provided an aerial half-time show that blows your socks off. It's still a big deal.

In the summer of 1955, as many as 350,000 people were in attendance at Seafair, sitting in bleachers along the shores of the lake, or in boats and yachts of varying sizes tied to a log boom surrounding the oval race course on the lake, a sort of party flotilla with ringside seats awaiting the roar of the unlimited hydroplanes.

Allen had invited several aviation industry VIPs to watch the hydroplane races from the vantage of a yacht tied to the log boom. A rumor had circulated that Boeing would fly the Dash 80 over the race course between heats of the hydroplane race. The huge, four-engine jetliner was so new that even in Seattle it was a rare and exciting thing to see it flying overhead, especially at low altitudes.

Tex was piloting the Dash 80 this day; Jim Gannett was his copilot and Dix Loesch was also onboard. The Seafair crowd heard the jet approach and looked skyward to the amazing sight of the big lumbering jet doing a slow flyby just 300 feet above them. That was exciting enough, but then, just after passing over the race course, Tex pulled the Dash 80's nose up and commenced a slow, easy, roll. A crewmember took photos from inside as the airplane was upside down. Seafair crowds on the ground were stunned. Many surely held their breath, thinking something had gone terribly wrong and the airplane would crash into the lake.

One spectacular roll wasn't enough for Tex the showman. Boeing's chief test pilot was known for being rough-around-the-edges, a bit of a cowboy and a show-off, but an excellent pilot. After completing the first roll, he circled back around, flew the Dash 80 low over the Seafair crowd again and executed a second slow roll before flying off and returning to Boeing Field.

Allen was as stunned as the rest of the crowd; he knew nothing of Tex's planned stunt. To Allen—a rather conservative attorney who became Boeing's president in 1945 and was not a pilot—it appeared reckless and dangerous. Had the airplane crashed, well, Boeing likely wouldn't have survived as a company. Tex was asked to visit Allen in his office the next business day. When Allen inquired what he thought he was doing over Seafair, Tex said, "I was selling airplanes."

Boy, did he sell airplanes. People couldn't stop talking about the stunt. They still talk about it today.

In 2005, I interviewed Jim Gannett. From 1950 to 1954, Jim was an Air Force test pilot stationed at Edwards AFB. He joined Boeing as a test pilot in Seattle in 1954, and after working on the Dash 80 and 707, he was named project pilot for the Boeing 2707 SST,[11] although he still flew test flights on the 727, 737, and 747. Jim handed me two copies of that famous photo snapped when the Dash 80 was upside down over Seafair.[12] Taken out of one of the small windows and aimed at a wing tip, the sky is down, and the Seattle city grid of homes and streets is up; the engine pods that hang under the airplane's wing are facing down and skyward. Confused? It's difficult to describe the photo and even more confusing to look at it; your eyes and brain insist that you hold it upside down, so that the cityscape is at the bottom of the photo instead of the top.[13] You have to remember that the photographer was upside down when the photo was shot.

---

[11] The Boeing 2707, a super-sonic transport (SST) design that received government financial support for development in the late 1950s, ultimately was not awarded the government funding that would have brought it into being after concerns about its environmental impacts were raised.

[12] Jim Gannett gave me two copies of this photo. I'm told that Bell Whitehead, the operations supervisor for the Dash 80 at the time, took the photo and he is given credit for it in Tex Johnston's autobiography. Brien Wygle told me that Jim Gannett once shared with him that Tex first did two practice rolls over Hood Canal before performing the two over Seafair. Jim also confided in Brien that it would be shame if all he was known for was being Tex's copilot that day.

[13] Don Cumming once chastised me for showing the famous photo upside down. He said that for years there was a big blown-up version of the photo framed and hanging on a wall in Flight Test, and it was hung upside down. Don fixed it, only to later see it upside down again. When Don retired from Boeing, Tex Johnston gave him an autographed copy of the photo, with his signature upside down. If you Google "707 roll over lake Washington," links to YouTube videos of the roll and a later interview with Tex Johnston pop up.

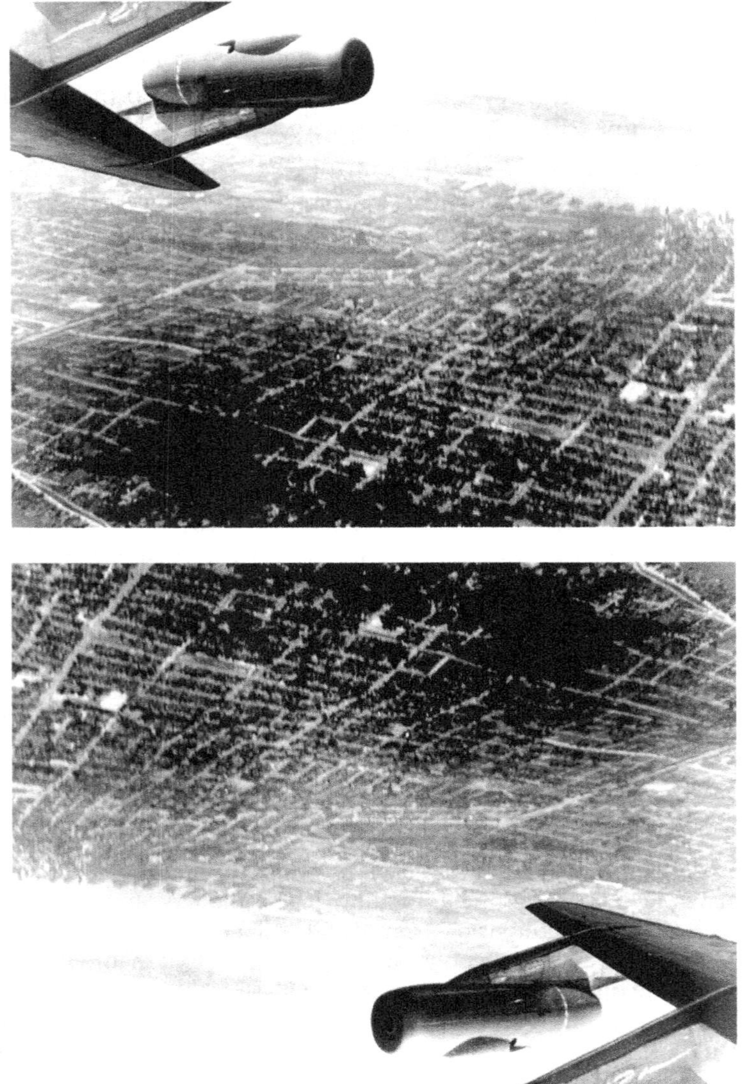

16A & 16B The famous Seafair roll photo, usual orientation on top, correct orientation on bottom.

I grew up hearing about the famous roll over Seafair, but always in an offhand way, for example being nearby when someone would ask my father about it. It was a story people would exclaim over at parties and it always got a big "Wow!" reaction. By the time I was old enough to understand the gist of these conversations, more than a decade had passed since the event occurred. Tex Johnston and the roll over Seafair had already become part of local lore and Boeing legend. Tex left Seattle for Florida in 1960, and left Boeing altogether in 1968. If I ever met him in person, I was too young to remember.

But this story—the roll over Seafair—had an enormous influence on me. It kept coming up, throughout my childhood and early adulthood. People seemed to think Tex Johnston was one of the coolest guys on the planet; as cool as any astronaut. My father was also a Boeing test pilot, like Tex. I wanted to know more. *Who are these guys, these test pilots?*

Every now and then—usually because I heard someone else talk about it—I would ask Dad about Tex's roll over Seafair. Beyond verifying that it had happened, Dad rarely elaborated. If my brothers or I asked Dad if *he* had rolled a Boeing jet, Dad would obfuscate or deny outright that he had. When I was in my twenties and older, if I shared with friends that my father was a Boeing test pilot, the Roll Over Seafair (by then it was discussed in ways that demanded capital letters) would invariably come up. Some would ask the inevitable: *Did your father ever do that*? I'd tell them no, because that's what I had always been led to believe. Of course, Dad occasionally did aerobatics in small private airplanes, including one called the Citabria (*airbatic* spelled backward). But never, as far as I knew at that time, did he roll a Boeing commercial jet.

At some point I thought to ask Dad what it might be like inside the airplane as it went through the roll. I imagined people and things that weren't strapped down being tossed all around. He easily answered that, if done correctly, the passengers wouldn't even know they were doing a roll unless they looked out the window. If a full drink was on a tray table, he said, it wouldn't spill. He explained that the *g*-forces were such that everything stayed in its place. This is why, he added with confidence, the maneuver as Tex performed it over Seafair was completely safe. The airplane was designed to withstand the minimal stresses of a roll; indeed, it was designed to withstand so much more. To my father and the other test pilots, the roll that Tex performed was certainly showy, but no big deal in terms of piloting. Clearly Tex knew that before he did the roll. Test pilots aren't stupid or reckless. But the general public? How were they to know that such a huge airplane—one that looked as if it shouldn't even be able to get off the ground, let alone fly—could safely roll? The public reaction to Tex's Dash 80 roll over Seafair was incredible.

✈

Soon after being transferred to Seattle, my father was checked out in the Dash 80 by Tex Johnston. The next day, Dad was the pilot in command of a routine test flight on the Dash 80. Some Air Force personnel, including a lieutenant colonel pilot, were sitting in the cabin. "The lieutenant colonel comes up into the cockpit and looks around," Dad remembered. "He asks, 'How much time do you have in it, Lew?' I turned to my copilot and asked him what time we took off. The lieutenant colonel scowled and walked back to his seat."

My father continued test flying the Dash 80 along with the B-47 and B-52. In those days, it wasn't unusual for employees from other areas of Boeing to be offered a ride on a routine test flight as a reward for a job well done.

The Movie Flight

Around 2004, my mother hired someone to come in and clean her house every couple of weeks. This woman was close to my age. The house cleaner mentioned my mother's name to her own father, who was retired from Boeing and living in Arizona. He wondered if my mother was related to Lew Wallick.

This sort of thing has happened too many times to count in my life. Someone with some connection to Boeing will learn my name and ask, "Are you related to Lew Wallick?"

In this case, the connection led to a wonderful story about my father and the Dash 80. The house cleaner's father—James Woodrow Day—hired on at Boeing in 1938 as a woodworker in the old Red Barn building.[14] He rapidly advanced through the ranks, retiring in 1978 after thirty-eight years, most in management.

On August 16, 1956, Jim took a very memorable flight on the Dash 80. "I was on cloud nine," he told me in 2004 when I called him at his home in Arizona. "It was my first jet flight." Jim had learned to fly at Smith Field in Kent, Washington, during World War II, doing spins and stalls and thoroughly enjoying flying. He had also flown on many piston-engine commercial airplanes for work, including the DC-3, DC-4, DC-5, the Lockheed Constellation, and Boeing C-97s and Stratocruisers. But this particular Dash 80 flight made such an impression that a few days later he wrote the story out in longhand. Jim's story provides the unique perspective of a knowledgeable and seasoned air traveler experiencing for the first time the incredible difference between propeller and jet commercial aircraft in a way few people are lucky enough to do: during an actual test flight. What follows—with Jim's gracious permission—is a slightly abridged version of the story he wrote in 1956.

> The phone rang one day. My boss, Joe Donnelly, seemed very serious. "If you get over to the B-52 flight test hangar right away, you may get to go up on the Dash 80 for a 'movie flight.'"
>
> [Jim reasonably thought "movie flight" meant obtaining footage for some sort of Hollywood film.]
>
> It didn't take long to drive from the Renton plant to the B-52 flight test hangar at Boeing Field. As I told the polite young man at the Operations desk that I was going up on the Dash 80, I wondered to myself, "Where are the pilots?" I was told to take a seat because there would be a short wait of ten to fifteen minutes as the airplane was

[14] The Red Barn is one of the original structures of Boeing's early airplane-manufacturing facility. Built in 1909, in 1975 it became part of the Museum of Flight after being moved to its current location at Boeing Field. The Red Barn hosts exhibits depicting The Boeing Story from its beginning in 1916 through 1958.

being readied for flight.

As I nervously waited for my first jet ride, I consoled myself with the thought that at least I would be in good hands, as I thought Tex Johnston or Dix Loesch would surely be at the controls. After all, Tex was the pilot who'd barrel-rolled the Dash 80 over the Seafair hydroplane races. And Dix Loesch was the pilot who, when the vertical fin [of a KC-135] was damaged during violent test maneuvers, with great skill regained control and brought the plane back to a safe landing.

The quiet man at the desk brought me back to reality with the words, "Okay Jim, the airplane is ready." He picked up a briefcase by the desk. I thought he was probably taking some important information out to the pilot. When we emerged from the hangar, there in the bright sunlight was the most beautiful airplane I had ever laid eyes on, gleaming aluminum lower body and yellow top with soft brown speed stripe. It appeared to be in motion even while parked on the tarmac.

As we approached the airplane, we were joined by my friend Logan Garrison of Facilities. He excitedly told me that he was also going up on the "movie flight."

The polite young man with the briefcase entered the airplane first, directed us to a triple-passenger seat 10 or 15 feet aft of the wing as he proceeded to sit in the pilot's seat!

Calmly and without any fanfare, he started giving instructions to the crew and very confidently flipping switches on the overhead panels, checking out the controls while at the same time visually reading all instruments on the panels.

To say that I was greatly impressed would be a tremendous understatement. Finally as we buckled up, I turned to Logan and asked if he knew the pilot. He saw my worried look and said, "No, he must be a recent hire."

Well, that didn't help any, and when the ground-support crew removed the two emergency escape hatches, one over each wing, I began to have a feeling of insecurity. "Well," I was wondering, "where are the movie actors?" when in walked two men with tripod-mounted cameras. I thought "Now we're getting somewhere." Imagine my chagrin when they pointed the cameras out over the wings, attached the tripods to fittings on the floor and then strapped parachutes on their backs.

**17 Lew Wallick in a 707 cockpit in flight, 1959.
Photo: Author's collection.**

When the main entrance doors closed, Hank Probst, the flight test engineer, came back to make sure we were securely fastened in our seats. A voice came over the PA system. It was our pilot, Lew Wallick, giving us a brief outline of our flight plan. He told us that the cameras would take moving pictures of the wings during various flight maneuvers. (So that's why it was a "movie flight!")

Lew did his thing in the cockpit and soon I heard the muffled whine of one jet engine after another coming to life. It was rather unreal: no propeller blades rotating outside the window, no vibration, no loud noise like the old propeller-driven airplanes currently in use.

As Lew increased the engine RPM and then released the brakes, the airplane started moving quietly and effortlessly to the north section of the field. As the throttles were advanced for takeoff, all that power moved us down the field, slowly at first, and then faster and faster as we passed by all the airplanes lined up for delivery. Lew held her on the runway until the speed was right, then he rotated it up. We left the ground at a very steep angle; we were climbing like a homesick angel!

I couldn't help thinking that if this were a piston-powered airplane at this steep takeoff angle it would already be in an uncontrolled stall. But this baby just seemed like it had power to burn, up and up with no letup in its angle of climb. Finally we leveled off, and the engine throttles were placed in cruise mode. It was so quiet in the airplane that there was the sensation of gliding, instead of flying, and I had a difficult time convincing myself that we were flying straight and level with such a low power setting.

Lew is back on the PA system telling us that the tests today will involve power-off, power-on stalls, near vertical turns, and emergency descents.

Wow.

So here comes the first power-off. The control wheel is pulled back until the nose comes up in the stall and the tail starts to shake. Then the vibration moves up the body and out to the wings that are now flapping slightly. Finally, the speed diminishes and no longer supports the flight of the airplane, and as with most good airplanes, the nose drops as the airplane goes into a clean dive with neither wing dipping nor resulting tail spin. In just a brief span of seconds, we have dropped several thousand feet of altitude, and I have the sinking feeling in the pit of my stomach like the rapid drop of an elevator.

Now we climb back up to the required altitude, and Lew comes on the PA to tell us this power-on stall will be more violent, with more tail and body motion and finally, wing flapping.

Well he sure had that right. As the nose came up in the stall and engines with full power, the whole airplane seemed to come to life with tail, body shaking, wings flapping about 10 to 12 feet at the wing tips. The engines on their pylons seemed to be rotating or contra-rotating like they didn't know which direction they were supposed to go. With all the shaking going on I was hardly aware of the sudden loss of altitude again.

It was a very frightening procedure. When it seemed like all hell was going to break loose, Logan looked at the cameramen with their parachutes and us without any, and said, "Which one are you going to piggyback with?" With my crew-cut hair standing up straighter than normal, I shouted, "The nearest one!"

Vertical turns were not too bad. One minute the airplane is flying straight and level, then the left wing is straight up, and I am looking straight down at the ground through my window, then back level. Once more, before I could say it, the left wing is straight down, and I am looking across the body to the opposite window and looking straight down at the ground on that side.

Now Lew is explaining that we have clearance to approach Sea-Tac Airport from the south (remember, no jet traffic there at this time), altitude about 8,000 feet. He says even though there is good visibility, we will pretend we are in heavy cloud cover. When we see a hole in the clouds, we will go into emergency descent mode. At the right moment, he lowers landing gear, extends flaps, raises speed brakes, pulls the nose up, and we are dropping like a lead sled. Before I know what has happened, we are almost down to ground level. He applies some power and cleans up the airplane to buzz the runway.

We are probably 50 to 100 feet above the runway heading north at about 200 knots when he applies full power and the airplane accelerates like we are taking off all over again. As I look over at the old airport terminal, there are hundreds of people on the balcony, waving frantically at their first glimpse of America's future commercial Jet Age.

As we accelerate, Lew pulls the airplane into a steep climbing turn and we see Vashon Island and lower Puget Sound below us.

Coming into Boeing Field is a breeze as Lew greases it onto the runway using brakes and engine reversers for its return to the nest (B-52 flight test hangar).

Before we leave the airplane, Logan and I both shake hands with Lew Wallick, congratulating him on an absolutely superb flight. (With my teeth chattering; what a superb pilot!) Coming down the stairs with my legs still trembling, I have an almost irresistible urge to kiss the ground, but I do resist.

Arriving back at the Renton plant, I made straight for Joe Donnelly's office. "Well, Jim, how did you enjoy your first movie flight?" he asked. I replied there was never a movie that could elicit the exhilaration and admiration I felt for the people that designed and built the airplane and the crew that flew it.

It's not surprising that Jim and Logan didn't recognize my father; he had just transferred from Wichita in 1955. As I came to realize, though, it wasn't long before *everyone* at Boeing knew who Lew Wallick was and admired him.[15]

---

[15] In 2013, I visited the Boeing Archives, located in a Boeing office park in Bellevue. I was instructed to check in at a separate building so that I could have clearance to get through the guard station. When I provided my name

Jim remembered that "movie flight" lasting about an hour. They went up to Bellingham, and out over the Olympic Mountains. "Lew was so cool and collected," Jim said. This story is one of my favorites because it shows the father I knew—friendly, modest, confident, and informative. Jim's vivid description of the flight also provides a good sense of what "routine tests" felt like to a non-flight-test person along for the ride. Commercial airline passengers will never feel the high bank turns or violent stall vibrations Jim experienced—which test crews experience all the time—precisely because the test programs find each airplane's limits and create airline flight manuals requiring operation well within those limits so that airline passengers are safe and never feel uncomfortable. Flight test crews routinely put the airplanes through maneuvers airline pilots should never find themselves in; they intentionally push the airplane's envelope to prove that even in some worst-case scenario where the airplane is flying beyond its flight manual limits, the airplane will remain structurally sound.

The Workhorse

The Dash 80 took a beating in those early years as Tex, Dix, Jim Gannett, my father, and others worked out all the bugs or experimented with new designs. Even before its first flight, the Dash 80's left main landing gear failed during taxi tests, leaving the airplane stranded on the runway, tilted to one side like a wounded bird. A month later, there was an incident with the nose gear at Boeing Field. Dix was in the cockpit with Tex and described it to me.

> We'd made a series of takeoffs and touch-and-go's. We'd used a lot a braking in one or more of them. On

---

to the sixtyish woman behind the reception desk, she said, "Wallick, Wallick... why do I know that name?" I offered that perhaps it was because my father had been a Boeing test pilot. "Lew Wallick? Oh my God, I loved that man! I'm so honored to meet *you*!" I was happily stunned by her reaction. Long after he retired, even after he had passed away, my father's good reputation at Boeing lives on with those who knew him and worked with him. It makes me so proud to be his daughter.

> about the third or fourth landing, there's no braking going on! Tex is saying, "The brakes are gone." He immediately switched over to the nose gear steering. By then we're so far down the runway, it's impossible to take off again. Then he did the exact right thing, he started turning off the runway and through the dirt and sod. I didn't even realize until we'd stomped off through the weeds that what he was trying to do was ground loop the airplane [get one wing to dig into the ground to slow the airplane down]. By God it was working. But just as he made the final turn at the end of the runway in the dirt, we hit a ditch and it broke the nose gear off. The funny thing was, Tex never was mad about the brakes failing. But he was mad about that damn ditch [being] there because he said he could have made it.

Dix added that what Tex did in that extreme situation was an example of his good instincts as a pilot. On one side of the runway were private airplanes, on the other, a row of B-52s; Tex chose the best option to minimize damage and injury to airplanes and people. Boeing had the Dash 80 back in flying condition in a matter of days, with better brakes.

There exists some Boeing film of another Dash 80 braking incident that has become one of those legendary stories that's often trotted out when the old-timers get together. Jim Gannett and my father were doing taxi runs to test the thrust reversers. Dad told me they *always* had it in reverse, never took it off. At one point, at the south end of the runway, they were told they had a fire under the wing. Hydraulic fluid was leaking onto a hot brake rotor. Jim shut the engines down and ordered the ten- to twelve-person crew to evacuate. They exited the airplane through the belly, the baggage compartment. My father, wanting to make sure everyone had left the airplane, was the last person off. While the others ran away from the airplane, the film shows my father… strolling.

Never let them see you sweat.

The Dash 80 was used for early autopilot and automatic-landing tests. The late 1950s saw the beginning of autolanding systems. Autopilot systems were just coming on during World War II, but those primarily worked to maintain level cruising during flight. The next step was to try to automate the approach to landing. The early systems used gyros; today they use inertial systems, which smooth out the ride.

By the early 1960s, in addition to the autolanding tests in the Dash 80, Boeing was testing autostability systems, or stability augmentation systems (SAS), that automatically actuate certain flight controls to damp buffeting (shaking or vibration) or correct for unintended movement in flight. For example, the most common type of stability system is the yaw damper. Swept-wing airplanes have a tendency to yaw (move slightly to the right or left while traveling forward) and go into a Dutch roll—a sort of swinging or rocking motion to one side or the other, as if the airplane was slowly wagging its tail side to side, making the nose swing as well. Passengers don't much enjoy the sensation. The yaw damper keeps the airplane from an unintentional yaw and eliminates the possibility of a Dutch roll by determining the amount of rudder input required to damp it in case the pilot hasn't already made the correction.

Auto*landing* tests were a new sort of beast, and could get pretty exciting, according to my father. The idea behind autolanding systems was to allow airline pilots to make landings in poor-visibility conditions, such as fog or heavy rain. Generally, the autolanding system follows ILS (instrument landing system) signals in to the airport, and a radar altimeter determines the height above the ground so that the system knows when to initiate the landing flare—that last moment before landing where the airplane's nose goes up slightly and the lowered flaps are slowing its speed while ensuring the rear gear touch first—like a duck coming in to land on a lake, putting its feet out just as its wings turn to act as spoilers and slow it down.

There are redundancies built in to the autopilot and autolanding systems to minimize to all reasonable extent the possibility that anything would fail at a critical moment. But think about this for a minute. The early—and by today's standards, crude—autolanding systems had to be tested by someone: a test pilot willing to take his hands *off* the controls as the Dash 80 or early 707 made the final approach for landing. A test pilot who, up to this point in his flying career, was used to being hands-on and in control of the airplane through all phases of a flight and most particularly during landing.

These tests involved many, many landings. Sometimes it seemed all they did was take off, circle around over Seattle, land, and repeat—at one point in time watching the Space Needle literally going up just north of downtown Seattle as it was being constructed for the 1962 World's Fair.

As my father explained, when they were testing the autolanding system, the pilots had to "let it go as far as you dared" because they needed the data. Sometimes, he said, the system might cause the airplane to swerve off the runway at the last minute. As they did those repeat tests—circling past the Space Needle—an engineer specializing in the autolanding system would be in the back of the airplane where the black boxes and wires of the system were housed. The engineer had a soldering iron. In between landings, he'd change things. "I was always a little concerned he'd make a mistake!" Dad said with a laugh.

All these tests, these discoveries, mistakes, misadventures, and successes, not only made the 707s, KC-135s and subsequent Boeing airplanes better and safer, but also gave the pilots invaluable experience along the way. Whether the airplane flew as expected or not, the pilots' level of competence grew with every flight, and that experience was carried forward—to the next flight, the next derivative, the next newly designed airplane built by Boeing.

Celebrity Demo Flights

The grueling testing regimen on the Dash 80 was occasionally broken by a celebrity demonstration flight. One such flight became part of my family's lore.

Arthur Godfrey was a well-known radio and television host in the 1940s and 1950s. An avid pilot, Godfrey was involved in a near-fatal automobile accident in 1931. His injuries didn't keep him from flying privately, but they did prevent him from flying on active duty during World War II. President Franklin Roosevelt knew Godfrey and enjoyed listening to his radio shows, so despite Godfrey's disability, Roosevelt gave him a commission in the US Naval Reserves. With that ticket, Godfrey was able to get demo flights on a wide assortment of military aircraft, and eventually he owned and piloted a private DC-3.

Godfrey was given more than one demonstration flight on the Dash 80. My father took him up on one of those occasions. During the flight, Dad happened to mention to Godfrey that my mother was in the hospital, with a broken leg from a fall while snow skiing. On his own initiative, Godfrey arranged for a dozen roses to be delivered to my mother's hospital room, with a card signed by him. My mother, in her mid-thirties at the time, was *thrilled* to have a dozen roses sent to her by a national celebrity. The nurses in the hospital had to be convinced they had really come from Mr. Godfrey.

18 Left to right, front row: Tex Johnston, Lew Wallick, and Arthur Godfrey, preparing for a flight in the Dash 80. Photo: Boeing Archives.

CHAPTER THREE: LAUNCHING NEW JETS

To put your life in danger from time to time... breeds a saneness in dealing with the day-to-day trivialities.

—Nevil Shute, British novelist and aeronautical engineer

How to Certify a Commercial Jet: Learning as You Go

The Boeing 707 first took to the air on December 20, 1957.[16] In fact, that day was such a typical Seattle-area rainy winter day that pilot Tex Johnston, copilot Jim Gannett, and flight engineer Tom Layne waited through the morning for sufficiently clear weather to fly. Once they did take off at 12:30 pm from Renton Field, the weather closed in so fast that they stayed aloft a mere seven minutes before landing at nearby Boeing Field. Later in the day, with better weather, they took off again and flew for seventy-one minutes, a more typical first flight.

Five years of hard work and significant financial risk led to that auspicious day—Boeing's first commercial jet—signaling the start of the equally daunting task of testing and proving the airplane's safety in order to obtain Civil Aeronautics Authority (CAA)[17] certification. That process was completed just nine months later when the 707 was certified for airline use on September 18, 1958.

---

[16] The 707 prototype—the 367-80, or Dash 80—made its first flight on July 15, 1954. Tex Johnston's famous barrel roll over Seafair on August 7, 1955, was in the Dash 80.

[17] The Civil Aeronautics Authority (CAA) later became the Federal Aviation Agency, or FAA.

Only time would tell if Boeing's big gamble would pay off, since there was no guarantee the 707 would be profitable. Boeing's previous passenger airplane, the 377 Stratocruiser, lost the company several million dollars before the military purchased it as the KC-97 Stratotanker. Several millions more had already been invested in the research and development of the Dash 80 and 707. The entire Puget Sound region's economic welfare depended on Boeing's gamble.

Working with the Feds

In early 1958, my father was designated project pilot for the number two 707, responsible for most of the aerodynamic certification testing. "My Dash 80 time paid off for me because it got me into the commercial program earlier than some of the other guys," he told me. From that time on, Dad flew almost exclusively commercial jets, although on rare occasions he still flew a B-52 or KC-135 to keep his fingers in those programs and his skill set diverse, and sometimes he flew the F-86 chase plane.

At Boeing, there exist several kinds of test pilots, each reflecting a career progression and thus the pilot's status within the organization. To get in the door requires an engineering degree and some military or civilian flying experience. Skill and experience are then acquired on the job—and assessed by senior pilots—often as a flight test engineer while waiting to be elevated to test pilot.

After promotion to test pilot but still early in one's career, a pilot might be designated a *production test pilot*. Such a pilot will handle the first flight of each newly assembled airplane and ensure it meets the standards of the certified original. *Experimental test pilots* are seasoned pilots at the top of their game, flying development and certification programs to validate the engineering concepts in each new type of aircraft. *Project pilots* are those few experimental test pilots chosen to be the chief pilot of a new aircraft type. They act as consultants to the engineering team, often during development and certainly during certification, and are a proxy for all the pilots who will eventually fly the airplane in commercial service.[18]

Sometimes, as with my father and Brien in the early 1950s, a tragedy can create openings that move a pilot along the progression a little faster.

My father described 1958 as a very intense time, getting the first commercial jet transport in the United States tested and certified by the CAA. While an airplane manufacturer's test pilots initially test new airplanes, the CAA also had pilots who had to fly the new planes alongside the manufacturer's test pilots, verifying that the airplane would do what the manufacturer claimed and could be operated safely by airline pilots.

The CAA came into being in 1938 when President Roosevelt signed the Civil Aeronautics Act. The initial goal was to promote commerce by regulating air traffic control and airlines, and ensure aviation safety by investigating aviation accidents and making safety recommendations. By 1940, the CAA was divided into two agencies. The Civil Aeronautics Administration handled air traffic control and safety enforcement, and certified pilots and aircraft, while the Civil Aeronautics Board investigated accidents and made safety and airline operation regulations.

In 1958, the Federal Aviation Act was signed, creating a new independent agency to promote the safe and efficient use of airspace: the Federal Aviation Agency (FAA). Then in 1966, Congress authorized a new Department of Transportation (DOT) to oversee all modes of transportation in the United States. The FAA became one of its organizations and was renamed the Federal Aviation Administration (still known as the FAA). The Civil Aeronautics Board also fell under the DOT and became known as the National Transportation Safety Board (NTSB), retaining its role of investigating accidents and

---

[18] Being named project pilot at Boeing is a prestigious thing. Over the decades, such designations created many legendary associations between a particular test pilot and an airplane model: Lew Wallick and the 727; Brien Wygle and the 737; Jack Waddell and the 747; John Armstrong and the 757; Tom Edmonds and the 767; John Cashman and the 777; and Mike Carriker and the 787.

promoting safety.

The Boeing 707 was the first commercial *jet* in the United States. Until 1958, the CAA had been evaluating and certifying propeller-engine aircraft. According to my father, "We were really breaking ground, because the CAA didn't know anything about jet transports. We knew quite a bit about jet airplanes, but we didn't have a very good idea how to apply regulations."

The CAA was trying to take old regulations and mold them into something that would work for jets. "I got involved two or three years before the 707 actually started flying because I had the Dash 80 experience. I'd go back to Washington, DC, with Joe Sutter and other engineering guys who were working with the government people, trying to write a set of rules that we could use to certify airplanes." Dad said that often he was the only person in the room who had actually flown a jet.

The "rules" were always a work in progress. My father remembers that time being akin to shooting at moving targets. The joke was that the CAA guys pulled regulations out of nowhere—"hip pocket regulations"—because there really weren't any. Boeing engineers were invaluable to the process because they had been working on design issues for years and had lots of experience with the early military jets—B-47s, B-52s, and KC-135s.

Accident rates in jets were high in the early days of commercial jet transport, mainly because the airline pilots didn't have any experience in jets. They were going from low speed propeller-driven airplanes into high-speed jets, and the training programs weren't adequate. The faster jets would "get ahead" of the propeller pilots at critical times, like approaches to landings, leading to crashes.

The airlines were trying to avoid spending more money than they had to, and in those days there weren't any simulators for training. All training occurred in the airplane, which was expensive, with Boeing pilots training key airline pilots, who then trained the rest of their pilots and crews. Boeing test pilot Jim Gannett was a real leader in pilot training and writing manuals for the airlines to use, learning from airline errors and accidents when commercial jets were so new, which in turn helped Boeing play a leading role in airline training systems.

Jim was project pilot on the number one 707. Tex Johnston, as Chief Test Pilot, didn't act as project pilot on an individual airplane, like Jim and my father, but he'd still fly quite a bit on top of his duties managing the entire Flight Test division.

Despite obtaining certification in September 1958, some nine months after the airplane's first flight, the 707 program was really a continuing series of programs as different derivatives of the 707 quickly came off the assembly line: the Intercontinental (a long-range version); the 720 (a shorter, lighter-weight version); the Qantas short body 707-138 (actor John Travolta currently owns and flies one of these); and several experimental derivatives with different engines, engine mounts, and so on. According to Peter Morton, who worked his way up from ground school instructor in 1958 to VP of Human Resources before retiring in 2003, "[With the 707,] if the customer needed something special to make their routes, we would modify the airplane rather than let Douglas get the sale."

The Dash 80 was still flying a lot during this time as well, as a test bed for many of these new designs. For instance, the leading edge of the wings that were developed for the 720, to give it higher speed, was tested on the Dash 80. My father and others were still flying the Dash 80 while they were also testing the 707 and its derivatives. Each new derivative took eight or nine months to certify. (By today's standards, nine months is very fast.) Much of the testing took place at Edwards AFB, where the crews often went for a month at a time. My father remembers most of the "senior" pilots of that era being involved in 707 testing: Brien Wygle, Jack Waddell, Ray McPherson, Jim Goodell, Sandy McMurray, and Don Knutson. Perhaps they were senior in terms of longevity with Boeing, but most were in their mid-thirties. "Between the testing and the training, just about everybody got involved," Dad said.

It was during this busy time of certifying 707s that my father was introduced to a CAA pilot out of Los Angeles, Walt Haldeman. The two men quickly became friends and shared many hours of flight time in various airplanes over the ensuing years. They also shared a wicked sense of humor, as an incident that occurred during Memorial Day weekend in 1958 illustrates.

"We got along really well and spent a lot of time together," Dad said. "One time, down at Edwards, we had two or three days off. He was building a new house in the Los Angeles area, so I went along with a couple of other guys, engineers who didn't have anything to do that had to be done right away. We worked a couple of days in his house, helped him stain ceilings, stuff like that. Kind of fun, a different sort of thing to do." Dad acknowledged that these days, that sort of conflict of interest would have gotten everyone fired. But things were much friendlier back then. Commercial jets were new and everyone was feeling their way through the certification process. It was a cooperative effort between Boeing and the CAA.

Like my father, most of the pilots working on certifying the 707 and its derivatives had previously tested and flown Boeing's military jets, working closely with military personnel to gain acceptance of military airplanes. There was no sense of a conflict of interest when flying and becoming friendly with military personnel because they were the customer.

With the 707—a commercial transport jet designed for airlines—the pilots found themselves in a similar working relationship with the CAA pilots, but now the CAA held the key to Boeing's success. Without certification, there could be no sales to the airlines. It was a new relationship for my father and most of the other test pilots, in an era with few workplace guidelines or regulations in terms of interactions between manufacturers and the federal government.

I think my father's approach to working with the CAA pilots was the same as with the military personnel: friendly and cooperative, with everyone working toward the same goal—a safe airplane. They were all engineers, a breed renowned for their honesty, integrity, and straightforward approach. While my father and some of the other Boeing pilots might have developed opinions regarding the flying abilities of some of the CAA/FAA pilots they worked with over the years, I never heard any of them complain about the requirements imposed on the Boeing pilots in terms of proving the Boeing airplanes. In fact, my father formed strong bonds with a few of the government pilots. I remember an FAA pilot from California—Joseph John "Tym" Tymczyszyn (1918–1999)—bringing his family up to our Lake Sammamish house on vacation at least twice in the 1960s. Today, that would be a clear conflict of interest. In the 1950s and 1960s, it was business as usual, and no one thought twice about it.

I'll go into more detail about how a commercial jet is certified for airline use and the sorts of tests done when I describe my father's work on the 727 and later models. Here, while talking about the 707 and that intense period of testing and certification in the late 1950s, I'll share one of my father's favorite flying stories, one that included his friend and CAA pilot Walt Haldeman.

In May 1958, Dad and other flight test crew members were at Edwards AFB, conducting certification tests of the second 707, painted in Pan American colors. Boeing wasn't the only airplane manufacturer trying to bring a commercial jet to market. Boeing always kept tabs on the competition, in this case, Douglas Aircraft in Long Beach, California. Douglas was close to launching the DC-8, a jet they claimed would be superior to the Boeing 707. A lot was at stake for both companies; it was a classic rivalry of aviation titans. At the dawn of the commercial jet age, both companies wanted to be Number One right out of the gate.[19]

The local news media were full of stories of the DC-8's upcoming maiden voyage on May 30, the Friday of Memorial Day weekend. Bleachers had been erected at the Long Beach Airport for employees and family to witness the first takeoff, which was set for noon.

That Friday was just another test day for my father and the rest of the 707's crew. The crew got up at 4:30 am, ate

---

[19] I grew up aware of the rivalry, but in an understated way. For example, my father and uncle Jesse both delighted in teaching the family dog tricks that went something like this: Place a treat on the end of the dog's nose and tell her it's a gift from Douglas. The dog doesn't move. "Oh, I was only teasing; it's from Boeing!" and the dog instantly gobbles the treat.

breakfast, drove to the base, and took off at 6:30 am for the first test flight of the day. Dad was piloting, while Walt had the copilot's seat. Also onboard was Don Archer, a Boeing flight test engineer. Don hired on at Boeing as a flight test analysis engineer in November 1957, after a stint at Edwards AFB as an Air Force flight engineer. The morning's test plan called for some low-altitude climb-performance tests over the Catalina Island area. They flew until about 9:30 am, when they'd burned so much fuel that they could no longer maintain the required gross weight and center of gravity needed for the tests. Leaving the test area, they climbed to about 15,000 feet and headed back toward Edwards AFB.

It so happened that the route back to Edwards AFB had them flying near Long Beach Airport. Over the flight-test radio frequency that both Boeing and Douglas used to communicate with their mobile radio stations, Dad and Walt could hear discussions among the various Douglas test support stations about the upcoming first flight. Dad and Walt decided they'd fly over the Long Beach Airport and take a closer look at Boeing's new rival, the DC-8.

"About 15 miles from Long Beach, I selected tower frequency, identified myself as N707 Papa Alpha, and requested to overfly the airport at 5,000 feet," Dad recalled. The tower acknowledged his request. There was a brief pause. The air traffic controller then asked if they were a Boeing 707.

"I confirmed that we were indeed a Boeing 707," Dad continued. "The tower cleared us to overfly at 5,000 feet. Shortly, the tower came back and cleared us to 3,000 feet, which I acknowledged. Very shortly, the tower cleared us to 1,000 feet, which I again acknowledged." The closer they got to Long Beach Airport, the lower the controller—on his own initiative—cleared them to fly.

Obviously, the guys in the tower were enjoying this. The 707's first flight had occurred just six months earlier, so it was still a unique airplane for anyone to see flying, including airport personnel. What air traffic controller could resist a closer look, especially if it might tweak some local noses in the process?

"When we were about three miles from the airport, without

any request from me, the tower cleared us to overfly the airport at any altitude we wished!" Dad said. Once again, he acknowledged the clearance. Lowering the landing gear and flaps, they descended to about 500 feet and flew the length of the runway, adding thrust at the end and climbing out with a roar of engines, leaving a thick trail of black engine exhaust in their wake.[20]

"As we were over the airport, there was absolute silence on the flight-test radio frequency," Dad laughed.

Flyby accomplished, Dad and Walt returned to Edwards AFB, landed, and planned a second flight later in the day. By the time they took off for their afternoon tests, the DC-8 had taken off on its first flight. Dad and Walt discussed that it might be nice to see what the DC-8 looked like *in flight*.

"Instead of going to our test points, we spent an hour or so looking for them," recalls Don. "We finally found them: the DC-8 with its landing gear down through the doors, in formation with a couple of fighter airplanes. Lew pulls up alongside and on their radio frequency says, 'Nice looking formation.' We never got a word back from them."

Don happened to know the DC-8 pilot in command that day, a guy named Bill Magruder. When Don asked him about it years later, Magruder admitted knowing they were there, but chose not to respond.

"I always wondered if those photographers in the chase planes ever took photos of us in formation," my father said.

"Nah," Don said. "I think they were too startled."

Dad thoroughly enjoyed showing off the 707 with that low overfly, perhaps stealing a little of Douglas's thunder and having a laugh at their expense, then flying in formation with them that afternoon. He thought nothing more of it. All in good fun, right?

The next day, Walt arrived at the base and told my father they were likely in trouble. Or at least Walt thought *he* was. Mr. Douglas—Donald Douglas, who founded Douglas Aircraft in

---

[20] Early jet engines emitted enormous amounts of black smoke, especially upon takeoff. Today's jet engines run significantly cleaner, with no visible exhaust.

1921—had called the regional CAA office in Los Angeles and raised hell with Walt's supervisor.

Apparently, the local media at the airport for the DC-8's first flight were still in coffee shops surrounding the airport waiting for the noon hour when they heard the 707 roar by. Running outside, all they saw was a jet with heavy black exhaust flowing from its engines climbing away. They ran to find telephones and reported to their radio stations that the DC-8 had successfully taken off. One result of these broadcasts was that many Douglas employees on their way to the airport to witness the first flight turned back for home, thinking they'd missed it all. Mr. Douglas was very upset. The DC-8's first-flight publicity had been spoiled.

Walt's supervisor had warned him that Douglas was thinking of filing a violation with the CAA against the crew.

"But we were perfectly legal," said Don.

The Boeing crew remained at Edwards AFB conducting tests for another three weeks.

"I later found out that Mr. Douglas also called [Boeing President] Bill Allen and apparently read him the riot act as well," my father said. "No one in Boeing management said anything to me, good or bad. Not a word from Tex Johnston, who was the boss then. I got back to the office and nobody said a word about it, period."

The Boeing crew wasn't done messing with the DC-8 pilots. Some months later, in April 1959, my father, flight test engineer Don Cumming, and other members of the Boeing crew were back at Edwards AFB with a 707-320, the stretched version of the 707. Douglas had a crew there with their DC-8, conducting their own tests. Dad found another way to one-up Douglas.

Word was out that Douglas was having trouble with their thrust reversers, and their use on the airplane was being delayed. The reversers on Boeing's 707 were working great. Though commercial airplanes were getting bigger, they still operated on airports designed for smaller aircraft, so it was important to be able to decelerate quickly when landing to avoid overshooting the runway. Thrust reversers temporarily change the direction of an engine's exhaust, directing thrust forward rather than aft. This helps the airplane slow down just after landing, reducing wear on brakes and allowing for shorter landing distances.

"Somehow, I'd been tipped off that Magruder was demonstrating the DC-8 to an Air Force general, some test pilots and engineers one morning," Dad said. Boeing's crew—with Walt Haldeman flying in the copilot's seat again—was out early, doing a series of takeoffs and landings. They would take off in one direction, do a 180-degree turn, and land the opposite direction, turning off the runway at the same end from which they'd started, holding there until they were ready to go again.

"I was keeping my eyes open for this DC-8," Dad continued. Just as the DC-8 landed, the 707 was ready to taxi out for another takeoff. The DC-8 was just leaving the runway as Dad starting taxiing out toward it. Seeing the conflict developing, Dad let it progress. According to Don, the tower airman was in a panic, but Dad told him not to worry, the 707 would get out of the way.

"Here we go, nose to nose!" Dad said. "I know he can't back up. I use the reversers, back up, open the window and wave him by." How better to show the Air Force generals that Boeing had working thrust reversers and Douglas didn't?

Magruder never said anything to my father about that incident, either. By now, Magruder must have either secretly admired my father, or hated him.

Apparently Dad was having a lot of fun showing off this capability of the 707. Don Cumming remembers Dad backing up the 707 several times during that particular trip to Edwards AFB. "We had little wands behind the wheels on the airplane that measured lift-off point," Don said. "They'd just drag down the runway, little whiskers. Every time Lew would back the airplane up it would bust the wands off. The instrumentation guys would have to build new wands during the night to get the airplane ready for the morning. One morning, after one of these episodes, we go out and see that the wands have little wheels." Luckily even the shop guys had senses of humor.

Later, Douglas was touting the use of their thrust reversers in flight, to slow and descend for landing. The DC-8 didn't have spoilers on its wings, which accomplished that slow descent task on the 707. "Walt and I were talking about that," recalled my father. "We wondered how this is going to work. So one day, we were flying our airplane and put the engines in reverse to see how it felt. We discovered there's a lot of buffet and noise, and increased drag. Of course, we didn't tell Douglas that. When they finally got their reversers working, they had the same problem." Turns out Douglas could only use reversers on the two outboard engines, rather than all four as originally planned, because the disturbed air flow from the inboard engines hitting the tail was too severe.

"If you've ever flown on a DC-8," said Don Archer, "you felt that rumble when they descended."

Ah, nothing like a friendly rivalry between industry competitors to keep one's job fun.

Douglas wasn't the only potential target. "When the Convair 880 was scheduled for its first flight [in January 1959], Walt and I joked about going to San Diego," said Dad, "but decided it was too far away."

In those early days of 707-120 testing, Dad and a Boeing crew took a 707 to Albuquerque, New Mexico, for high-altitude testing. It was January 1959. Don Cumming was along as part of the crew and remembers a good deed done on their way back to Seattle. "There was a young airman in the terminal, just walking around as long-faced as anything," said Don. "We found out that this kid [had] had a ride back to Seattle in a T33 [two-seater jet trainer used by the Navy and Air Force], and he'd just gotten bumped by a colonel. We tell Lew the story. Lew says 'Put him onboard, we'll take him to Seattle.' We all chuckled about, here's this guy, he's going to go back to Fort Lewis and tell everybody he flew the 707 from Albuquerque to Seattle."

Pan Am had just started service with the 707 in the United States a couple of months earlier. That lucky young airman was one of the earliest jet age passengers. "The colonel had to ride all the way back in a T33. The kid was all over the airplane, people talking to him and showing him things," said Don.

Selling Boeing Jets to Howard Hughes

By 1958, Boeing had already sunk a lot of money and time into the development of the 707. They needed a significant order from a large airline to get the sales ball rolling. TWA was interested. Howard Hughes was its majority stockholder. Boeing was wooing him.

In early October, Brien Wygle, Harley Beard, and a ground crew of several men took the Dash 80 to Los Angeles to give Hughes a demonstration flight. They expected to be in LA for a couple days. Their expectations were quickly dashed by Mr. Hughes's quirky personality; yet when they finally did return to Seattle, it was with stories they enjoyed telling for years to come.

Douglas and Convair were designing competing commercial jets; it was important for Boeing to get orders for its 707 before their competitors' airplanes hit the market. The goal was to show Hughes the 707's capabilities and convince him to buy. All available 707s were tied up in testing, however, so the Dash 80 (the 707 prototype) was taken to LA. Brien's instructions from Boeing management were to bring the plane back to Seattle as quickly as possible, but to avoid alienating Mr. Hughes. These directives turned out to be incompatible.

By the 1950s, Hughes was a very successful businessman and extremely wealthy. He was tall, lean, and handsome, with long dark hair slicked back off his forehead. He had owned RKO Radio Pictures, the movie studio. He dated famous movie stars, including Jean Peters, whom he secretly married in 1957.

Brien and Harley knew of Hughes's general reputation in aviation—he had set speed records flying around the world (ninety-one hours in 1938) and had designed and tested various airplanes. They were aware of his role in TWA. They also knew and appreciated that he had produced several movies with flying themes in the 1930s and 1940s. They admired him, and assumed he was a skilled pilot. The man they met and flew with, however, turned out to be not at all what they anticipated.

Things got strange even before the crew left Boeing Field. They planned to depart at 9:30 am on Thursday, October 8th. "Two engines were already started when the tower called and said, 'Shut down; we'll send somebody out to explain it to you,'" Harley recalled. "We shut down, and the deal was, Howard had called and he did not want us to arrive before 12:30 pm. He would call back and tell us when we could start the engines." Harley—a balding, burly former Air Force pilot who had survived bailing out of a B-24 over the Black Sea during World War II—wasn't used to being told how to fly an airplane by a stranger, even if it was Mr. Hughes. Approval to start engines eventually came, and they took off, heading for LA. Because of a tail wind, they still arrived early, at 12:15 pm.

When they taxied to their parking spot, they spied Boeing's advance man, Bob Brown, on the tarmac. He was waiting with several rental cars to transport the crew to their motel. By the time Brien and Harley completed their paperwork and stepped out of the plane, all the cars had disappeared. As Harley looked around, wondering what the hell was going on and where the cars had gone, a man in a dark suit approached him, introducing himself as one of Hughes's staff.

"We've dismissed all your rental cars," the man informed Harley.

"Why?" Harley asked, puzzled.

"Well, we've also cancelled all of your motel reservations," he replied. "Mr. Hughes would appreciate it if you would be his guests while you're here."

What the man didn't say, but what Harley now began realizing, was that Hughes had taken over complete control of this demonstration trip.

Harley and the ground crew got into cars provided by Hughes and rode to the Sheraton Hotel in downtown LA, where they checked in. When Harley looked around, he realized Brien wasn't with them.

Brien had been whisked off separately by another member of Hughes's staff to the Beverly Hills Hotel, the most elite hotel in LA at the time, favored by celebrities and movers and shakers. Brien was provided one of the private cottages in the gardens.

Like most Boeing employees, Brien was used to modest motels, so it seemed quite luxurious to him. Hotel staff came in each night to lay a fire for his comfort.

Shortly after Brien arrived at the hotel, a man named Bill Gay, one of Hughes's personal staff, contacted him. "Howard chose his staff out of a group of Mormons," Brien recalled, even though Hughes wasn't Mormon. "I think he selected Mormons because he felt they wouldn't drink and carouse and they'd be reliable." Some referred to Hughes's staff as "the Mormon Mafia."

Gay told Brien that Hughes wanted to fly the next day, October 9th. A car would pick Brien up at 11:00 am to take him to the airport, where Hughes would meet him. "We never, ever, made a schedule, or even close," Brien said. "When 11:00 went by and I hadn't heard from anybody, Gay or one of the other staff would call and say, 'Mr. Hughes is running a little late today and instead of 11:00 am, we'll make it 1:00 pm. Stay in your hotel room.'"

And Brien would wait, unwilling to leave for fear of annoying Mr. Hughes. This became the routine nearly every day—a set start time that would be delayed, often more than once, followed by more waiting alone in his cottage. Usually on the final delay, Hughes would come on the phone to speak to Brien directly, as he did on October 9th.

"Oh Brien, are you there?" Hughes started. "I'm sorry about the delays, but I'll have a car around for you." There was a pause.

"What time do you have?" Hughes asked. Brien replied it was 4:30 pm.

"Okay," Hughes said. "There'll be a car there at five o'clock, and he'll pull up to the side street. Now don't you go out ahead, don't wait there, but step out onto the sidewalk there, the curb, at exactly five o'clock."

Brien agreed to do this. He would check his watch, hang back in the shrubbery for some minutes and then emerge precisely at five o'clock. Just as he stepped onto the sidewalk, a Chevrolet pulled up to the curb with only a Mormon driver inside. "It was like cloak and dagger, except there wasn't anything to be cloak and dagger about," Brien said. This became the standard routine for transporting Brien to the airport.

Hughes was also living at the Beverly Hills Hotel, in one of the other cottages. Brien didn't know it at the time, and Howard never let on that they were neighbors. Nor did he ever offer to have Brien ride with him to the airport.

When Brien finally did reach the airport and the Dash 80 that day, the crew had already been alerted and had prepared the airplane to fly. Harley had completed the preflight checks. Everyone was ready and waiting for Hughes, who arrived a few minutes later. When Hughes got out of his plain, old, chauffeured Chevrolet, he spent a good ten minutes giving the driver precise instructions on the route he should take on the return drive.

Hughes then introduced himself to Brien, asking to be addressed as Howard. Brien found Hughes to be very affable. But Hughes's appearance was a bit shocking. "He was tall and gaunt," Brien recalled. "Thin. He told me he'd been ill. Sometime later I heard that he'd had a nervous breakdown and had been hospitalized around that time. That was not generally known."

There were other unique aspects of Hughes's appearance. He had a scraggly beard. He wore an ordinary white dress shirt. His trousers were rolled up at the ankles and were held up with an old necktie he had woven through the belt loops and knotted. He wore dress shoes, but there were no laces, and he didn't wear socks. Brien remembers thinking that his attire was quite odd for a man reputed to be a titan of industry.

Harley also took note of Hughes's unusual appearance. "He really needed a shave," Harley recalled. "I heard later he'd had a beard and decided to cut it off with a pair of scissors and that's why he needed a shave." Once Hughes got into the pilot's seat, he kicked off his shoes. Harley vividly remembered noticing that his toenails were extraordinarily long.

Hughes's obsession with germs and cleanliness—more commonly known in later years—was also evident. "He turned around and asked me if I could put the air conditioning on recirculate," Harley said. "It was hot, still summertime. Well, there was no way to do that, but I said, 'Yes sir, I've got it on recirculate now.' He also had a cloth and lighter fluid that he used to wipe off the control column."

Brien and Harley weren't regular readers of celebrity news and gossip, so they were unaware that in some circles, Hughes's germ phobia and obsessive-compulsive behaviors were frequently commented upon. There was also speculation that he was taking a lot of pain medication because of injuries received in the aviation crashes he'd been in during the forties.

With Hughes in the pilot's seat, Brien sat in the copilot's seat while Harley occupied the flight engineer's seat behind Brien. Hughes didn't want anyone else in the cockpit, except his valet, George. George constantly hovered right behind Hughes. He would spread paper napkins on Hughes's lap and then provide him with a constant supply of sandwiches, Hershey bars, and milk. "The sandwiches were mostly carrots and celery and stuff like that," Harley said. "And he complained about them. He'd say, 'You're lucky you don't have to eat this stuff.'" George rarely said anything.

Because Hughes refused to allow anyone else on the airplane, the rest of the Boeing crew was left behind on the tarmac, including the regular flight engineer; Harley assumed that job for the flights.

Hughes always wanted to talk prior to actually starting the engines. Harley wasn't included in these conversations, perhaps because he was merely the flight engineer in Hughes's mind, but he often listened in as Hughes and Brien talked. These preflight question-and-answer sessions would last about an hour. Brien wasn't inclined to cut the sessions short, despite the waning daylight, remembering his overall objective to get Hughes to place an order for 707s. Hughes didn't ask many questions about the airplane, and he didn't seem to be after technical information. Instead, he'd quiz Brien in a general way. Often Hughes's questions were phrased in a way that seemed to avoid having to admit he might need the information for himself. For example: "What would you tell a person, who was a pretty good pilot, had flown airplanes, but hadn't flown any jets—what would you tell him about...?" Brien would patiently answer all of his questions, but the next time they flew, Hughes would ask the same questions all over again.

Those roundabout questions were asked because Hughes had yet to fly a jet. He'd most recently been flying the Lockheed Constellation (the "Connie"), a propeller plane. Yet Hughes seemed relaxed about flying the Dash 80 his first time. Eventually, they started the engines and took off. Brien had heard that Hughes liked to "shoot" lots of landings—touch-and-go's—and indeed, that's what Hughes wanted to do on this flight. They flew over to the Mojave Airport, in the desert approximately 100 miles northeast of Los Angeles and about 25 miles west of Edwards AFB. In 1958, there was little activity left at Mojave Airport. The Marines no longer used it as a base, leaving it nearly abandoned, with only a few light airplanes remaining. The only nearby town, Mojave, was very small. To Brien and Harley, Mojave Airport seemed like a ghost airstrip in the middle of nowhere.

By the time the Dash 80 with its three-pilot crew plus valet arrived over the Mojave Airport, it was nearly dark. "I think he may have gotten in his first landings in dusk," Brien recalled, "but it was getting dark, and we went on and on, and on. He had difficulty flying the airplane on approach." Brien knew that pilots coming off propeller-driven airplanes had a tendency to want to point the nose of the Dash 80 down, toward the end of the runway, because that was the normal attitude for a prop airplane on landing. But the swept-wing Dash 80's landing attitude was more nose high. It had to be settled onto the runway.

"I'd get him to slow down, and get the nose up, then he'd keep trying to lower the nose, like he was uncomfortable with it there," Brien said. "I tried to explain this to him, but he was a man of habit, and such a solo guy all his life, I'm sure that he didn't take instruction very readily from anybody. He was never rude to me. But as he kept lowering the nose, the plane would get lower, so we were way below the glide [approach] path. I'd keep telling him, 'Bring the nose up, bring the nose up' and he'd bring it up a little. Harley was sitting there, sweating bullets. It was tougher on him; at least I was in the copilot's seat and could have done something about it."

The repeated approaches were miserable for the Boeing pilots. Because the area was devoid of towns, there were no lights or other objects on the horizon to provide ground reference. There were no electronic aids to guide the pilot onto the glide path for landing. And it was *dark*—like dropping the airplane into a big, black hole in the earth, not sure where the bottom is. Flying under such conditions was like walking in a dark room full of furniture, wearing a blindfold. The pilots couldn't judge the airplane's altitude over various land formations. The repeated touch-and-go's made for nerve-wracking flying for everyone but Hughes, who wanted to go around and do it again and again. Finally Brien and Harley conspired to tell him they were running low on fuel, just to get him to relent and return to Los Angeles Airport.

This first flight with Hughes ended with a nasty surprise for all. The Dash 80 had a structural speed restriction of 140 knots when landing with full flaps, and Brien wanted to use full flaps to keep the nose up to counter Hughes's tendency to point the nose down. Brien wasn't watching Hughes carefully enough, and his speed got over 140 knots on the final approach to LA Airport. Harley noticed the excessive speed, though, and he quickly snapped the flaps back up to 30 degrees, but it was too late. One of the fore flaps (a metal wing structure approximately one foot wide and 10-12 feet long) came off and fell onto a car that, as luck would have it, belonged to a CAA official.

No one onboard felt or heard anything unusual, however. Once they were parked on the ground, a CAA official approached the airplane. Harley went down to greet him on the tarmac while Brien, Hughes, and George remained behind in the airplane. Hughes did not want to be seen.

"Somebody has dropped an airplane part," the official informed Harley. "We think it's you."

"I don't think so," Harley responded. He was nervous about keeping Hughes's presence on the plane a secret, as Hughes had requested. And he certainly didn't want Hughes to receive any negative publicity or be publicly embarrassed, which could jeopardize the sale. Good pilots don't drop airplane parts when landing.

The two men made an inspection walk around the airplane and didn't notice anything missing. The CAA official then asked Harley to put the flaps down. Harley went back up into the cockpit to do so, and then rejoined the CAA official on the ground. They walked around the airplane again. This time, sure enough, no fore flap—it was missing. Harley went back to the cockpit. Brien and Hughes were standing there, and Harley announced the bad news.

"George, do you have some money?" Hughes asked. George told him he did. "Find out how much the guy wants," Hughes commanded.

"You can't bribe the CAA!" blurted Harley.

"The hell I can't!" Hughes responded.

Harley went back down to the tarmac and told the CAA official they were sorry and made sure no one was injured. Harley asked what the CAA was going to do about the incident.

"Well, I guess nothing," the man responded. "We know the spot you're in." He then left. Harley understood that somehow the CAA official knew whom they had onboard and the difficulties they might be encountering with Hughes at the controls. Harley returned to the cockpit and told Brien and Hughes to forget it, everything had been settled. As soon as the CAA man left, so did Hughes. "Howard was secreted off the airplane," Brien said. "He barreled out of there as quickly as he could."

It took the ground crew a couple days to repair the airplane. About a month later, Brien was fined $500 by the CAA for careless flying. He paid the fine and was eventually reimbursed by Boeing. To this day he feels the fine was justified, as he was the captain and should have prevented Hughes's too-fast approach that led to the flap's structural limits being exceeded. Harley had seen it coming, so Brien feels he should have as well. The incident was never again addressed by Hughes or his staff.

To his credit, Brien had several distractions to deal with whenever Hughes was landing the plane at Los Angeles Airport. Not only was there the issue of making sure Hughes kept the nose up and the airspeed down, but Brien also had the task of relaying the tower's landing instructions to Hughes. Air traffic was relatively light at Los Angeles Airport in 1958. Still, the tower would give pilots specific approach and landing instructions, and failure to follow them could lead to fines or license suspension, not to mention a collision.

"Howard didn't like to follow instructions," said Brien. "We always had a little struggle when coming back to the airport, because I would contact the tower about 10 miles out, and they would tell me, okay Boeing such-and-such, take up a heading of 090 or whatever. Howard was kind of deaf, or claimed to be deaf. He wouldn't wear a headset, anyway, so he didn't know what the tower was saying. I'd relay the headings, saying, 'Howard, take up 090,' and maybe he'd grudgingly do that. Then I'd say, 'OK, turn to 120,' and he wouldn't—he'd refuse to do that. So I'd say, 'Well, Howard, the tower wants us to turn to 120,' and he'd reply, 'Tell them to go fuck themselves.' I didn't follow that advice! Don't get me wrong—he wasn't given to obscenities, he was very well spoken, but he was irritated."

Eventually Brien realized that the Los Angeles air traffic controllers became aware of exactly whom they had onboard, because after two or three approaches and landings, they became more lenient of Brien's surprising inability to follow instructions. They realized Brien's feeble excuses, such as some warning light or other, were a cover, and accommodated him. "They never said anything, but I could tell they were quite puzzled at first, you know—what's wrong with this Boeing guy?" Brien said.

The biggest struggle, however, for both Brien and Harley, was an internal one: how to reconcile the Hughes of legend, the world-record-setting aviator as famous as Charles Lindbergh, with the disheveled shell of a man sitting in the cockpit whose flying skills were appalling. Harley, more than Brien, felt betrayed when Hughes didn't live up to his reputation, losing respect for Hughes as a pilot after that first night of flying with him. Yet they had to hold their tongues, because Boeing needed a big order from TWA to ensure the viability of the 707 program.

And unbeknownst to both of the Boeing pilots, they still had eight more days of catering to Hughes's whims and piloting peculiarities. As seasoned test pilots, Brien and Harley were both accustomed to putting their lives on the line testing new airplanes. Providing demonstration flights was part of an airplane's sales program and so also part of their job. What didn't occur to them was that launching the 707 with a big order from TWA would involve risking their lives flying with aviation icon Howard Hughes. Their professionalism and patience in handling Hughes and his poor piloting allowed Boeing to get the TWA order, which in turn helped launch the commercial jet age.

Seattle's Love Affair with Unlimited Hydroplane Racing

For two weeks in October 1958, Brien Wygle kept Howard Hughes happily interested in Boeing's Dash 80, days spent waiting to fly, nights flying a seemingly unlimited number of takeoffs and landings with Hughes at the controls, making even Brien's experienced test pilot knuckles a little white. Despite Brien's dedication to pleasing both Hughes and the bosses back in Seattle, eventually he asked for a substitute test pilot to handle Hughes so that he could tend to another obligation. "I said I'd like to be relieved because we had a race on Lake Mead, near Las Vegas," said Brien. My father was dispatched from Seattle with the directive to quickly finish the demonstration flights with Hughes and get the Dash 80 back home where it was needed for continued testing.[21]

Brien's race? Unlimited hydroplanes, affectionately known

---

[21] Dad flew with Hughes just one time before he and Harley brought the Dash 80 back to Seattle. Dad didn't have any of the drama experienced by Brien, although by the time Dad arrived, Hughes had logged several hours under Brien's tutelage. Dad did tell me that he felt Hughes was on pain-killers, that he seemed to be a bit drugged.

to fans as thunderboats.[22] The Lake Mead race was one in a series of races across the country—from Detroit to Seattle—each summer. Brien was driving the *Thriftway Too*, and this was to be its final race of the 1958 season. Finding a last-minute substitute hydroplane driver was much harder than securing a relief Boeing test pilot to finish the demonstration flights with Howard Hughes.

Hydroplane racing was a huge community event for Seattleites in the 1950s and 1960s. Imagine combining the hype of all the professional sports teams of any major city and compressing it into a nucleus of boundless energy devoted to just one sport, played out over the course of a few summer days, and you begin to appreciate Seattle's attachment to hydroplane racing. It's still wildly popular, although it now competes with several professional sports franchises that have moved into Seattle. From 1950 through most of the 1960s, however, hydroplanes were *the* sports game in town, thoroughly embraced by the populace, young and old.

Around 1950, two forces combined, entwining Seattle and hydroplane racing in the population's minds for good: the will of an incredibly talented local boat designer named Ted Jones to build the world's fastest hydroplane, and Seattle's desire to create a summertime festival with a maritime theme to celebrate its centennial. Already touting itself as "the pleasure boating capital of the world," Seattle lured Walter Van Camp, director of St. Paul, Minnesota's water carnival, to create an even better festival here. The festival was christened "Seafair." A tradition was born.

Seattle is, indeed, a city obsessed with water and boating. We claim more boats per capita than anywhere else in the United States. Lakes, rivers, and Puget Sound are all within easy reach, allowing Seattleites to enjoy all types of boating

---

[22] Gottlieb Daimler is given credit for originating power boating when, in the 1880s, the automotive inventor strapped a gas-powered engine to a row boat and trolled the River Seine. Two decades later, American's first Gold Cup Race saw the *Standard* win with what was then a blistering speed of 23 mph. In the 1940s, surplus WWII Allison V-1710 jet engines were used to power the hydroplanes, a significant boost to speed and leading to the nickname thunderboats. Today, speeds exceed 220 mph.

activities year-round. In the 1950s, ferries capable of carrying over 100 cars and 1800 passengers, such as the MV Kalakala—whose steel skin and art-deco style made her look like a giant slug plowing across the water—plied Puget Sound to destinations on the Olympic Peninsula.

The post-war era was one of immense innovation and growth for the Puget Sound area. Boeing, leading the way, was testing the latest jet engines on bombers (the B-47 and B-52) and doing more of its building and testing in Seattle rather than Wichita. Boeing boomed and prospered. It had 16,000 employees at the end of World War II and added some 40,000 more during the 1950s.

Seattle and its surrounding suburbs also boomed and prospered. Seattle's population grew from 467,391 in 1950 to 557,087 in 1960, an increase of nearly twenty percent. Jobs in aerospace and ship and boat building were attracting a skilled workforce from across the country. Positive, can-do attitudes abounded in the region, spilling over into hydroplane design and racing.

Seattle was ripe for this new love affair with unlimited hydroplane racing. It mixed so much of what makes Seattle unique: water, boating, roaring aircraft engines, engineering know-how, heroic men—some of them test pilots—willing to drive the dangerous hydroplanes, and the love of a good family show in the great outdoors, with iconic Mount Rainier as backdrop. Hydroplane racing benefited from innovative boat design, incorporating powerful aviation engines for maximum speed, and knowledgeable mechanics to keep the boats running. It's no accident that skilled Boeing employees played a major role in the early years of unlimited hydroplane racing on Lake Washington.

The first Seafair, held in 1950, had many of the features that would become staples surviving to this day: small boat races on Green Lake, invading pirates kissing unsuspecting ladies and frightening children, the crowning of a Seafair Queen and her court, amateur athletic events, Aqua Follies and "swimusicals" at the Aqua Theatre on Green Lake, and smaller community events like the University District Kid's Parade and the Ballard

Festival. The first Seafair Grand Parade had an estimated 250,000 spectators lining downtown Seattle's Second and Third Avenues.[23]

That same summer, a newly designed hydroplane called *The Slo-Mo-Shun IV* debuted on Lake Washington.

Seattleite and Boeing mechanic Tudor Owen "Ted" Jones first began racing boats in 1927. Obsessed with building ever-faster hydroplanes, he introduced himself to Stanley Sayers, a successful Seattle automobile dealer who dabbled in hydroplane racing. Jones told Sayers he had designed—on butcher block paper—an unlimited hydroplane that would blow the rest of the boats out of the water. Sayers agreed to back Jones in building the boat. Construction on the *Slo-Mo-Shun IV*, a "three pointer" that would ride on two sponsons and a propeller, started in the fall of 1948.

On June 26, 1950, the *Slo-Mo-Shun IV*, with fifty-something owner Stanley Sayers in the cockpit, literally flew across the chop of Lake Washington. Sayers set a new mile-speed record: 160.3235 mph (just under twenty-two seconds over a 1-mile stretch), almost 20 mph faster than the previous speed record set in England eleven years earlier. The July 10, 1950, issue of *Time* magazine described the *Slo-Mo-Shun IV* and its record-setting run this way: "Head on, the thing suggested an amphibious flying saucer with rudder trouble. From the rear it looked like Old Faithful on a rampage. To the motorboat experts who got up at 6:00 am one day last week in Seattle to see it perform, it looked like the fastest thing afloat."

The *Slo-Mo-Shun IV* was the first prop-riding hydroplane to race successfully, becoming the darling of Seattle. These three-pointer hydroplanes with powerful aircraft engines were given a new and exciting nickname: *thunderboats.* The Unlimited Hydroplane, or Thunderboat, Class began drawing more

---

[23] The Saturday Grand Parade would eventually give way to a Friday Night Torchlight Parade with beautifully lit floats. The Aqua Theatre at Green Lake hosted water-themed shows through 1965. After a Grateful Dead concert there in 1969, the seating portion of the theatre was determined unsafe and slowly dismantled; the ground-level structure now houses public restrooms and a boat house for rowing clubs.

spectators than any other boat-racing division.

But breaking the world record wasn't enough. The *Slo-Mo-Shun IV* had to prove its worth in the city that was then the hydroplane racing capitol, Detroit, home of the Gold Cup. The speed record put Detroit on notice.

At a 1950 Gold Cup pre-race press conference at the Chrysler Boat Well in Detroit, Sayers had this to say about his odd-looking boat. "It's really a backyard-built boat, a rule-of-thumb job that has been perfected by what you might call seat-of-the-pants experiences in test runs." Sayers, himself a seasoned private pilot,[24] credited Jones's design, which helped the audience appreciate an airplane mechanic's ability to strap a jet engine onto a revolutionary and aviation-influenced hull design that did, in fact, blow the other boats out of the water. When Sayers set the speed record on Lake Washington, he promised Jones the job of pilot in the Gold Cup race. "I don't think a $5,000 check would [have gotten] Ted out of the seat," Sayers concluded.

Jones piloted the *Slo-Mo-Shun IV* to victory in all three heats of that year's Gold Cup race on the Detroit River. Jones's 1950 Gold Cup win in Sayers's boat set in motion what would become the biggest fan-supported sporting event in Seattle for the next few decades: Seafair's Gold Cup race. The importance of Jones's 1950 win in Detroit can't be overstated. The location of the Gold Cup race was based on the sponsoring yacht club of the previous year's winner. Detroit had won this honor for several years running. The Seattle Yacht Club-sponsored *Slo-Mo-Shun IV* brought the Gold Cup west. Seattle and Seafair would get their chance to host the coveted event, beginning in 1951—Seattle's Centennial.

Sayers's *Slo-Mo*, as she became affectionately known, made Seattleites unlimited hydroplane enthusiasts overnight, and they came out in droves every August to watch the thunderboats race on Lake Washington in the Seafair Regatta. Thunderboats quickly became synonymous with summertime in Seattle. In their heyday, nearly half a million people would

---

[24] Ironically, Sayers's wife thought airplanes were too dangerous, so he returned to hydroplane racing.

pay to line the shores of the lake, many wading into the water to stay cool and get a closer view of the hydroplanes. Others vied for space on the log boom surrounding the three lake-side lines of the oval race course, tying their yachts, motorboats and rowboats to the logs or to boats already tied there, creating a colorful floating garland of boats and people around the racecourse. Those not attending in person tuned in to radios or TVs, making a full day of the festivities. We were a city enthralled with thunderboat racing—the boats, the drivers, the owners. We became racing fanatics. The boat races—just one part, albeit a very large part of Seafair—were our Kentucky Derby or Indy 500, *the event* Seattleites eagerly anticipated, watched and talked about for days.

This devotion to Seafair and the Gold Cup races increased exponentially in 1955 when Tex Johnston barrel-rolled the new Boeing Dash 80 right over the Gold Cup race course before the very surprised and awestruck crowd. Seattle—and Boeing—were definitely now on the national map. We were no longer just a bunch of redneck loggers. The rest of the country had to stand up and take notice. So much so that by 1959, both *Time* and *Sports Illustrated* ran features about Seafair's Gold Cup races. In the August 17, 1959, issue, *Time* described the event in an article titled *The Water Monsters.*

> The world's fastest racing boats are the unlimited hydroplanes. As much airplane as boat, they are bellowing giants powered by World War II fighter-plane engines, ride on two hand-sized patches of hull and the submerged half of a whirling propeller, skip along the water like a flat stone thrown from shore, tossing spray with the sting of buckshot. No one knows how fast the top boats will go because no one has ever had them wide open, and for good reason: at speeds around 180 mph, the slightest swell can send them hurtling into the air. Last week Seattle's Lake Washington reverberated like a fighter strip as the nation's 14 fastest hydroplanes roared off in the top race of the year: the Gold Cup.

In a *Sports Illustrated* article dated August 10, 1959, writer Wilbur Jarvis captured the peculiar fanaticism that by then gripped Seattle every August. The title of his article was *Gold Cup Madness: The Annual Epidemic*. The piece opened with this teaser: "The sober citizens of Seattle go slightly daffy every year when the time comes for the roaring hydros to defend the city's proudest possession—the Gold Cup."

Let's admit something: part of the allure of these races is the prospect of seeing a boat go airborne, maybe even flip in midair. Unlimited hydroplane racing is dangerous. Spectators hold their breath through each heat, wondering whether their favorite boat will make it to the finish line. *Sports Illustrated* once described thunderboat racing as, "A sport—'the hairiest sport of all,' say some—where shattered boats and sudden catastrophe are commonplaces." The magazine noted that most hydro drivers admit to some fear driving the thunderboats, quoting one driver as saying the sensation of driving one is "like racing over railroad ties on a motorcycle with solid tires."

Given all that, who would be brave—or crazy—enough to get into the driver's seat of such a beast and push it to speeds well over 150 mph, when a single unanticipated wake or gust of wind could suddenly flip you ass-over-teakettle? In the 1950s, drivers sat in open cockpits and had only a helmet and life vest for safety in the event of an accident or fire. It's a rare breed of driver who willingly takes such risk in order to enjoy the thrill. Brien Wygle was of that breed.

The *Times* article described some of the drivers in the 1959 Gold Cup race: Bill Stead, 34, a cattle rancher from Nevada, sporting burn scars from an earlier crash; Mira Slovak, who flew a C-47 out of communist Czechoslovakia in 1953, came to the United States and worked as a crop duster and eventually as private pilot for Bill Boeing, Jr.; and Bill Muncey, 30, a former professional hockey player and local disc jockey. Jack Regas, 1958's winning driver, was not even there; he was still in the hospital with severe head injuries suffered the previous month when he'd spun into a wall of water on Idaho's Coeur d'Alene Lake while driving *Miss Bardahl*. Taking Regas's seat in defending champion *Hawaii Kai* was Brien Wygle, 32.

Brien wasn't the only test pilot racing hydroplanes. Russ Schleeh—"The Flying Colonel" as he was called by the press—a military test pilot who also flew B-47s and B-52s, introduced Brien to Ted Jones, opening the door for him to become a driver. Schleeh was tall and muscular, resembling a linebacker and exuding confidence and strength. In 1957, Schleeh became the only unlimited hydroplane driver to grace the cover of *Sports Illustrated.*

19 Brien Wygle and Russ Schleeh, test pilots and unlimited hydroplane drivers. Photo: Wygle collection.

In many ways, Brien was a natural for this "hairiest sport of all." He had the right look: tall and lean in racing coveralls that looked very much like a flight suit, crew-cut hair, strong features, and a steady, intelligent gaze. His training as a multi-engine pilot in World War II, his work as a fighter pilot after the war, and his ensuing career as a test pilot for Boeing meant he understood the demands and risks of propelling himself in a "monster" with incredible speed, whether a jet airplane through the sky or a thunderboat skimming the chop on a body of water.

Brien was as fascinated with the hydroplanes and races as any other Seattleite during the 1950s, perhaps even more so because he'd flown the airplane engines used in the boats. In 1956, when Schleeh introduced him to Jones, Brien didn't realize that Jones was seeking a driver for a boat with a radical new "cabover" design—putting the driver *in front* of the engine, rather than behind as in all the current boats. Jones feared experienced drivers would refuse to drive his new design, the *Thriftway Too*. Brien, a thirty-two-year-old adrenaline-junkie test pilot eager to join the racing circuit, was Jones's ideal candidate and was selected to drive.

As Brien raced the *Thriftway Too* through the summer of 1957, he realized its fatal weakness. "It would lose its way in the turns; it was unable to keep up its speed," he says. Once a hydroplane loses too much speed, it comes off "plane"—the ability to skim on the water's surface, which creates less drag and greater speed. But on the straightaways, the *Thriftway Too* showed her rivals what she was made of, going as fast as 170 mph. "She would accelerate extremely rapidly," Brien remembers. "I'd pass people on the straightaways and they'd pass me on the corners. It was frustrating." Not wearing a seat belt, Brien used both hands to firmly grasp the steering column in the turns to counteract the centrifugal forces. None of the drivers wore seat belts, because in 1951, a boat that crashed had nosed in, plunging to the bottom of the lake and drowning the driver and his mechanic who were both strapped in. Better to be thrown free than to drown strapped to your seat.

Racing didn't pose the only danger to thunderboat drivers. Like test pilots testing innovations to airplanes, between races the boat drivers tested new equipment. In 1958, during a test run on the *Thriftway Too*, "I lost a rudder," Brien says. "It came off at 150 mph, making me lose steering and stability. My boat swapped ends so quickly... I remember thinking I don't want to be thrown out because the back end could swing around and kill me. It was a huge *g*-force because I went from 150 mph to minus ten. I held on to the steering column to stay inside the boat. I was stunned." When he came to a rest—right side up—Brien raised his hand to signal he was okay. His crew towed him back to shore, remarkably unhurt.

By the late 1950s, Bill Muncey—driver of the *Miss Thriftway*, owned by the same local-grocery-chain owner as Brien's *Thriftway Too*—was the best-known hydroplane driver in Seattle, a local hero. For reasons unknown to Brien, Muncey gave him the cold shoulder, rarely speaking to him, despite racing for the same team. "Muncey was a great racer and competitor," says Brien. "But he had lots of ego, and probably some envy of the easier route the test pilots had to top racing positions."

Brien left the Thriftway team in 1959, becoming driver for the *Hawaii Kai* team. In 1958, the *Kai* won the Gold Cup, its only race that year. The boat had proven potential. Driving the *Hawaii Kai* in the 1959 Apple Cup, Brien didn't have a great first heat. The second heat brought out old rivalries. Muncey was driving a new *Miss Thriftway* and at the top of his game. "That second heat was a terrific race because Bill didn't like me very much. He certainly didn't want me to beat him in that race. And it was close for a while but I beat him. And in doing so, in the first lap, I set a world's record for the fastest competitive lap ever run. Muncey didn't take very kindly to that. He didn't like to lose to anybody, and he particularly didn't want to lose to me."

Most envelope-pushing, high-risk endeavors involve the strong possibility of unintentionally short careers. Just three years in, Brien decided 1959 was to be his last year as an unlimited hydroplane race driver. Designs were changing and improving, boats were gaining power and speed, but they weren't any more stable on the water. "It was getting more and more dangerous," Brien says. "Up until then, there had been only a few bad accidents, but I could see it was getting too dangerous. I had a wife and four small children. I didn't think it wise to continue." He informed the *Hawaii Kai* crew that the 1959 Seafair Gold Cup would be his final race.

One of the exciting features of any unlimited hydroplane race is the strategic start. As the boats leave the pits and warm up by running the course, they're jockeying for position amongst themselves *and* against the start clock. The starting line is midway up the straightaway closest to shore. As the race clock counts backward to the start, each driver wants to be going full speed just inches behind that starting line when the clock hits zero; misjudge and cross the line too soon, you're given a penalty lap. Think of it as a NASCAR rolling start but without pre-assigned positions.

As racers gauge their speed and timing in their final pre-start lap, they're closely watching each other and choosing a lane. There are no buoys designating "lanes" on the water, but the drivers follow rules regarding how to position themselves as well as unspoken rules—gentlemen's agreements—regarding competing with courtesy and honor.

Drivers set up in a lane well before the start so that no one takes their place. As a child watching the races on TV, I clearly remember this being a really exciting part of each heat, hoping "your" boat's driver jockeyed well for position because if not, if he didn't hit the starting line well, it was almost impossible for the boat to finish high enough in the standings to move on to the next heat. On the edge of our seats, we'd yell at the TV set, "Come on, come on… not too fast… okay, gun it… *yes*!" Starts were the pins-and-needles, make-or-break part of each heat, with late starters getting slowed by the rooster tails and wakes of faster boats for the balance of the heat. Turns were almost as exciting, for that's where boats bunched up, dangerously close to each other as they bounced over wakes, seeming to skid around the turns, nearly colliding.

Brien knew he had to do well in the first heat. "I come around the turn toward the start, choose my lane. We're going about 100 mph, on plane, around the last turn, then you accelerate to the starting line," Brien says. "We were all close.

I'm in the #1 lane. I was good at this—flooring it, full-speed throttle, 150 mph within a second of the start. Everyone knew to do this, so everyone's coasting for that moment to floor it. Suddenly I hear a roar and I think, 'It's way too early.' A boat goes by me, pulls in front, and slows down." A flagrant violation, blocking another racer's lane, which Brien felt was done deliberately. "I had to slow way down—hard on the engine—or hit him," Brien continues. "I ended up last over the line, and I never was before." By crossing over into Brien's lane and making sure Brien had a bad start, the other driver destroyed his own chances of winning the heat as well. It was bizarre.

Recovering from his surprise, Brien hit the throttle to speed up. He arrived at the first turn. "I got to the turn and hit a hole in the water left from another boat's wake." Drivers refer to the cleft between two wakes of a boat as "a hole in the water" because if your boat launches over one wake and lands there, it feels like dropping into a hole. Brien hit the hole so hard that his boat's wooden seat smashed. He instantly knew that his back had been injured by the impact, but he managed to finish the heat. Returning to the pits, Brien carefully climbed out of the boat and tried to assure everyone he was fine, but when his crew saw the damage the boat had taken, they weren't convinced. Up on its trailer, the crew discovered that the boat's drive shaft was actually bent. The race was over for Brien *and* the *Hawaii Kai*.

Brien's respect for the other driver went to zero after that incident. Cutting someone off deliberately was cheating, petty, and dangerous; in short, ungentlemanly.[25]

To this day Brien does not want to name the driver publicly. It's precisely this sense of honor that epitomizes the Boeing test pilots I grew up around. If they say something negative about a person—and that's a rare event in itself—they have good reason to, yet they ask me to not name him or her because they don't want to publicly besmirch someone's name, especially all these decades later.

---

[25] My father always emphasized that cheating was despicable, a sign of someone utterly lacking character. There are no shortcuts to earning respect.

Brien's sense of increasing danger in the sport of unlimited hydroplane racing was prescient. Fellow test pilot Russ Schleeh hadn't raced since 1957, sidelined by injuries resulting from an accident on the Potomac. In 1960 he returned, racing in the Seafair Regatta at the wheel of Brien's former boat, the *Thriftway Too*. That race was, unfortunately, another bad one for Schleeh. In the final heat, the *Thriftway Too's* engine caught fire. Schleeh went to the hospital to be treated for burns. Despite that, Schleeh continued driving various unlimited hydroplanes until finally retiring from the circuit in 1963. In the decade following Brien's retirement from racing, seven drivers were killed racing unlimited hydroplanes.

Eventually, unlimited hydroplanes would be designed with more driver-safety features, saving many lives, but racing unlimited hydroplanes will never be without extreme risk to the drivers. Which is why we unwashed masses, the spectators, consider them heroes and worship them.

Seattle kids in the 1950s and 1960s remember well the noise and the thrill of the summer's hydroplane races. Devotion to a boat, and hero worship of the drivers, was encouraged in several ways. When Brien drove the *Thriftway Too*, his caricature appeared on the side of Thriftway grocery store paper bags for children to color.

In the weeks leading up to Seafair, we kids would beg our fathers to create model hydros from plywood and wood scraps in their shops. We painted them in the colors of our favorite boat. These wood models had sponsons and tail fins, and an eye bolt screw in the center of the broadly curving bow threaded by several feet of string. Tied to a bicycle's rear fender or seat post, the hydros would drag across the pavement behind us as we rode.

My bicycle was a Schwinn Stingray with a deep-blue frame, a white banana seat, and butterfly handlebars. I often added playing cards to the spokes of the front wheel, clipped with clothespins, to gain that special *whap whap whap* sound that increased in frequency and volume the faster I rode, vainly trying to imitate the sound of a real hydroplane engine. Along with my brothers and other neighborhood kids, we'd "race" our boats around an oval course set on the street in front of our house, trying to keep our boats from flipping on the curves or from hitting some obstacle.

Sometimes, for variety, we'd build a jump out of a sheet of plywood propped on one end with two-by-fours, scraps we'd find in Dad's shop. Accelerating toward the jump, we'd ride right alongside it, turning our bike at just the right moment to cause the hydro to swing out and over the jump, soaring through the air and crashing upon landing. Wipe out!

Come race day, if we weren't already on shore or on a boat tied to the log boom, we were gathered in front of the TV for an afternoon of racing thrills, fueled by barbequed hotdogs and hamburgers and homemade ice cream. TV and radio coverage lasted for hours on race day, with color commentary about the boats, owners, and drivers, much like today's Super Bowl or a NASCAR race.

In my family, before each heat began, one of the adults would write qualifying boat names on slips of paper, which were then put into a bowl. We'd each draw a name and cheer for "our" boat. Sometimes your boat didn't even make it to the starting line of a heat; sometimes it won the Gold Cup (or the Seafair Trophy in the years Seattle wasn't hosting the Gold Cup race). Results didn't matter as much as participating in all the excitement and rituals associated with Seafair and its hydroplane mania.

For the four Wygle daughters, those rituals carried more personal meaning. Jan Wygle was eight when her father raced his last hydroplane event in 1959. Sometimes the girls visited the race pits on Lake Washington's shore to watch the mechanics work on the boats. At home, Brien helped Jan and her sisters make wooden hydros to pull behind their bikes, just like all the other kids, but in their case they painted them in colors matching their father's boat. Jan thought it was very cool that her father was on the Thriftway shopping bags, and was even on TV! "It was a popular, competitive sport," she recalled. "To hell with his day job flying airplanes—he raced hydros! Dad was a hero!"

Proving to the Airlines What the 707 Could Do

With all new airplanes, Boeing's test pilots flew what they called "proving" flights for airline customers. An airline's senior or training captain would be onboard, in the cockpit as copilot or simply observing as the Boeing pilot flew a typical leg of that airline's routes. This allowed Boeing to show off a new airplane's flying characteristics: capacity, range, speed, and—especially if the airline's route included a "tricky" airport—takeoff and landing abilities. Proving flights are an example of that place where the Boeing pilot's testing and selling duties blur.

One trait of a successful test pilot is creative problem-solving. Whether the problem arises during a proving flight or while the airplane is parked at some remote airport, possibly in a foreign country, the Boeing pilots and crew will need to address it immediately with whatever tools they have at their disposal, including ingenuity. A big sale could be on the line.

By January 1959, Boeing's stretch version of the 707—the 707-320 Intercontinental—took its first flight, a little over a year after the first 707 took to the air. As its name implies, this jet would be used by airlines with intercontinental routes. Bigger wings allowed the jet to carry more fuel, extending its range beyond the original 707 Transcontinental. The interior comfortably seated 189 passengers. The first Intercontinental was delivered to Pan Am in August 1959.

To demonstrate the airplane's expanded range, Tex Johnston, Dix, and my father decided to fly nonstop to Rome. *From Seattle.* This may sound normal and straightforward to readers today, but in 1959, this was extraordinary. Airline flights from the United States to Europe typically left from the East Coast. On October 26, 1958, Pan Am made history with its first trans-Atlantic jet service between New York and Paris with a 707 Transcontinental (707-120). If you were in Seattle and wanted to get to Europe, you first had fly to the East Coast, say New York City or Washington, DC, then take another flight to Rome or London or Paris. The 707-320's extra fuel capacity expanded its range by 1,600 miles, a significant distance. As Tex famously said, the 707 was shrinking the world. It is 5,830 miles from Seattle to Rome.

This nonstop flight occurred on May 28, 1959, two days after my father's thirty-fifth birthday. His aviator's flight log notes the flight took eleven hours, nine minutes; he recorded "5:48" as pilot time on that flight, so apparently he, Dix, and Tex shared piloting duties on that long haul.

There were forty people onboard, including Boeing President Bill Allen, some FAA pilots, and at least one airline president.

Also onboard was a Boeing engineer named Dudley Nichols, the man responsible for the design and engineering drawings that put the 707 together. "I swear he walked all the way from Seattle to Rome," Dad laughed. "He never sat down. He was up pacing around, looking at things, looking out the windows, listening, walking up to the cockpit. The only man I know who walked nonstop from Seattle to Rome!"

Two days after landing in Rome, Dad flew the 707-320 from Rome to Paris, then Frankfurt, and finally London. Then on May 31, 1959, he piloted the 707-320 nonstop from London to Seattle, a flight that took nine hours, forty-eight minutes. That particular flight stood out in his memory. The story of their departure from London is a good example of my father's trademark creative problem-solving that also allowed for some good laughs and a little nose tweaking.

Onboard for the hops across Europe and for the London-to-Seattle flight was a Pan Am captain named Jim Fleming. He was Pan Am's chief technical pilot in their San Francisco division. The first Intercontinental delivery was going to the San Francisco base. A Pan Am navigator was also onboard. Fleming had flown earlier versions of the 707, but not the Intercontinental; he was onboard to observe, get acquainted with the airplane, and see up close how the Intercontinental would work on Pan Am's international routes. For Dad, it was nice to have someone familiar with the European airports and procedures onboard.

When the Boeing jet landed at London's Heathrow Airport on May 30th, they were directed to park way out on the taxiway, away from the terminal. A little odd, but they weren't a commercial flight, and the airport transported them to the terminal by car, so Dad didn't think more about it. The next morning, as they arrived at the airplane to prepare to fly back to Seattle, it became obvious why they'd been directed to park there: overnight, Heathrow personnel had erected scaffolding and towers right behind the 707-320, with anemometers attached to measure wind velocity when they started the engines. Dad figured the scaffolding probably had noise sensors as well. Boeing's big 707s, with four loud jet engines that belched lots of black smoke upon takeoff, were of concern for many airports in the late 1950s, especially those in urban areas, because the jets were larger and noisier than anything the airports had hosted before.

Captain Fleming was well aware of Heathrow's concerns about noise and brought my father up to speed on the issue. Heathrow had already instituted a noise limit upon takeoff for airlines, and had measuring equipment set up at several points for a few miles beyond the runway to monitor an airplane's noise while climbing away from the airport.

The Intercontinental had compressed air bottles built into the nacelles (the covers housing each engine) so that pilots could start the two inboard engines. Generally, the airplane's engine-start procedure was to start the inboard engines first, using the air bottle's compressed air, run them up to medium power, then bleed the air off their compressors to start the outboard engines; each engine's starter was an air turbine that required compressed air to start. Dad's concern was that running that first two engines up to medium power right in front of the anemometers might give Heathrow an argument for preventing Pan Am's operation of the 707-320 there, which would hurt sales of the airplane.

Dad and Fleming took in the scaffolding and its meaning, thought about the problem, discussed some options, and came up with a plan. "We decided we'll just sneak out of here without using any power!" my father said.

The 707-320 was parked on the slightest of downhill slopes. They pulled the chocks away from the wheels, got everybody onboard, and closed the doors. Using the compressed air bottles, they started the two inboard engines, but left them at idle rather than running them up to medium power. When they released the brakes, there was just enough thrust from the two idling engines to let the airplane roll away.

"We rolled about 100 feet and turned up the wick [power] on those two engines, bled the air off them to the outboard engines, started them and taxied on out," Dad continued. Because the Pan Am guys were familiar with the noise monitoring system set up beyond the airport, they contacted a Pan Am radio crew member on the ground at Heathrow, asking him to give them a countdown as they flew over the recording area right after takeoff.

"This airplane being bigger, loaded up to go nonstop to the West Coast rather than the East Coast of the United States, with bigger engines and everything else, we were just... really loaded for bear," Dad said. "We took off, doing everything by the numbers, very precisely, making sure we got the gear up, the flaps in the right position, had the right speed and climbed the best we could to get the maximum altitude. Then, when we got the countdown from the Pan Am radio guy, we throttled way back until we were just powered essentially for level flight. We tooled along like that for two or three minutes, got past the sensitive area, and then climbed on out of there. We were hanging on by the skin of our teeth to maintain our altitude and airspeed."

The rest of the flight was uneventful, and they landed in Seattle nearly ten hours later. Fleming then continued on his own down to San Francisco. A couple of days later, my father received a message from Fleming: *You made the quietest jet takeoff that's ever been made out of London!*

Ego and Its Consequences: The Braniff Crash

In addition to flying proving flights for airline customers, Boeing pilots also often had the task of training airline pilots on how to fly the 707. There were no simulators in those days. Providing instruction to outsiders was new for the Boeing pilots, who until this point had only instructed and provided check (qualification) rides to each other. Learning to fly 707s—commercial jets—was new for the airline pilots, who were used to flying piston-engine aircraft. It was probably inevitable that at some point, a disaster would occur.

"Don't date anyone with little-man-itis," my father frequently admonished me throughout my high school and college years. Occasionally, he would elaborate on what that meant. "Someone short, with a chip on his shoulder, always trying to make up for his lack of stature," he'd say. "A big ego." I had certainly encountered men with outsized egos and didn't find their bravado enticing, so I was quietly amused when my father continued to make such a big deal about this over the years. But at just 5'4" myself, who am I to criticize anyone's height?

I got that Dad wanted me to be safe, to be smart about the guys I dated. I was, after all, his only daughter, the youngest of his four children. When I was in college, my friends avoided dating Boeing engineers because their job title screamed BORING. But I always assumed that my father would prefer I date someone safe and predictable, someone who would treat me with respect: a Boeing engineer or someone equally non-flashy. Everyone else was suspect. Still, I was always puzzled by the short-man prejudice.

Then, as I started researching my father's career, I learned about the Braniff 707 training flight that crashed near Arlington, Washington, in 1959. After hearing the full story of that crash from one of its survivors—Bill Allsopp, a Boeing test pilot and my father's colleague—Dad's advice finally made sense. I began to truly appreciate how my father's experiences as a test pilot affected how he parented me.

"That was an accident caused by ego," Bill Allsopp told me when I sat with him and his wife in their Normandy Park dining room in 2003. By then, Bill had had over four decades to reflect on the Boeing 707 training flight crash that nearly ended his life. Of the eight pilots and engineers onboard, Bill was one of four to survive. Time and emotional distance finally allowed Bill the freedom to be blunt, to point the finger of blame where he always felt it rested: on Boeing test pilot Russ Baum. Still, all these years later, Bill could barely bring himself to use Baum's name, instead simply referring to him almost exclusively as "he" throughout our conversation. To say something negative about another test pilot to outsiders would violate the unwritten code they all observed, so trying to avoid using Baum's name was Bill's compromise.

The opening paragraph of the official Civil Aeronautics Board's Aircraft Accident Report filed on June 13, 1960, was also blunt: "On October 19, 1959, at 1620 PST, a Boeing 707-227, N7071, crashed and burned in the Stillaguamish River about 10 miles northeast of Arlington, Washington. Four of the eight occupants aboard received fatal injuries; one of the four survivors received serious injuries."

The official cause of the accident: pilot error. The pilot in command: Boeing test pilot Russ Baum.

Bill was the seriously injured survivor referred to in the CAB report. He sustained a broken clavicle that left him with uneven shoulders for the rest of his life, a severely twisted left knee, and a concussion. He spent a week in the hospital, and it was weeks more before he was cleared to fly. "I had to do pushups, and I had to do knee bends. When I could do those, I went back flying," he said.

This particular 707 was a new model. CAA certification flight tests had just been completed and final certification awaited verification of the test results. Meanwhile, it had an experimental certificate, so Boeing was able to use it to train commercial airline pilots. Jim Gannett assigned Bill to go along with Baum on the Braniff training flight that day, to learn how to instruct. Four of the eight crew members onboard were employed by Braniff.

Just the day before, Don Cumming, Boeing flight test engineer, had been aboard the same airplane on a similar training flight with many of the same crew. Don's job was to gather data. Jack Waddell was the Boeing test pilot in command when Don flew, with a Braniff pilot in the copilot's seat. Don remembers that Braniff pilot Frank Staley was also onboard, observing from the cockpit jump seat; he would fly again the day of the accident as an observer.

"The purpose of both these flights was customer guarantee," said Don. The airlines contracted with Boeing for a certain number of hours to prove performance. This earlier flight wasn't specifically for training, but to demonstrate to the Braniff pilots various handling characteristics, such as engine-out takeoff and a couple of touch-and-go's—routine stuff as Don remembered it. There were eight or nine people onboard, including Don; no CAA personnel were on his flight. Don knew that there would be a training flight the next day. "Baum was strictly a training pilot," remembers Don. Bill was an experimental pilot, but all pilots ended up doing some training, which is why Jim wanted Bill to tag along as an observer.

On that fateful day, Baum was thirty-two years old and had been employed as a test pilot by Boeing since June 1957. He had a wife, Bobbie, and four young sons. Baum's colleagues considered him arrogant and aggressive. As the pilot in command on this training flight, he conducted the preflight briefing of the crew, discussing what maneuvers would be performed. The airplane carried five hours of fuel. In addition to Baum, the crew consisted of Braniff Airlines Capts. Frank Staley and John Berke; George Hagan, Boeing flight engineer; A. C. Krause, Braniff flight engineer; F. W. Symmank, Braniff technical instructor; W. H. Heubner, CAA Air Carrier Operations Inspector, and Bill. They expected to be aloft just over four hours.

Captain Berke, age forty-nine, was making his first flight in the aircraft. He was in the pilot's seat and Baum sat in the copilot's seat. Krause acted as flight engineer. All eight crew members were in the cockpit area for most of the flight. At first, everything proceeded normally—Baum demonstrated the maneuvers, and Berke executed them. For many airline pilots at that time, the 707 was both their first jet and their first swept-wing-design airplane. Airplanes of this type handled very differently from the straight-wing propeller-driven airplanes they had been flying.

Eventually, Baum's training reached the demonstration of recovery from a Dutch roll, a wallowing motion in which the airplane rolls right or left while also yawing (a situation in which the airplane's nose moves to the right or left on the horizon). In normal flying conditions, a Dutch roll is caused by turbulent air, or lateral/directional over-control by the pilot. Because it tends to make passengers both nervous and queasy, it is avoided whenever possible, and corrected quickly when encountered. The ideal, of course, is to keep the wings level during flight. When the airplane is rolling one direction or the other, input to the aileron and/or rudder is usually sufficient to stop the roll and keep the wings level. The pilot must apply the rudder correction in the correct direction, however, or the roll becomes worse.

Baum set up the first Dutch rolls in a clean configuration—flaps and landing gear up—and demonstrated proper recovery. Berke made several recovery attempts. Next, airspeed was reduced to 155 knots and flaps were lowered to 50 degrees, simulating approach for landing. Baum set up more Dutch rolls in this configuration; Berke's attempted recoveries were done poorly. During this series of rolls, bank angles exceeded 25 degrees. Bill, knowing the bank angles went beyond Boeing's restrictions, voiced his concerns to Baum.

"I'm standing or sitting in the position of the jump seat, following the flight all along," said Bill. "He [Baum] showed them how to recover from a Dutch roll. And then he set it up for the Braniff pilot to do it, and he did it wrong. So he did it again, and the student did it wrong again."

With each attempt, Baum set up the maneuver with increased banking, causing Bill serious concern about the airplane's ability to handle the stress. "While we're doing the maneuver, I told him, 'We have a letter in the file that we are not supposed to do that, to that degree,' and of course his answer was, 'Well, I've done it a thousand times, I'm not worried.' And I said, 'Damn it, Russ, either let me in and I'll do it, or stop.' He said 'No, I'm the instructor.' So, yes sir, yes sir...." Feeling both angry and powerless, Bill—nearly ten years older and more experienced than Baum, but fully aware that Baum was the captain on this flight—moved to the back of the flight deck and remained silent.

All the Dutch roll recovery attempts made by Berke to this

point had been from the nose-left position. Despite Berke's struggles, for some unfathomable reason, Baum suggested he try one from nose-right.

"And then [Baum] did it *again,*" Bill continued. "He went... well, we had a rule, you weren't supposed to go over something like 10 degrees bank, and he went up to at least 40 degrees bank, and flipped into it. And the guy did it wrong, *again.*"

According to the CAB report, Baum set up the Dutch roll with a bank of 40 to 60 degrees, far exceeding Boeing's restriction of 10 to 25 degrees. Berke allowed the aircraft to complete several oscillations, each time with a roll bank angle reaching 40 to 60 degrees; when he finally initiated recovery, the right bank continued to increase. Berke applied full-right aileron, which caused the airplane to yaw and roll heavily to the right, well beyond a 90-degree bank.

Baum took the controls and applied full-left aileron as the plane was continuing to roll to the right. After the wings passed vertical, the roll to the right finally stopped, but because of Baum's actions, the airplane rolled swiftly and violently back to the left—a snap roll. The exact number of rotations is unknown, but when the left roll finally slowed to a near stop, the airplane was *upside down*, nose pointed toward the ground. Baum allowed the airplane to continue slowly rolling to the left until it returned to an upright position but still in a medium downward dive.

During the snap-roll recovery executed by Baum, crew members heard sounds—loud, confusing, alarming sounds. Horrified, they watched the thrust levers on the floor stand between the pilots' seats snap, their cables going slack, leaving the levers dancing wildly on their own. Each engine had a fire sensor; the engine 2 fire alarm began ringing and the fire-warning light was flashing.

As Baum pulled out of the dive, everyone on that flight deck could see that the instruments showed a complete absence of thrust on engines 1, 2, and 4; the thrust and start levers for those engines were slack and there was no electrical power to them. After the initial shock at the violence of the maneuvers and the complete roll, each member of the crew began his own internal damage assessment. They quietly scanned the instruments while Baum focused on flying the crippled jet.

As any Boeing flight test crew member will confirm, when things in the cockpit get "interesting" as they put it, everyone shuts up and focuses on doing the critical functions of their assigned job so that the pilot can do his. Engine-fire alarm blaring and warning lights flashing, useless engine-thrust levers moving on their own, anything not strapped down or clipped on having been randomly thrown through the air—the cockpit was barely controlled chaos, thick with human tension and dread.

Heubner, the CAA representative, raced back into the body of the airplane to try to visually confirm what was going on with the engines. He reported back to the flight deck that engines 1 and 4 were *gone*, and small fires were burning in their place; engine 2 was also on fire. Its forward wing mount had failed and it was hanging front end down, with the tailpipe pointed into the wing flap, burning it. It didn't remain attached to the airplane much longer.

Bill also went back to see what was going on with the engines. By the time he looked out a window, engine 2 was gone. "When number 2 came off, apparently the drag link that held the engine came up and hit the spar. The spar is the front ring of the fuel tank. It cracked and leaked fuel out onto the engine; it caught on fire, and eventually, it was going to burn the left wing off." Bill saw a *lot* of fire. He rushed back to the cockpit and reported to Baum what he'd observed. "We had started at 14,000 feet, and we're descending all the time. We had engine 3. He was controlling it very well," said Bill. They broke through the overcast. "We came out over Lake Cavanaugh, by Bellingham," remembers Bill.

"Jeez, that's great—put it in the lake!" Bill said to Baum.

"No, I'm not going to put it in the lake, I'm going back to Seattle," Baum said.

"Seattle? You're never going to get there, your left wing's burning off!" Bill said. "Put it in the lake, we'll put the fire out, we'll maybe even save the airplane—and save us."

"And he said no," Bill recalled with disgust. "He said, 'I'm gonna land this thing. If I have to, I'll go to Arlington, but I'm going to go back to Boeing.'" Bill kept trying to convince Baum they'd never make it, but his pleas fell on deaf ears. Precious time was passing. Baum undoubtedly was so intent on trying to get the 707 safely on the ground that once he had a plan in mind, he wasn't going to deviate. Or maybe Baum was hoping to avoid any bad publicity by making it back to Boeing Field.

"I would have taken over, but he wouldn't let me," said Bill.

Baum continued circling and descending east of Lake Cavanaugh. Hagan, the Boeing flight engineer, took over the flight engineer's post in the cockpit from Krause, the Braniff flight engineer. Hagan was twenty-eight years old, and had hired on at Boeing just five months earlier.

They eventually came out over Deer Creek, near Oso, just north of the Stillaguamish River. Flying in a southeast direction, they had low mountains on their right and high mountains on their left, all densely forested.

Despite being a sparsely populated part of Snohomish County, at least twenty people on the ground witnessed the airplane's harrowing descent. Even before it broke through the cloud cover, several heard an unusual sound, like an airplane breaking the sound barrier. That alarming boom was quickly followed by the bizarre sight of three big objects falling from the sky: engines 1, 4, and then 2. Once the airplane descended through the clouds, witnesses could see it was on fire. Others reported that as the 707 made a sweeping left turn over the south end of Lake Cavanaugh and headed southeast toward Oso, they heard an explosion, then a loud whistling sound. Baum had shut down his last remaining engine so that he could better control the airplane's descent and path. The 707 had become a glider with one wing on fire.

Precious minutes ticked by—one, two, three, four—as the crippled airplane steadily descended, searching for a place to land, a chance at survival.

Baum made a final right turn, heading west over Oso and the Stillaguamish River. At that time of year, after a long summer, the river was very shallow, its rocky bottom mostly exposed. Not a soft landing option. But there were few options left. "There was a big field there, and I could see what he was gonna do… land in that field," said Bill. "I suggested, 'Russ, that's a hell of a field to land in, it's full of stumps. At least try for Arlington, up at the point of the river….'" Baum said he didn't think he could make it.

Having now descended to nearly treetop level, everyone knew that they were about to crash land. They did what they could to prepare for impact. Four of the eight crew members—Krause, Symmank, Huebner, and Bill—took ditching positions in the back of the airplane. The rest—Baum, Berke, Staley, and Hagan—remained in the cockpit, doing everything they could to crash in a controlled way. No one wanted to die that day.

"One of the guys turned to me and asked what he should do," Bill said. "I told him to go to the back end and sit in the far aft. He went and sat in the stewardess chair [left side, extreme rear of the airplane], facing forward. He used the left shoulder strap from the right-hand seat, so nobody could sit next to him; I don't think he thought about that at all. So the next guy to get back sat down on the floor against the bulkhead, facing him. And the next one sat on the right hand side, in a passenger seat, next to the aisle." Bill was the last of the four to get back to the tail section, waiting to the last moment to prepare himself. He started to sit on the left passenger side, but the heat from the fire created by the loss of engine 2 was so intense that he quickly moved to the right side of the aisle. By this point, the fire had burned a hole in the flaps, consumed most of the inboard aileron, and burned through so much of the top wing surface that Bill could see the interior structure of the wing.

Bill barely made it into his seat. "I picked up my safety belt, and that's when we hit," he said. "I hammered into the ceiling, came down, unconscious."

Baum was unable to get the 707 to the open field. Perhaps five to six minutes after the fateful Dutch roll and snap-roll recovery, the left wing clipped some treetops, then 400 feet farther, hit more trees at a height of 90 feet, cutting a swath the width of a wing span. The wings were level at this point, no mean feat given the lack of engine power, loss of hydraulics, and added drag caused by the fire damage to so many flight-control surfaces. Trees severed a 16-foot section of the left wing tip, and the remaining portion of the wing, dropping rapidly, cut through more trees and finally gouged several trenches into the sandy soil of the river bank, breaking up as the fuselage finally struck the ground and literally broke in two, right behind the wings. The aft portion of the airplane skidded away and came to a stop in the shallow water of the river.

"The water woke me up," said Bill. "I found I could sit up, or kneel, and my head was out of the water. The seats were above me, slanted; the airplane was tilted a little bit. I reached up to take the seat, but I couldn't pull it down. I didn't realize I had a broken shoulder. So I used my other arm, and I got standing up. A pair of feet walked by on the hat rack." When Bill asked the owner of the feet if everyone had gotten out, he was told, "If you get out, that'll be all of us." Bill took a look around the back compartment of the airplane, now lying on its side, to make sure no one else was back there. "I walked out of the thing. Somebody said I must have been stunned, because I was standing outside the end of the fuselage to see if there was anybody on the ground. There was a hell of a fire going on—a fuel splash." When an airplane noses in, the fuel in its tanks splashes forward. "The front of the airplane was all in gasoline," Bill said.

All four crew members in the cockpit died on impact.

Back at Boeing Field, Don Cumming heard right away about the crash. Don and Jack Waddell had been on almost every flight that N7071 had taken, including performance testing at Edwards AFB. Jack came charging through the office saying "They crashed our airplane!" But they didn't know why it crashed. Jack and others went to the crash site to assist with the investigation. "I remember wanting to find my wife and son before they heard the news on the radio," Don said, fearing they would think he was onboard.

The scene of the crash was horrific. It's truly amazing

anyone walked away, and Baum is to be commended for bringing the airplane in level, given all the damage it sustained while still in flight. The forward portion of the fuselage was almost completely destroyed upon impact and by the intense fire that followed. The severed left wing tip landed across the river, about 50 feet from the first gouge in the sand made by the remaining wing structure.

The fire from engine 2 caused extensive in-flight damage to the left wing, the entire left side of the aft fuselage, the left side of the tail, up and over the fuselage top, and back along portions of the right side of the tail. The left aft windows were covered with small cracks from the intense heat. Three of the four engines, with most of their pylons still attached, broke off the wings during flight and were found one-and-a-half miles from the main wreckage.[26] Engine 3, shut down in flight to aid in keeping the airplane level, remained on the airplane until impact.

The Civil Aeronautics Board made a full investigation of the accident. The official report states, in part:

> There is little question that the violent gyrations of the N7071 which followed the improper Dutch roll recovery attempt resulted in the separation of the three engines and the in-flight fire.... It is equally clear that the Dutch rolls being performed reached angles of bank far in excess of the limitations established by the company. Responsibility for the safety of this aircraft rested solely on the instructor-pilot. The Board can find no valid reason for Mr. Baum initiating the final Dutch roll so violently. No training advantage could be gained by conducting these maneuvers at the extreme angles of bank reached. Baum certainly should have been aware of this and he was admittedly aware of the company's restrictions. In

---

[26] The 707's nacelle pylon structure was designed to fail in the event of abnormal loading (such as those that occurred when the airplane went into a snap roll) so that destructive loads would not be transmitted to the wing. The fact that the engines separated in this extreme situation was to be expected.

addition, it was surely less than prudent to permit a pilot with no previous experience in the airplane to attempt a recovery from this extreme maneuver.

After this accident, Boeing re-emphasized the roll-bank angle limitations for the 707 with all company personnel. In training, the Dutch roll was no longer demonstrated in the flaps-down configuration because recovery techniques could be demonstrated equally well in the clean configuration. Finally, the point at which a Dutch roll recovery was demonstrated was moved back in the training program, allowing trainee pilots to acquire more familiarity with the airplane before attempting this maneuver.

Four decades after the crash, despite feeling he did all he could that day, Bill nursed some regrets. He knew enough about fuel splash to tell others to get to the back of the airplane; he followed them at the last possible moment when there was nothing else he could do up front. "Three of them came back, and we all walked out. Thinking on it, I should have got everybody but the pilot out of there, to go aft." When I pointed out that wasn't his job, that it was the job of Baum, the pilot in command, Bill still felt responsible. "I should have gotten them out of there."

Bill paused, shaking his head. "Ego," he continued, refusing to speak Baum's name out loud. "He didn't want me telling him, because he already knew everything. That shows what a neophyte he really was. If he'd been listening to the aerodynamicists and flight-control people, they would have told him we've destroyed models in the wind tunnel doing this. So he did it, his last time. And that was that."

Like the CAB investigators, all of the Boeing pilots blamed the crash on pilot error—on Baum. In their view, this wasn't a test crash or an issue with the airplane, it was a training crash. Before the accident, test pilot Harley Beard spent three months with Baum in Australia on a Qantas Airlines 707 training and certification program. "Russ was a little guy, and it just seemed like he had to prove something to everybody," Harley told me in 2004. Harley, Baum, and the rest of the Boeing training crew had returned from Australia just two days before the fateful Braniff training flight.

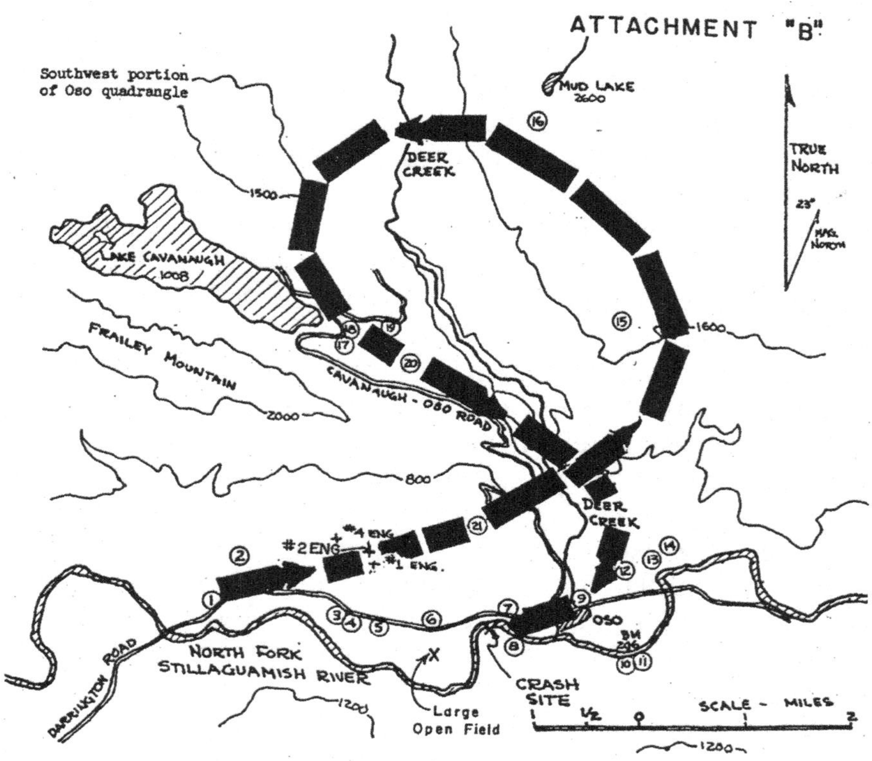

CIRCLED NUMBERS INDICATE
LOCATION OF EYE WITNESSES.

Accident involving Aircraft N 7071
occurred one mile west of Oso,
Washington, on October 19, 1959

Prepared by
Civil Aeronautics Board
Bureau of Safety

USCOMM-DC-25360

20 CAB Accident Report diagram of flight path just prior to crash, showing where engines 1,2 & 4 were found and where witnesses on the ground were located.

21 & 22 Tail section of Braniff 707, in Stillaguamish River. (Photos from CAB Accident Report)

Harley was running errands, picking up his car from the repair shop. "I hear on the radio that a 707 has crashed near Arlington," he said. At first, Harley assumed the reporter meant Arlington, Virginia, and wondered who had taken a 707 back there. His wife convinced him the reporter meant the small rural town of Arlington, *Washington*.

"I called out there [to Boeing] and asked, 'Did we lose an airplane?'" Harley said. "A guy said, 'Yeah. We've been trying to get you. It was Russ. We called him in because he's flown that airplane before. And he was the only one around. We'd like you to go around and tell his family.' I said, 'You mean he's dead?' He said, 'Yeah, they're dead.'"

Harley shook his head sadly as he recalled that awful day. "But of course, they weren't all dead, just half of 'em," he continued. "So I had to get in the car. The wife and I went over to Russ's house, and when we walked in, his wife Bobbie knew. The room was full of eight or nine women, all from the neighborhood. And she had told them, 'If Russ is dead, the guy that'll tell us is Harley because they'll send him over.' We didn't live too far away. So I walked in, and they knew. She asked me to come back the next morning and tell the boys; they were already in bed. I had to go back the next morning and tell the boys their dad was dead."

After talking to Bill, then Harley, years of my father's warnings were put in proper context. I realized that at a very deep level, that accident had affected my father's view of human nature. I now understood why the single word "ego" had such negative connotations when he used it to describe someone's character. To him, a big ego could have deadly consequences. He didn't want me to become involved with someone whose outsized ego might put me in danger.

The B-52 Crash: An Earlier Tragedy

The Braniff 707 training crash was the second crash with fatalities for Boeing in 1959. The other involved a B-52 conducting low-level radar testing for the military and killed five Boeing men, two test pilots and three flight-test engineers, on June 23, 1959. That crash had nothing to do with ego or lack of pilot skill, and everything to do with stressing an airplane beyond its limits. To make the accident even more tragic, it turned out the crew didn't need to make what turned out to be their last flight that day.

The B-52 was designed to fly at high altitudes. The military wanted to see if it could tolerate the stresses of violent turbulence at low altitudes when flying at high speeds. The Boeing crew was to fly just 500 feet above the ground at a near-maximum speed of 638 mph—simulating a nuclear bomb run deliberately flying under enemy radar detection. (Remember, this was during the Cold War.) Somewhere outside Burns, Oregon, the tail of the B-52 sustained structural damage during the test, and at such a low altitude, the crew had no way to maintain enough control to land. The airplane crashed and burned, killing all five crew members instantly. Sadly, the data the military needed had been obtained from a similar test conducted days earlier, but hadn't been reduced from the oscillograph and other raw data to meaningful information by the engineers right away; the flight that ended with a crash wasn't, in fact, necessary.

The two pilots killed that day were Joseph "Joe" Quentin Keller and Lewis "Lew" Moore, both friends of my father. Keller worked alongside my father at Beech Aircraft in Wichita, and followed him to Boeing. Also killed that day were flight engineers Charles K. McDaniel and Neil Johnson, and navigator Gerald Green.

"I'll never forget that funeral," Harley said, remembering. "I was one of the pallbearers. Walking into church and there's five caskets. Unusual."

When I asked my father years later whether that accident had any impact on how the rest of the Boeing test pilots approached their work, he said it didn't because the crash had nothing to do with pilot skill, or pilot error. He did say, though, that they made sure data was reduced as quickly as possible so that no unnecessary flights would be made, and so that any problems with the airplane's structure would be seen before the next flight.

One of the widows told me that after the B-52 crash, the rest of the pilots at Boeing made sure they had wills.

The Widows

Some of my mother's closest friends when I was young were Jane Stewart, Bobbie Lang, and Lorraine Moore. They and their families were part of the greater Boeing "family" I was so familiar with growing up.

I now think of those three women as "The Widows." Bobbie was married to Russ Baum, killed in the Braniff training flight crash in October 1959. Jane was married to Quentin Keller, and Lorraine was married to Lew Moore, both killed in the B-52 crash in June 1959. Growing up, I didn't know they'd lost their husbands in those crashes. By the time I started forming memories of them and their children, Jane and Bobbie had remarried. I didn't fully understand the tragedies they survived until I began researching this book.

When I look at family photos and films from the 1950s, I often see Quentin and Jane Keller and their kids, or the Moores, in scenes from group camping trips and picnics, often before I was born or when I was just an infant.

Harley Beard was the bearer of the awful news for Bobbie Baum. For Jane Keller, my parents had the sad duty of telling her that her husband was gone.

Quentin and my father knew each other from the Navy Reserves. Jane told me that Quentin had asked my father to help him land a job at Boeing. He did, and Quentin hired on in September 1955. Quentin and Jane moved to Seattle and settled into the Sherwood Forest neighborhood of Bellevue.

"Your Dad and I were the ones to tell Jane that Quentin had died in an accident," Mom remembered. "My parents were out visiting, so we were able to leave you kids with them and spend time with Jane and her kids. I spent four or five days there, and Lew spent quite a bit of time as well. Lew had to tell the media people to leave. They wanted to interview and take pictures of Jane. I was so impressed with how Jane handled it. She never broke down in front of anyone. She was so strong. We were all in our thirties then."

After a pause, Mom added, "I saw your father cry for the first time at Quentin's funeral."

The three widows leaned on each other, as well as the greater Boeing Flight Test family. As time went on, they ended up throwing parties for their Boeing friends and entertaining airline pilots in town for training. In May 1960, the three of them went to a pawn shop and bought a used guitar to present to my father as a birthday gift. "He was always saying he wanted to learn to play," Bobbie told me. He did learn to play, teaching himself. I have fond memories of sitting in our basement, singing along with Dad as he played songs like "Red River Valley,"[27] "On Top of Old Smoky," and "Tom Dooley," recorded in 1958 by the Kingston Trio, one of my father's favorite groups.

Bobbie ended up marrying Bill Lang, a friend of my father's at Boeing who worked in customer relations. Bill adopted Bobbie's four boys, so that by the time I remember hanging out at their family's summer cabin on Lake Sammamish, I just assumed Bill was their father. Bobbie loved entertaining, and the Lang's summer cabin, though small, was often crammed with families invited to enjoy the lake and a barbeque. I loved spending time at the Lang's cabin; it was a happy place.

Jane also remarried, to a man named Bill Stewart. Jane's children joined Bill's children, and eventually they added children of their own for a yours-mine-ours blended family of eight kids. They also lived in Bellevue, and I distinctly remember visiting their home because they had some acreage where they'd set up badminton and volleyball nets, and... they had goats! The Stewarts' house was a kid-friendly place to play and be wild, and Jane was always happy and outgoing and fun. Growing up, all I knew is that all of the children in Jane's house had the same last name, so I was unaware that some of the older ones had lost a parent. I just thought it was an awfully

---

[27] The song's melody was used by British pilots in their song "Hurrah for the Next Man Who Dies" in the 1938 film *The Dawn Patrol*. I'm not sure if that influenced my father's favoring the song, but it wouldn't surprise me if it did. Woody Guthrie recorded the song in 1944.

big family.

It wasn't until I was in college, possibly later, that I truly understood that three of the families we socialized with regularly when I was a child consisted of the widows and children of pilots who died in those two 1959 crashes. No one talked about how the men died, at least not that I heard or understood. The tragedies were handled seamlessly within the Flight Test family. The widows and children were cared for and watched over by the other pilots and their families until new families were established. Even then, all three women and the "new" families of the two who remarried continued to socialize with the greater Boeing family. As was common in that era, the tragedies of the past were not openly discussed or dwelt upon. People moved on.

Dad, Where Should I Sit on a Commercial Flight?

The two 1959 crashes were the only fatalities within Seattle's Boeing Flight Test group during my father's entire thirty-five-year career,[28] and they had many far-reaching and often subtle effects on the pilots and families who remained.

Asked whether, after those two accidents, anything changed about the way test or training flights were conducted, Harley's reply focused on the B-52 crash. "Well, not from a pilot's standpoint, but I'm sure things changed as far as the engineers were concerned—data was reduced on time! But from our standpoint, I don't recall any big changes, although we were probably looking at the data a whole lot closer." Brien Wygle told me that because the Braniff training flight crash was pilot error, the other Boeing pilots didn't need to do anything differently, the unspoken inference being that they didn't suffer from big egos and would never have allowed such a dangerous training situation to arise.

When we spoke all those years later, Harley hinted that

---

[28] There was, however, the 1951 midair collision of two B-47s in Wichita, which killed four Boeing test pilots, the tragedy mentioned earlier that led to my father and three other flight test engineers being promoted to test pilot while still based in Wichita.

maybe Baum shouldn't have been allowed to fly for Boeing. "Especially when they found out that... Dix [Loesch, Boeing's Chief Test Pilot at the time] was really mad because he got reports from Australia that the Qantas students were afraid to ride with Russ from the hotel to the airport because of the way he drove. His reputation was pretty bad."

It turns out that another piece of advice my father often gave me relates to the Braniff crash. Whenever I'd ask Dad about the safest place to sit on a commercial flight, he'd advise me to sit in the back, even though the engine noise is loudest there. "If that's not possible, sit over the wings where the emergency exit doors are," he suggested, even though the wings block most of the view. When I asked why the back of the airplane, he'd just say it was safer; I never got a more detailed explanation than that.

Bill's vivid description of the Braniff crash and the effect of fuel splash on the 707's cockpit made the basis for my father's advice to sit in the back abundantly clear. And on January 15, 2009, my father's decades-old advice about sitting over the wings was made obvious when Captain Chesley "Sully" Sullenberger ditched his Airbus A320 on the Hudson River after both engines lost power just after takeoff because of bird strikes.[29] Passengers exited the floating airplane onto the wings and were rescued from there.

In both instances—warnings against "ego" and suggestions to sit in the back of the airplane or over the wing—my father's advice came without the emotional baggage of the actual accident from which it derived. I don't remember my father ever talking about the 707 crash when I was growing up. It wasn't until I started collecting stories and specifically asked him about crashes that resulted in fatalities within Flight Test that it came up. By that time, he was in his seventies. He simply suggested I talk to Bill Allsopp for the specifics.

---

[29] I chafe when I hear this incident referred to in the media as "the Miracle on the Hudson." While Capt. Sullenberger exhibited the aw-shucks humbleness of pilots of his experience and vintage, the safe landing of that airplane on the water was the result of *his* skill as a pilot, not divine intervention.

Still, hearing the details of these stories, I finally began making connections between long-ago incidents and the way I was raised. None of the pilots, my father included, dwelled on things that went wrong or were the result of someone else's error. If they had, they wouldn't have been able to climb into those cockpits day after day, risking their own lives while taking airplanes to extremes in test programs. Their families wouldn't have been able to grow and thrive without worry. It is the nature of successful test pilots to have confidence that their skill will keep them safe, and that confidence in turn allows their families to relax and carry on with their own lives. I grew up knowing that worry was pointless, that calculated, smart risk-taking was acceptable and even encouraged, but one should do everything possible to minimize exposure to unnecessary risk or to those whose behavior could put one at risk.

The 707 Intercontinental model that my father flew to Rome was the last of the 707s designed for passengers; later derivatives were cargo versions, or in one case, a "convertible" design that could quickly be configured for passengers or cargo. By 1960, Boeing was moving ahead with the 727 and named my father its project pilot. Boeing did, however, later use the 707 for two unique military purposes. The Boeing E-3 Sentry is a United States military airborne warning and control system (AWACS) aircraft based on the 707. It has a huge saucer-like disc (a rotating radar dome) sitting atop two tall pylons attached to the upper surface of a 707-320 fuselage, between the wings and tail. The radar is able to detect vehicles, aircraft, and ships at long ranges to help direct air battles; it's also used to carry out surveillance.

Since 1977, the AWACS airplanes have been providing communications, all-weather surveillance, and command-and-control functions for tactical and defensive missions to the militaries for the United States, the United Kingdom, Saudi Arabia, France, and NATO.

I asked my father if he'd ever flown an AWACS airplane. His reply cracked me up. "No, never did," he said. "They used to go out and fly for twelve hours in circles, which I didn't find very exciting. Seriously, they just flew a big circle pattern." This answer was similar to those I would get when as a child I'd ask if he'd ever wanted to be an airline pilot or an astronaut. He'd always smile, shake his head no and say something like, "Airline pilots are just hauling passengers over the same route day after day. Too boring."

As for any interest in being an astronaut when NASA first recruited test pilots for the job in 1959, his answer was even more dismissive, noting that the first astronauts didn't use any flying skills, essentially having the same job as Enos, the first chimpanzee to orbit the earth in Mercury Atlas 5 on November 29, 1961—strapped into a capsule, having no control, and simply hoping to return home alive. Why leave Boeing, when he was having so much fun testing cutting-edge commercial airplanes?

The other unique use of the 707-320 was as Air Force One, the secure airplane the Air Force uses for transporting the president of the United States (if the airplane is carrying anyone other than the president, it's not referred to as Air Force One for that flight) and as a US Strategic Command Airborne Command Post. Boeing 707-320s were used in the 1960s and 1970s; thereafter, Boeing 747s continued in that role. Having such a presidential airplane and command post has become an enduring symbol of our country's power and status. My father did fly the first 747 version of the Airborne Command Post, when that 747 was undergoing testing, before it was delivered to the Air Force for the president's use. It's still disconcerting to see film of that big white 747 with UNITED STATES OF AMERICA painted on its side, landing gear on fire on the runway at Edwards AFB after failing a refused takeoff test in 1974, prior to certification. Rest assured, Boeing fixed that problem before delivering Air Force One to the military for presidential use.

Tex Johnston's Secret: How He Flew in All Conditions

Alvin "Tex" Johnston had an out-sized personality, which

he often put to good use. He had a huge impact on Boeing's success and the reputation of Boeing's early jet airplanes—and the tests pilots who flew them—when he twice rolled the Dash 80 over Seafair in 1955. Throughout his career he promoted his cowboy showman persona by wearing cowboy boots in the cockpit, a Stetson hat, and maintaining a pencil mustache à la Errol Flynn and Clark Gable.

23 Tex Johnston and Lew Wallick, late 1950s. Photo: Boeing Archives.

And of course, he was an excellent pilot. "A very good stick and rudder guy," is how my father and others usually described him. Good instincts.

Tex's biography reads a lot like my father's and Brien Wygle's, probably like those of many test pilots of their era. Born in Kansas in 1914, Tex was ten years older than my father. His first experience flying was at age eleven when a barnstormer landed near the family farm. That encounter set his life's course. He took flying lessons and soloed at age fifteen. After leaving high school, he became a barnstormer himself. He did eventually return to college with the intention of getting an engineering degree, but dropped out in 1939. Starting in 1941, Tex flew for the US Army Air Corps Ferry Command, getting airplane parts to Britain before the United States officially entered World War II.

In late 1942, Tex joined Bell Aircraft in Buffalo, New York, as a test pilot. It was on Bell's flight line that wearing cowboy boots and a Stetson earned him the nickname "Tex." At Bell, Tex helped design and was the second man to fly the rocket-propelled Bell X-1.

Joining Boeing as a test pilot in July 1948, Tex worked on the B-47 in Seattle and Wichita, returning to Seattle in 1951 as project pilot for the B-52. In 1952, Tex piloted the first flight of the B-52 with Lt. Col. Guy M. Townsend, of the US Air Force Flight Test Center, as copilot.[30] Soon after, Tex became Boeing's Chief of Flight Test.

I asked my father what Tex was like to work for. "He was okay," Dad said. "The main thing was, don't try to be too close to him." I took this to mean Tex was distant with his colleagues, but Dad quickly corrected me. "He was friendly enough. I've seen more than one guy get bit because they tried to brownnose him." According to Dad, Tex would tolerate that

---

[30] According to Boeing test pilot Dix Loesch, despite having already flown as Tex's copilot on other first flights, Loesch wasn't selected for the B-52's first flight because he was a former Navy pilot, and the Air Force wanted one of its own in the cockpit. Townsend eventually joined Boeing in 1970—after retiring from the military as a brigadier general—as Assistant Operations Director of the SST program.

for a little while, then turn on the person. "I got along with him fine," Dad continued. "I just did my job, was friendly with him, but didn't try to go party with him."

Tex was the boss when Dad arrived in Seattle in 1955. They worked together on B-47, B-52, Dash 80, and eventually 707 testing and certification programs. By the late 1950s when the 707 was flying, Tex wasn't flying as much, Dad said, but he was interesting to fly with because he didn't have an instrument rating.[31]

When Tex first started flying, pilots didn't fly with instruments. And then, he just never got the rating. Dad said Tex didn't want to go through the trouble of learning about instruments and taking the written tests. "He could fly instruments—fly into clouds on instruments, which didn't bother him a bit. He could sit there and hold altitude and air speed, heading, flying level, and descending, whatever you wanted him to do. But he had a mental block about procedures."

Dad would fly with Tex on cross-country and demonstration flights to be his "instrument ticket" especially in the Dash 80. Jim Gannett also filled that role for Tex, but less often. "I turned out to be one of his favorites," Dad said, "I guess because I never embarrassed him. Flying around on instruments on demonstration flights, we'd be wearing headsets with boom mics on them, using the interphone so no one else on the airplane could hear. I'd give him what I called a cockpit-controlled approach, rather than doing a radar-based ground-controlled approach. I'd tell him, 'Okay Tex, turn to such-and-

---

[31] An instrument rating allows a pilot to legally fly through clouds or in the dark when visual references to the ground and obstacles aren't available for navigation, under what is called IFR (Instrument Flight Rules). Using visual references is referred to as VFR, or Visual Flight Rules flying. An instrument rating is required for all flights in air space above 18,000 feet. Obtaining an instrument rating requires additional training beyond a Private Pilot certificate or Commercial Pilot certificate. A pilot must pass a written exam and a practical exam (check ride); the practical portion includes an oral component to verify that the pilot understands the theory of instrument flying, and an actual flight during which the pilot demonstrates the skills required for IFR flight.

such heading and descend to such-and-such altitude and speed.' He'd level off and hold that speed. When time came to turn, I'd say, 'Now make a 20-degree bank turn to the right and level off to such-and-such heading....' I'd talk him through the approach. He'd fly it precisely, as long as he didn't have to do the mental work of the procedures." Tex wasn't required to have an instrument rating for his job at that time; there were plenty of pilots who did and could fly copilot with him.

Test engineer Don Cumming remembers an early demonstration flight of the 707 to an Air Force general. Tex was pilot, my father copilot. They were flying from Seattle to Minneapolis. "Lew asked me to go along because the test director was often asleep," Don said. "Tex wasn't instrument rated. As we neared Minneapolis, it was snowing. Lew took it down until the runway was in sight."

I wondered whether my father got an instrument rating while he was in the Navy. "No," he replied, "you didn't have to back in those days. But you would get some instrument training. When I got out, I didn't have an instrument rating. I got it on my own, while I was working at Beech."

While at Beech, Dad was also in the Naval Reserves, which had SNJ's, a two-seat trainer Dad had flown during his Navy training. He'd get someone to fly in the front seat while he took the back seat and practiced instrument flying. He knew what he was supposed to do; it was just a matter of practicing.

When he felt ready to take the test—with permission from the Navy Reserves to use an SNJ—Dad contacted the CAA inspector in Kansas City. The inspector happened to be a former Army Air Corps pilot and he agreed to fly with Dad. "I flew up there," Dad continued, "picked him up and put him in the front seat. He took off, and I went under the hood in the back seat to do this check ride. I got my ticket." Dad got a civilian instrument rating check ride using a Navy airplane—something that would never happen today.

As for Tex's cowboy persona, Dad said that Tex promoted that. "His attitude was that there was no such thing as bad publicity. I heard him say that more than once, and he was serious. He knew that it was better to have good publicity, but he felt there was nothing so bad that it was bad publicity." Dad did feel, though, that Tex rolling the Dash 80 so publicly over Seafair had less to do with publicity and more to do with Tex's showman attitude toward flying. He loved to roll airplanes; he'd already rolled an XB-47 in front of the airport tower in Wichita.

Don Cumming described Tex as technically competent, a guy who put a lot of thought into things and was well respected. However, he said Tex was wild when socializing, something he never saw in my father. Brien Wygle made a similar comment about Tex, so I think that was the general perception in Flight Test.

In 1960, Tex was named assistant program manager for Boeing's X-20 Dyna-Soar program. The "Dynamic Soarer" was an Air Force program to develop a spaceplane that could be used for military missions—reconnaissance, bombing, satellite maintenance, and sabotage of enemy satellites. So by 1960, Tex was no longer flying Boeing's new commercial jets as part of Flight Test. He had a short yet ultimately very public and famous career as a Boeing test pilot.

When Tex went to Florida for the Dyna-Soar program, Dix Loesch was promoted to Chief of Flight Test.

CHAPTER FOUR: THE SIXTIES

Experience is that marvelous thing that enables you to recognize a mistake when you make it again.
—Franklin P. Jones, reporter and humorist

Roll, Roll, Roll Your Plane, Gently Through the Sky

I described my surprise when, at my father's retirement party in 1986, my suspicions regarding his having rolled a Boeing jet were confirmed. Knowing my father as I do, I was pretty certain he didn't stop at one roll. In fact, how could Harley Beard have known to have the movie camera ready in the F-86 unless he was pretty sure he could taunt my father into rolling the 707? Harley already knew Dad enjoyed rolling the big jets.

Dad eventually gave me the details behind that roll captured on film. It was 1960 or 1961. Dad was piloting the 707-300 with a minimum crew of copilot and flight engineer. They were doing routine tests, somewhere high over Washington State with Harley shadowing them in the F-86. Dad and Harley were communicating directly via radio. Harley had a mischievous streak. A former Air Force pilot, he loved flying the F-86 for its speed and maneuverability and was skilled at executing aerobatic maneuvers.

On this particular day, after they'd run through all their tests, Harley said over the radio, "Hey Lew! Watch this!" and flew up fast from behind and underneath the 707, performing a roll right in front of its nose.

"Nice, Harley," my father responded as Harley flew back around into position alongside the much slower 707.

Then Dad said, "Hey Harley, watch *this*!" as he rolled the 707.

What Dad didn't anticipate was that Harley was prepared, ready to film the roll. Harley knew my father well, knew his goading might just get the desired result. My father saw the film one time, shortly after it was made, but had forgotten about it until the stills taken from it appeared in his retirement party presentation.

When I began interviewing my father's colleagues in 2003, I always asked about rolls. I also went to the Boeing Archives for information. I discovered that even as the current millennium dawned, the common belief inside and outside Boeing was that Tex Johnston was the only pilot to roll a commercial jet, and that he did it only that one time over Seafair.

I knew differently, but I didn't know all the details nor the full extent to which my father may have rolled jets. I finally got Dad to admit to me that he not only rolled the 707 shown in that retirement party slide show, but he rolled a 707 *several* times over the years. He also rolled the KC-135 (a military refueling tanker that, like the 707, was derived from the Dash 80), the 727, and the 737. He wouldn't say how many times, exactly, probably because he lost count. He also emphasized that a roll isn't a violent maneuver. In fact, my father said that one time he rolled a 707, and two guys standing in the cabin didn't even realize the airplane had rolled.[32]

I also learned that my father and Tex weren't the only Boeing test pilots to roll those babies. Yet getting *any* of them to admit it to me, for public disclosure, was like pulling teeth. I resorted to pleading, telling them that these stories would die with them if they didn't tell me. Because I'm Lew's daughter, they trusted me and shared some of their stories.

I always wondered why they were so reticent. Why not admit they'd rolled these airplanes? They were all long into retirement by the time I asked.

Then I interviewed Harley. His cautionary tale about rolling 707s helps explain why the pilots never talked about it, why

---

[32] If you find this hard to believe, I invite you to view this YouTube video: http://www.youtube.com/watch?v=uw2qPLEgKdQ (or Google "Bob Hoover airplane roll") and watch as a glass of tea is poured while the airplane does a barrel roll, nary a drop spilled.

they did rolls very quietly and secretly, and why my father likely did feel a little embarrassed by the revelation during his retirement party.

I sat with Harley in his kitchen one day in early 2004, tape recorder and pen ready. Harley still looked much like I remembered him from my childhood: stocky, mostly bald, a commanding presence, a bit gruff yet ultimately friendly and warm. He showed me the small aerobatic airplane he'd been building in his garage for a number of years. Recently widowed, Harley had put the project on hold as he'd nursed his wife through her final illness.

Mentioning the story of goading Dad into rolling the 707 and filming it, I asked Harley if he, too, had rolled the 707 or other jets. "Oh yeah," Harley said without hesitation.

"You all did, didn't you?" I asked.

"Well, I don't know. I know Lew did, and Brien [Wygle] did, but I'm the only one that got caught!" he replied with a quiet chuckle.

In the early 1960s, Boeing sent Harley to Germany to train Lufthansa pilots in the 707 and 720 (a shorter version of the 707). During that time, he met and worked with a Lufthansa pilot named Werner, a former fighter pilot. "Werner and I got along really well," Harley said. "He was an excellent pilot. When I'd go to Germany, I'd go out to Werner's house. The last time I saw him, he had a party at his house. He said, 'Harley, that airplane is so nice, every time I'm on a training flight, I always roll it.' And he could do a good roll." Harley knew this because Harley showed him the maneuver. It wasn't part of the training curriculum, but, well... *they all did it.*

Then, on July 15, 1964, a Lufthansa Boeing 720 crashed during a training flight, with all three crewmembers onboard losing their lives. The instructor pilot in charge of the flight was Werner. Harley's friend was dead.

Boeing sent Harley over to assist with the investigation. He arrived about thirty-six hours after the crash. "They were digging the engines out of the ground," Harley said. "They were still hot." The black box was recovered and the data extracted. "We looked at the traces. It looked like Werner had done a roll," Harley said. "And the pilot he was checking was also a student of mine, but he was not a very shining pilot; he was not all that good. It looked like Werner let this guy try to roll the airplane, and they dished out, and pulled a lot of *g*'s, and the tail pulled off the airplane, so they crashed and it killed them," he said.

That was just the beginning of Harley's own ordeal.

"There was a German mechanic who testified, 'Oh yeah, Captain Beard—I was on a flight with him from Homburg to Frankfurt, and he rolled it all the way,'" Harley said. "Well, that was an exaggeration; I only made about five of them. That testimony got me in a whole lot of trouble. It looked like my career at Boeing was over." Harley's career survived, but he was penalized. Dix Loesch, Chief Test Pilot, cut Harley's pay by half for six months. Harley was a little miffed because when he did fly, he was in charge of the very expensive airplane, but everyone else onboard was making more money than him. "But at least I was still employed," he said, remembering that during that period he would say to himself *this will pass.* And it did.

It was after the Lufthansa incident that Dix issued a firm decree: *No more rolls.* Harley explained that even before the crash, Tex Johnston had issued the same order. "Tex called us all into the office before he left [in 1960] and said we were not to do any more rolls," Harley recalled. "It was a case of 'Do as I say, not as I do.'"

Which helps explain why some of the pilots continued doing rolls. Harley had previously done a roll in a 707 *with* Tex. "One day, he and I were in a Qantas airplane which I was certifying," Harley said. "Tex says, 'Let me show you something,' and did a roll. I asked if I could try one and he said sure. Well, I'd been flying every day, and he hadn't been flying. My roll was better than his, so he made a remark about my ancestry, saying 'You son of a bitch; let's go home.'" Harley smiled as he told the story. "Tex knew we were doing them." Tex's prohibition didn't stop Harley when he trained Werner, the Lufthansa captain.

"The prohibition was still in effect, which I had ignored," Harley admitted. "It cost me." Harley, my father, Brien, and many others continued to occasionally take the airplanes out for a roll—literally—albeit secretly, and in Harley's case, despite nearly losing a job he loved. "It didn't stop me, but it made me think about it," Harley said.

The same was true for my father. That's how Harley knew he could goad Dad into doing a roll and capture it on film. Had it been anyone other than Harley in the chase plane, I doubt my father would have done the roll. It also explains why my father was embarrassed to have that photographic proof displayed at his retirement party, and why—even well into retirement—he was loath to admit to me that he had rolled any of the jets. It had been prohibited—first by Tex, then by Dix, his mentor, boss, and friend—and had he been caught while employed, he could have been fired. Beyond that, I think he felt that it was unprofessional to have ignored company policy just for sheer fun.

Rolls, and the prohibition against them, became so ingrained in the company DNA that on June 12, 1994, when test pilot John Cashman was preparing to take the 777 on its first flight, Boeing President Phil Condit offered his best wishes for a successful flight, concluding with "No rolls!" John knew exactly what Condit was referring to.

Still, most of the test pilots of my father's era did roll those beautiful jets. They couldn't resist.

Along Comes the 727

In 1960, my father was named project pilot for the 727. The airplane was still in its design phase at this time, so Dad continued testing the 707, 720, and the Dash 80 while attending meetings on the 727. He thoroughly enjoyed being involved in the design of a new airplane from the get-go, working with all the engineers and going to the various meetings. This was the first time he was able to be involved from the earliest stages of a program and have significant input in the design of the cockpit.

The 727's design was a radical departure from the 707 in terms of engine placement: three engines mounted near the tail—one in the center and one on either side—rather than four engines on the wings.

24 Publicity photo of Lew Wallick in the 727's not-quite-ready cockpit. (Note the plywood seatback and missing instrumentation. Everything was completed for the first flight on February 9, 1963.) Photo: Boeing Archives.

To test design theories, Boeing engineers and mechanics installed an engine on the side of the rear fuselage of the Dash 80. It looked like a big brown lamprey sucking on the airplane's fuselage, its tail (exhaust pipe) bent in a wiggle as if swimming alongside. They also designed and installed a set of flaps that were scaled to be like the inboard flaps on the 727, which were huge on the Dash 80. All this was done so they could test the air flow from the wing into the side engine inlet. Engineers were concerned that there might be air distortion, creating engine surge problems. (An engine surge is like a car backfire.) The extra engine mounted on the Dash 80 mimicked the anticipated placement of one of the side 727 engines.

25 Modified Dash 80 with test engine. Tom Edmonds, Lew Wallick second and third from left. Photo: Boeing Archives.

"I flew a lot of the flights on the Dash 80 in this configuration—a five-engine jet!" Dad said. "Everything was fine. We didn't run into any surge problems. I figured everything was going to be fine on the 727." The day before the first flight, Boeing took some publicity photos. My father posed on the tarmac, the 727's three engines and tail behind him. He also posed in the cockpit, in the pilot's seat, a huge grin on his face as he looks over his shoulder at the camera. Dad pointed out that he was leaning against a temporary plywood seat back; the real seat back was installed before the first flight.

February 9, 1963, dawned a beautiful clear morning, perfect for the 727's first foray into the skies over Puget Sound. Pilots describe this sort of weather as "severe clear"—brilliant blue skies with unlimited visibility. "A test pilot's dream weather conditions for the first flight of the new Boeing 727," my father said. "The airplane was ready, so we flew it." No big deal, right?

My father was the pilot; his boss and Chief of Flight Test Dix Loesch was copilot, and M. K. "Shuly" Shulenberger was flight engineer. They each wore lace-up boots and a flight suit, like those worn by military aviators—a one-piece jumpsuit of light green that zipped up the front and had a plethora of zippered pockets on the legs, arms, and chest for stowing pencils, maps, writing pads, and so on.[33]

After a preflight briefing with engineering to go over the test plan, they headed out to the airplane, painted Boeing yellow with brown trim. Standing on the tarmac near the airstair leading up to the airplane's main door, confident and relaxed with their bulky flight helmets nestled under crooked elbows, they stood for publicity photos while commenting on the remarkable weather. Pleasantries with the flight-line crew and several members of company management were exchanged. My father, at just under six feet, was the tallest of the three and sported the longest hair—jet black, cropped close on the sides (where a little gray was just starting to show), the longer-on-top hair parted at the side and combed back from his forehead with a bit of a wave. Dix's hair was closely shaved, showing a receding hairline, and Shuly sported the more typical Boeing

---

[33] Starting with the 747, first flight crews wore jackets and ties, which I always thought was a mistake; losing that romantic aura of the test pilot. Business attire didn't allow them to look like the true aviators they were. John Cashman, Boeing's Chief Test Pilot and in command of the 777 on its first flight in 1994, told me that he and copilot Ken Higgins compromised: they changed into flight suits once onboard, then changed again before getting off at the end of the flight. I so loved those flight suits, that for years, as a Halloween costume, I wore an orange one of my father's with his Navy leather jacket, leather helmet, and goggles.

engineer crew cut. All three men were smiling broadly, exuding confidence with the subdued and controlled excitement of an experienced test crew about to fly into history.

The maintenance supervisor, quality-control supervisor, and flight-test operations supervisor reviewed the work items completed after finishing the previous day's taxi tests as well as the status of the airplane for this day's test flight. When those supervisors signed the flight release and presented it to my father, he signed it, accepting the airplane for flight—a formality making him responsible for the airplane.

"We had a pretty nice turnout at the Renton Airport," Dad remembered. "It was a Saturday. The weather was clear, a nice breeze out of the north right down the runway. Perfect conditions for what I wanted." The three days of taxi runs completed a few days earlier showed him that the airplane was ready.

Once inside the cockpit and while going through checklists and checking instrumentation, the pilots went over some emergency procedures, some "what if" scenarios. For example, if they had an engine fire midflight, since they planned to be flying north of Seattle, they'd want to land at Paine Field or Whidbey Island Naval Base. But if something happened right after takeoff, they'd want to land at Boeing Field because it had a good runway and Paine Field didn't have a Boeing facility. They didn't envision any emergency that would prevent them from landing *somewhere,* so they didn't even discuss the possibility of ditching into Lake Washington immediately after takeoff.

The interior of the 727 looked more like the inside of a warehouse than that of a commercial airliner. The entire length of the cabin was full of instruments for recording test data. The interior of the fuselage was covered in thick padded sheets of material to keep crews from bumping heads and elbows on sharp surfaces. Once inside the cockpit and strapped into their seats, the crew conducted their preflight check of all the systems and started the three engines. They couldn't hear the engines inside the cockpit, but the instruments and a faint hum told them all three were running smoothly. Flight-test radio cars were in position on the runway, and Tom Edmonds in the company's F-86 chase plane had just taken off; he would be shadowing the 727. Thousands of people lined Rainier Avenue, waiting to watch the takeoff.

Taxiing to the south end of the runway, checking the brakes and steering as they went, they turned onto the runway. Dix described this moment as "the 727 settled into position like a sprinter into the starting blocks." A Coast Guard rescue chopper and "crash boats" moved into position because the 727 would be taking off to the north, over Lake Washington, as required by the FAA.

Then, the moment of truth arrived. With takeoff clearance from the tower, Dad said to his crew, "Alright, let's go!" Moving the throttles forward to full thrust, he let go of the brakes.

26 Takeoff, first flight of the 727. Photo: Boeing Archives.

Here's how my father later described that memorable first takeoff:

> We release the brakes and go charging down the runway, get to rotation speed, rotate, lift off, nose is up, and I can't really see the end of the runway anymore—all

> I see is water and Mercer Island off in the distance. When we're about 50 feet in the air, we hear BANG! **BANG!** It was really loud; you could *feel* it. It was a big backfire—surges. Shuly said it was the center engine; he saw it on his instrument panel. I reached up and pulled all three engines back a little bit; we still had plenty of power to climb. I just left the throttles there and climbed out to a higher altitude. We let our radio crew know it was surges. Then we started experimenting with it.

The crowd on the ground, watching that initial takeoff, surely heard those backfires, but probably only the engineers in attendance realized what it was. The sounds were loud but quick, like two shotgun blasts, or as my father said, the backfire of an old Kansas farm tractor. It's doubtful anyone would have thought it was an engine exploding or similar disaster. Still, it was *completely* unexpected. Dad and his crew knew what surges sounded like because they'd had them on the 707, and in fact the whole reason for mounting a side test engine on the Dash 80 was to determine whether surging would be an issue on the 727. "It's just that we weren't expecting it on takeoff," Dad said. "Normally when you have an engine surge, you're doing reversing and you suck exhaust gas up into an inlet and that causes distortion and surges. I figured I knew what it was, but I didn't know which engine, so I pulled back on all three throttles. Shuly knew, saw it, and said it was the second engine. I was looking out through the windshield; I wasn't watching the gauges." An example of a test pilot's instant reaction to an unexpected occurrence, using gut instinct and experience to address it while remaining calm. Pulling back on all three engine throttles sufficiently to stop the surges while giving enough thrust to maintain a reasonable climb rate bought them time to figure out what was going on.

Dix wrote a piece about the first flight for the March 1963 issue of the Boeing News. He didn't mention the engine surges.

> The 727 came off the ground easily as Lew pulled back on the column, and we went out over Lake Washington

> in a shallow, easy climb to the north. Edmonds came whipping in behind us in the chase plane and we continued our climb at about 150 knots and 2,000 feet per minute. This is well below the airplane's capabilities, but in those first few minutes you might say that the 727 and its crew were just getting acquainted and we didn't want to be too forward.

That's one way to put it. The climb was shallow and easy, well below capabilities because the surges were a surprise, causing my father to throttle back.

Once at cruising altitude, the crew continued with their test program for that first flight, the program they'd been planning for days. They leveled off at about 15,000 feet, flying between Renton and Port Angeles while performing mild maneuvers on all axes—sideslips, turns, rolls, nose up, nose down—with flaps in takeoff configuration and gear still down, getting a feel for the airplane. Once satisfied with what they saw and felt, they brought flaps in to cruise configuration and brought up the gear. They then met up with a Boeing photo airplane, flying formation at 9,000 feet over Port Townsend. First-flight photos done, they went back up to 15,000 and continued testing, including some initial stall work and shutting off primary control systems so as to operate on the secondary systems. After approximately two hours of flight, they landed at Paine Field near Everett, Washington. This was the first time a Boeing first flight was required by the FAA to land at Paine Field—at the time, a fairly rural airport, before the enormous Boeing 747 production plant was built—rather than Boeing Field. It had been several years since Boeing had had a first flight. Now, the FAA was requiring at least ten hours of flight time on a new airplane before allowing landings at airports in more densely populated areas.

After landing, taxiing, and parking the 727 at Paine Field's terminal building, the crew shut down the engines and prepared to exit the airplane. Dix described their final moments in the cockpit in his Boeing News article.

As we closed up the "office" for the day I thought that these first two hours might be likened to skiing an unfamiliar course. We take the first part easy and then when we break into the open we're still careful, but know that the rest of the run will be all downhill and fast.

"Thanks for the ride, Lew," I said as I climbed out of the seat.

Lew looked out the window at the bright sunny sky where we had just been. "It sure has been a good day, hasn't it, Dix?" he said.

I knew that he wasn't referring entirely to the weather.

27 The 727 crew celebrates first flight: M. K. Shulenberger, Lew Wallick, Boeing President William Allen and Dix Loesch. Photo: Boeing Archives.

A news conference was held in a small office building belonging to the airport. Then everyone left. No big celebration, as happens after first flights today. Dad, Dix, and Shuly had all left their cars at the Renton Airport. Luckily, Boeing had a station wagon waiting at Paine Field and hauled them back to Renton to retrieve their cars. "There was a restaurant right across the street from the Renton Airport," Dad said. "We really hadn't had anything to eat, so we went over there and decided to have lunch and a celebratory drink or two. Then we went home."

An anticlimactic ending to an exciting and historic morning.

If my mother, brothers, and I were present for the 727's first takeoff—and we most likely were—I don't remember. I was only six.

Surges at takeoff weren't the only mishap during that first flight. Most of the flight was routine, except for one other thing: if you look at a true in-flight photograph of the 727's first flight, the leading-edge slats are extended; they couldn't retract them. Dix didn't mention this in his article, either. The leading-edge slats issue wasn't completely unanticipated. Wind-tunnel tests had indicated there might not be enough muscle in the hydraulic actuators to pull them up. Larger actuators had been built and stocked, but according to my father, the VP of Engineering at that time, trying to save money, instructed them to test the smaller actuators first. The fact that the slats wouldn't retract wasn't a big deal in terms of the airplane's handling. Extending leading-edge slats allows an airplane to obtain more lift from the wings on takeoff or landing; in regular flight they're retracted to reduce drag, but if not retracted, the airplane still handles well. Before the 727's second flight, the larger actuators were installed.

Engineers also temporarily fixed the surge problem before subsequent flights by locking the bleed valve in the center engine in the open position so that the engine had lower compressor pressure. Then they went back to wind-tunnel testing and created a pattern of vortex generators[34] in the S duct of the center engine to smooth out the airflow for a permanent fix. "We were back in business," my father said.

---

[34] A vortex generator is a small vane that disrupts airflow over a surface, creating a vortex. Vortices are a major component of turbulent flow. Vortices form in stirred fluids, including liquids, gases, and plasmas. Common examples are smoke rings; whirlpools in the wakes of paddles and boats; and winds surrounding hurricanes, tornadoes, and dust devils. Vortices form in the wake of airplanes. Vortex generators can be found on many devices, but are most often used in aircraft design.

While the general public rarely heard about these "minor mishaps" during first flights or early tests in those days, I know from hearing the stories told by my father and the other pilots and test engineers that they were actually quite common. It seemed something always went wrong, but rarely was it something the experienced pilots couldn't handle. These were the stories they swapped with each other when socializing, the stories I'd hear bits and pieces of as I grew up, prompting my desire to record and preserve at least a few of them.

Each early flight on the 727 lasted from ninety minutes to two hours. Within a week, they had the requisite ten hours and were able to bring the 727 to Boeing Field, where the flight test facilities were located. "Jack Steiner was the first 727 passenger, on the flight from Paine back to Boeing Field," Dad said. "He was the program manager for the 727. We started a tradition, a way to say thanks, we [the pilots] appreciate your work and the airplane."

Now, with the 727 back at Boeing Field, the real work for the test pilots and crews began. The goal: certification, in under a year. Things were going to get intense again, just like during the 707 certification program. Everyone would be spending lots of time at Edwards AFB as well as at airports around the world, proving just how versatile the 727 could be.

The Water-Skiing Wallicks

The year the 727 first took to the air stands out in my mind for a completely different reason: 1963 is the year I learned to water ski. That summer I was six, and we were living in our cabin on Lake Sammamish. Granddad Wallick and Uncle Ed and his wife, Sharon, were visiting from Kansas, a rare event and something to look forward to. Granddad always brought us shiny collector's silver dollars[35] and lots of candy. Uncle Ed's

---

[35] I once had a pristine 1888 silver dollar Granddad gave me. Throughout my childhood, I carefully stowed it in a safe place in a cabinet, along with the beautiful diamond solitaire ring in an intricate antique white gold setting that my father's mother left me. I cherish that ring because of its back story: Her parents gave it to her when she was in her early twenties, fearing she

Kansas accent and slow speaking style always made me smile; he also had Dad's mischievous sense of humor. This particular summer, Granddad offered me a dollar if I learned to water ski while he was visiting. That was huge sum compared to my allowance of a quarter a week. I was determined to succeed. Granddad was a tall, lean man I hardly knew; he was already a widower, my father's mother having died when I was just one year old. Granddad died shortly after this trip out West, so I'm happy this was my last memory of him.

Dad had devised a way to teach people to water ski, and he used it that day to teach me. Sitting in a small inner tube, in water two to three feet deep close to the shore, Dad carefully put two wide "double" skis on my feet—we called them banana skis. Gently inserting my toes into the front tunnel-like part of the soft, white rubber binding on each ski, he slid the movable heel cup up as far as it would go, but the bindings were still too big for my feet. My uncle, driving the boat, positioned it in front of us, pointing toward the center of the lake. One of my brothers, riding shotgun, tossed the tow rope handles to Dad. The slack tow rope floated on the water's surface as Dad gave me the handles. I grasped the handles tightly in each hand, nervous. Dad, his usual calm and positive, reassuring self, said, "Don't worry, Becky, you'll do great. You won't sink."

My three older brothers had already learned to water ski. And of course we could all swim. Mom made certain we knew how as soon as it was clear we'd be spending time on the lake. For some reason, despite loving the water and wearing a life belt, I was convinced that if I let go of the tow rope, I'd sink to the bottom, where the creepy crawdads scurried among the bigger rocks. I didn't want to fall or let my feet touch the bottom where they might get pinched.

Reminding me to hold my arms out straight, to not pull back on the handles as I started to stand on the skis because that would make me fall backward, Dad signaled my uncle to start pulling the slack out of the line. Standing in the water beside

---

would never marry and would become a spinster. The ring was a sort of consolation gift. She did marry, and had five children. I've since lost the 1888 silver dollar but not the family heirloom ring.

me with one hand on the inner tube, feeling the inner tube being pulled forward, Dad yelled "Hit it!" The boat accelerated. Dad steadied me on the inner tube until I got too far away, the water too deep for him to walk through. He let me go. As I gained momentum and felt the skis under me, the inner tube fell off my butt back into the water. Forgetting to keep my arms straight, I did what almost every beginner does—I pulled back on the handles without straightening my legs, which threw my weight back and to one side. As I fell, the skis were immediately pulled off my feet because I refused to let go of the tow rope! I held on for dear life. My father, seeing what was happening, yelled to my uncle to stop the boat. Thanks to the life belt, I bobbed to the surface, sputtering from the water that had gone up my nose, and gasping for air. I finally released the handles, but only because Dad asked me to.

28 Learning to water ski: Dad, Aunt Sharon, and brother Tim helping the author. Photo: Author's collection.

Unfortunately for me, this learning-to-water-ski drama was recorded on 8-mm film. At family and holiday gatherings, *Becky the Human Submarine,* as my brothers named it, was shown for general laughs and much teasing.

I did earn Granddad's dollar that day. I succeeded in getting up on the skis and going a short distance. I also learned a valuable life lesson with Dad's encouragement: always get back up on the horse, even when it's scary; keep trying until you succeed. Never let a misstep or minor failure scare you off. We learn from our mistakes. We learn with gentle encouragement and positive reinforcement. Dad was great at providing all the tools and rewards.

29 The Wallicks ready to take the Pacific Mariner ski boat to the cabin on Lake Sammamish, 1961. Left to right: Ruth, Rick, Sam, Becky, Tim, & Lew, with my aunt Annette sitting on lawn. Photo: Author's collection.

My brothers and I loved to water ski. On good-weather weekend days, with Dad offering to drive the boat, we often tried to be first out on the lake before other boats added chop to the surface. Dad bought four rubber wetsuit tops—short sleeves with "beaver tails" attached to the lower back that could be pulled between the legs and attached with two snaps above the pelvis. With those wetsuits, we skied in colder weather and water, or played in waves tossed by storms until we simply couldn't stand the cold any longer. When water skiing, we all took turns skiing, riding shotgun, and driving, although Dad usually drove; sometimes we'd talk Dad into skiing as well. He'd always wait until last, after we kids had our fun.

A couple of years after I learned to water ski, Dad taught me to ski on one ski. The Kansas farm boy, who didn't learn to water ski himself until he was an adult, reasoned with an engineer's logic that when skiing on a single ski, one's dominant leg should be in the *back* position, contrary to popular methods at the time. When slalom skiing, the strength of a carved turn comes from the weight the skier puts on the rear foot, so this made sense. My brothers all learned this way—dominant right foot behind the left—but everyone else we knew skied right foot forward.

Lake Sammamish had a couple of slalom courses set out for anyone to use. My brothers got better and better at running the course. As Sam and Rick got bigger, and gained skill, it became apparent that a better ski boat was required if they were to continue improving as slalom skiers. Riding in our original ski boat—a Pacific Mariner with a 75-hp engine and a top speed of maybe 35 mph—while pulling either of them through the course, I could feel the tug on the boat whenever they cut a sharp turn on their slalom ski, pulling hard on the tow rope. It felt like they were bringing the boat to a standstill for a second. Nor could that boat pull them fast enough for slalom competition; its engine simply wasn't powerful enough.

Dad went shopping. He came back with, well, the perfect ski boat for a test pilot: a flat bottom, purple metal-fleck-paint Muffler City ski boat, 18-feet long with a 210-hp inboard engine, a marine version of a Ford Mustang engine. It had a low, sleek profile, designed for speed. The sun made the flecks in the paint sparkle, as if the boat were dancing on the water. It had two black vinyl bench seats; if you wanted to get from the back seat to the front, you climbed over the back of the front seat because there was no gap between the driver's and passengers' seats. The ski rope tied into a silver metal post just behind the back seat, in front of the engine hood, keeping the rope free of the propeller. That boat literally skimmed the lake's surface at high speeds, leaving minimal wake while easily pulling my brothers through the slalom course at 34 to 38 mph. Full out—not towing a skier—the boat could go 45 mph. For a time, we had the flashiest boat on Lake Sammamish. Dad christened it The Purple People Puller.

Eventually I also learned to ski through a slalom course, joining my brothers in trying to increase the speed at which we could successfully run the course. I'd give it a go less frequently, but would join in if called upon to help make up a team for annual "competitions" held in conjunction with parties hosted by the Langs (the widow Bobbie Baum and her new husband, Bill, who adopted her four children) and other friends living on the lake or by the Lake Sammamish Water Ski Club.

Sam and Rick wanted to learn ski jumping. Dad got them the appropriate flat-bottomed, wide skis and found someone living on the lake to give them some initial tips. Then, with Dad as driver, they learned together how to jump, taking those initial tips, watching others do it, and practicing. Lots of trial and error. My father's approach to so many things in life.

Water skiing was a great family activity. Whoever wasn't skiing was driving or observing, or swimming near the dock while waiting for their turn. Today, I marvel at the amount of free time, money, and enthusiasm my father invested in our recreational activities.

Turns out my father took advantage of every opportunity to water ski when working in foreign countries for Boeing. He told me stories of a day of water skiing while in Australia training pilots in the early 1960s, and another time in Greece when he had a day off between demonstration flights.

Occasionally, when we had friends over for water skiing and socializing, with sufficient goading from us, Dad would do a showy jump start off the dock, with his own special twist. One of my brothers would drive the boat, slowly pulling out the slack in the ski rope. Left foot snug in the slalom ski binding, all his weight on his right foot, Dad would balance, his left leg bent slightly to hold the ski an inch or two above the dock, tip out over the water. The last several feet of the tow rope were coiled like a lasso in his right hand, the handle in his left, a lit cigarette clenched in one corner of his mouth. "Hit it!" he'd yell between clenched lips, and my brother would gun the boat at full throttle. Just before the slack disappeared—timing it perfectly—Dad would launch off the dock, leading with the ski, landing on the lake surface just as the rope got taut and pulled him smoothly forward. The cigarette, of course, remained lit because he created so little splash with his expert timing. Slipping his right foot into the rear binding of the ski, he would proceed to cut turns across the boat's wake, cigarette remaining lit between his lips until he returned to the dock.

Even in play, Dad was always pushing the envelope in a way that was entertaining, fun, and just a little competitive, as if silently saying with a sly grin, *Try that!*

Mostly, though, Dad was the one driving the boat, not skiing; or he'd be filming us from the dock as we took off or came back in. He didn't get to ski much himself, but I don't think he minded. Tom Edmonds remembers this to be true. "Your dad enjoyed seeing you ski," he said. "He taught Dale and Alan to ski using that same method." Tom eventually bought our Pacific Mariner, and sometimes brought it out to Lake Sammamish and over to our dock for a summer day of fun. Tom himself used the inner-tube method to teach a daughter-in-law and others to water ski. At some time or another, virtually all of the extended Boeing Flight Test family members—test pilots, flight test engineers, even CAA/FAA pilots, and their families—came to enjoy a summer day at our house on the lake.

Water skiing wasn't just fun. It helped me gain confidence as a child and young adult. Whether Dad realized it, or simply intuited it, allowing me to stretch my athletic wings gave me confidence in all aspects of my life.

Killing Time by Sacrificing to the Wind Gods

Throughout their careers, Boeing test pilots and crews frequently found themselves at Edwards AFB for tests. What an exciting time the 1950s and 1960s were to be there, with the likes of Yeager, Crossfield, and others regularly breaking speed and altitude records in their fantastic rocket-powered aircraft. As the 1960s dawned—the Age of Aquarius—Edwards AFB was increasingly focusing on space flight, and the Test Pilot School on training future astronauts. In 1961, more "firsts" were occurring in rapid succession—first aircraft (the X-15) to exceed Mach 4, then 5, and 6, and to reach near space by soaring 67 miles above the Earth's surface (354,200 feet).

With the Happy Bottom Riding Club no longer, the Boeing crews found their own fun at other local bars, including a cozy one called the Amber Room at The Desert Inn in nearby Lancaster, where they typically stayed when working at Edwards AFB.

Some context is in order here. During the 1950s, '60s, and '70s, regularly drinking alcohol was accepted, even fashionable in the United States. Business people had drinks with lunch or to celebrate the close of a sale; many executives had wet bars in their offices. Cocktails with dinner—in restaurants and at home—were common for middle-class people, as were cocktail parties on weekends. Hard liquor and beer ads, along with cigarette ads, were in all the American newspapers and magazines. I remember, as a young girl, asking to taste my mother's then-preferred drink, the Stinger, which she made with vodka and crème de menthe. I thought it was fabulous and often asked for a sip when she made herself one in the evening after dinner. When Mom hosted bridge parties during the weekdays, I'd come home from school to a group of four or eight ladies getting giggly on Bloody Marys or gin and tonics. At home, Dad seemed to drink only when we had company over, occasionally a cocktail when he got home from work or a beer while barbequing hamburgers on a weekend evening. I never saw him drunk. And to my knowledge, he *never* drank when he knew he was going to fly within eight hours, emphasizing to me that to do so was not only foolish, but also forbidden by FAA regulations.

It was common during the 1950s and '60s for the Boeing pilots and crews to spend their Friday evenings drinking at a restaurant across the street from Boeing Field called the Sky Room. They also had "check out" parties: when a pilot got checked out to fly a new airplane, he had to throw a party for the rest of the guys. Some of those parties involved heavy drinking.

One such party was hosted by test pilot Ray McPherson at

the Sorrento Hotel in downtown Seattle. My father's younger brother Jesse had just come out to Seattle from Kansas, fresh engineering degree in hand, and had obtained an entry-level job as an engineer at Boeing. He was living with us until he found his own place. Jesse remembers that the day after Ray's party, Brien Wygle called my father. "Brien said, 'We gotta go help Ray; Ray couldn't find his car last night.' So we go downtown and start driving around looking for Ray's car. We found it." A few years later after another such drinking party, one of the test pilots had some trouble getting to work, according to Jesse. "He was hung over. He finally got to work and said, 'I found out I can't get through the toll booth [on the Evergreen Point floating bridge] with my Boeing badge.'" That pilot lasted about fifteen minutes before he returned home to nurse his hangover.

What is considered heavy drinking today was simply the norm in the '50s and '60s. Books and movies depicted drinking and smoking as common behaviors without negative consequences. Men who could throw back a few and hold their own were real men. Even getting drunk on occasion—for example, when at Edwards AFB with time to kill—was not considered an issue or a sign of trouble, so long as it didn't interfere with your work. And apparently it didn't; I never once heard of an instance when a *pilot* tried to fly under the influence of alcohol or while hung over. Flight test engineers, however, were another matter, often nursing a hangover on early morning flights. Almost everyone in the Boeing crews drank too much while at Edwards AFB. To them, at the time, it was harmless fun and a way to blow off steam. And, since they usually drank in the bar of the Desert Inn where they were staying, there weren't any concerns about drinking and driving.

In fact, the Boeing guys created an initiation ritual for anyone new to working with the flight test crews at Edwards AFB or any of the other remote testing sites Boeing used. They called it *sacrificing*. Calm air is critical for most of the tests done at Edwards AFB, and the calmest air occurs right at sunrise, before the sun has a chance to heat the atmosphere and cause turbulence. Catching this calm air necessitated setting alarms for 3:30 am so that everyone would be on the flight line and the airplane and crew ready to go as the sun peeked over the distant hills. "Sacrificing" referred to picking on the newest guy in the group, getting him to drink way too much and become ripping drunk as a sacrifice to appease the wind gods for the next morning's tests. If the wind gods were successfully appeased and the flight was a go, and if the sacrificed newbie was onboard (having survived the night's festivities), lots of tormenting of the poor sod—who was invariably feeling nauseated and had a splitting headache—ensued. I guess this could be compared to college fraternity hazing.

Paul "Pablo" Bennett, a test pilot who joined Boeing as a flight test engineer in 1962 after a stint in the Air Force during the Korean War, introduced the Boeing guys to a drink called the After Burner. According to Dennis Mahan, another flight test engineer and good friend of Bennett's throughout their careers at Boeing, the After Burner was an Air Force thing. It's a shot glass of Drambuie. "It's a sweet, sticky, Scotch-based liqueur that's a little like napalm when on fire," says Dennis, who made his first trip to Edwards AFB in early 1966. "You set fire to the shot glass. Then the object of the game is to drink the shot and set the glass down with flame still in the bottom. This is usually done after way too many other drinks. Many people have been seen immediately afterward with their teeth on fire or a burning stream of 'napalm' down their chin. Not for the fainthearted but mostly for drunks and fools."

My uncle Jesse remembers the first time he was included on a testing trip to Edwards AFB, in the mid-1960s. He was one of several relatively new flight test engineers at that time.[36] Jesse and Pablo and another young engineer named Tom Edwards were sharing a room. Everyone realized that the per diem Boeing gave them wasn't generous enough to pay for all the partying unless they shared rooms, so most of the engineers did. As bad luck would have it, the young engineers' room was directly above that of Jack Waddell, the test pilot they'd be flying with the next day. The next morning Jack arrived at the flight line and boomed, "Boy, have I got a bunch of eager test

---

[36] My uncle Jesse would eventually become a test pilot after paying his dues as a flight test engineer.

engineers! I heard them up fifteen minutes before I got up." What Jack didn't know, according to Jesse, is that they were just coming in from a long night of partying.

Jesse Pablo, and Dennis were contemporaries, all three roughly a decade younger than my father, Brien Wygle, and most of the other test pilots they were flying with. Of course, as a kid I knew my uncle Jesse well and adored him—when I was five I was flower girl at his wedding to my aunt Annette—but I also have fond memories of Pablo and Dennis. The three of them were always laughing, joking, and at weekend boating parties usually had a beer in hand. Sort of "The Three Amigos" in my memories. Jesse remembers when Pablo was introducing them all to After Burners down at Edwards AFB. "Pablo went to toss it down and he missed!" says Jesse. "A bunch ran down the sides of his mouth and that stuff was sticky. He had a big burn down his neck. After that, when we'd go into that bar, the ol' bartender would pull out his fire extinguisher." Dennis, never one to miss an opportunity for a joke, made name tags for Jesse and Pablo to wear at Edwards AFB. "It was like a Boeing badge, with a picture," says Jesse. "It said something like, 'My name is Jesse Wallick. If found drunk and disorderly, please return to the Desert Inn.'"

The Desert Inn's original owners were Carl and Mary Fischer. They built a thirteen-room motel in 1947—the same year Yeager broke the sound barrier in the skies above Edwards AFB—on the corner of a former chicken ranch owned by Mary's mother. By 1962, the motel had around seventy-five rooms, its growth fueled by income from Boeing and other corporations that had business at Edwards AFB. Mostly Boeing, according to Gary Fischer, who, in 1962 at the age of twenty-three and with a new college degree in hand, took over operation of the motel as general manager. "It was terribly exciting," Gary recalls of being near Edwards AFB as a child and young man. "That's when NASA and the early astronauts were there. Compared to them, the Boeing people were pretty corporate." Still, Gary did reserve some admiration for many of the Boeing people. "I noticed that the test pilots were an untamed bunch. There was more freedom then." He said my father wasn't one of the really wild ones, describing him as the "professor" of the bunch. Jesse, Pablo, Dennis... well, they were closer to Gary in age and weren't as reserved as my father and the other pilots. "As years went on, they had to rein it in," Gary said, probably due as much to the fact that everyone was aging as a change in corporate culture.

Gary befriended many of the Boeing pilots and flight test engineers who frequented the Desert Inn in the '60s and '70s. "I felt like an insider. I saw them at their best, as professionals, having fun. I knew the various types of tests. It was exciting." As an insider, Gary was occasionally invited to fly on a low-risk test flight. And, when business duties allowed, he partied with them. He remembers many within the Boeing ranks being hung over a lot, unless of course the next day's test was particularly technical or demanding. "When the Boeing crews left, it was forty-percent quieter," Gary said.

30 Lew Wallick and Joe Sutter relaxing at the Desert Inn. Photo: Author's collection.

Dennis—tongue very much in cheek and with his own brand of engineer humor—eventually wrote a satire of the testing experience at Edwards AFB in the early days of the 747 program. The sorts of events he describes had already become longstanding tradition by the early seventies. Writing in a style mimicking the medieval time of lords and serfs, Dennis assigned aliases to the people and organizations involved. Boeing becomes the Everett Glider Works (EGW). The FAA people are the King's men. Pablo is the Earl of Watusi, Dennis is the Reader of Curves (and the narrator), and Jesse is the Keeper of Cabin Temperature. Boeing crewmembers were serfs, and pilots or management, Lords.

After detailing a few weeks worth of tests, most of them having gone awry, The Reader of Curves describes "sacrificing" and how the serfs spend their downtime:

> Of those many days that tests could not be made of the huge airplane some were because the huge airplane needed healing and some were because the gods of wind and temperature were angry. It was often decreed that these gods must be appeased so that the tests could continue. Each of the Lords and serfs of the EGW and the King's men were prevailed upon to make sacrifice to these gods in whatever manner they might choose. A few tried obtaining great quantities of sleep and much good food. Most felt, however, that the only true and valid sacrifice was to rid the hamlet called Lancaster of all of that evil liquid called alcohol and to ignore food and rest. Many valiant attempts were made by the Earl of Watusi, the Keeper of the Cabin Temperature and the flight test Reader of Curves and many more. Ferocious attacks were made on the drink called martini and the drink called scotch, sometimes with success and sometimes with none. Probably the most valiant of all was the flight test operations serf called the Drinker of Coors. His method of appeasing the gods was to rid the hamlet called Lancaster (and possibly the entire land) of the ale called Coors. This valiant serf could be found daily dressed for battle in his multi-colored swimming pants thrashing through trash baskets by the concrete pond searching for that last can of the ale called Coors.
>
> It also came to be that after the Keeper of Cabin Temperature had been at the place called Edwards and

> away from his mate for about a fortnight, he drank great quantities of ale and lurked in the bushes by the concrete pond to attack the most desirable of all beasts—the orange *golfus cartus*. But alas, he chose a *golfus cartus* of the highest virtues and was trod into the ground by the angry beast. Many injuries were inflicted on the Keeper of Cabin Temperature, and the innkeepers of the inn called Desert Inn, the Earl of Watusi, one of the flight test Lords and the Reader of Curves, after much argument, took the Keeper of Cabin Temperature to see a healer at the big castle of sick peasants. The healer shot the Keeper of Cabin Temperature with many of the rays called X and bandaged his wounds and told him to return to the inn and lay off the ale. Shortly thereafter the Keeper of Cabin Temperature's mate arrived so that he would not be tempted again by the orange *golfus cartus*.
>
> It should be mentioned that the day most feared by all was the dreaded scheduled day off, for these were the days that many fell victim to the plague of headaches and foul stomachs. This was no doubt caused by the quantities of wine and ale consumed the night before.
>
> But at these places called Edwards and Grant County Airport [Moses Lake], many friends were made and probably a few enemies (mostly husbands of the friends). But alas, these tales are too numerous and one must stop sometime so let it be here.

Don Cumming, a flight test engineer who came to Boeing as a summer student in 1957, then hired on full time in 1958, remembers being impressed that my father remembered him from his student days. Don also recalls that at Edwards AFB in those early years, my father invented a drink he called the Double Double martini. This was at another favorite drinking hole, the Antelope Valley Inn, where according to Don, they had sufficiently large martini glasses. There was also a bowling alley they frequented, not to bowl but for the drinks. "They had a two-for-one happy hour," says Don. "Pablo was always in a hurry to get there because the longer we waited, he said, we were losing money. And Lew was able to 'con' or shame new arrivals from Seattle, particularly management types with expense accounts who just came to observe, into buying us all a round, saying 'fresh money has arrived.' That helped us on per diem. It was all part of the camaraderie there." Don added that, as a friend, my father was interested in their families and invited them to our house. "He took us skiing behind the Purple People Puller," Don said.

By the mid-sixties, Don would have to manage a group of flight test engineers he refers to as "the misfits," including Jesse, Dennis, and Pablo. I don't know how he managed to supervise them—it was probably a lot like herding cats—but he did. In addition to working together, they socialized on weekends with their families, and today, long after they all retired, those still alive remain close friends and see each other regularly.

Don's favorite drink during those times at Boeing: a martini. Still is, he says.

Don shared another tidbit during that time that is quintessentially my father. "The Antelope Valley Inn is where Lew taught me to clean up my Roquefort salad dressing with crushed soda crackers," says Don. "Eat salad, crush crackers somewhat, use back of fork to further crush crackers while smearing around plate soaking up dressing so that the mix sticks between the tines, then consume. Repeat as necessary until plate is clean. I was a Roquefort virgin until I was introduced to it at the Antelope Valley Inn—they had a super chef's salad that was also easy on the per diem." Confession: I am addicted to soda crackers. Clearly it's my father's fault. As a child, he taught me that crushed soda crackers were a necessary garnish to a fresh bowl of chili or any kind of soup; that peanut butter is best consumed smeared between two soda crackers and eaten like a sandwich; that the proper way to eat an apple is to quarter it, cut away the seeds and core, and follow every bite with a bite of soda cracker. I've often said that if it were possible, I'd live just on soda crackers. They are and always have been my favorite food.

Attire for the pilots and engineers working at Edwards AFB in the 1960s and 1970s consisted of short-sleeve dress shirts with pocket protectors and open collars, khaki or light-colored slacks, desert boots, and… aviator sunglasses. If the winds were good (the wind gods having been suitably appeased) and testing took place, a day's worth of tests were usually completed before noon. That left a lot of extra time in the afternoons and evenings, in a place with few cultural amenities and even fewer natural amenities. If the winds were too strong and tests were delayed for another day, the crews had the entire day to kill and often donned swim attire. I've seen numerous photos of my father and some of the other pilots and engineers sitting around the pool at the Desert Inn, wearing swim trunks and working on their tans, and in my father's case, demonstrating his signature half-gainer dive.

Dennis says that because they stayed at the Desert Inn so much, he got to know the owners, the Fischers, pretty well. The Inn's bar, the Amber Room, was Dennis's favorite haunt. "A couple of the X-15 pilots hung out in there occasionally," he recalls. "Through my friendship with Gary Fischer, I had dinner (in a large group) at the Lancaster home of John Young, an astronaut who was on the moon." Dennis also was invited to spend some time on the Fischer's 58-foot yacht in San Diego, including a swordfish fishing trip. "Swordfish are harpooned," Dennis learned, "so it's more like whaling in a way. We brought a 350-lb fish back to Lancaster for the Desert Inn restaurant."

The Boeing test crews hung out together as a close-knit group when at Edwards or other off-site locations. They spoke the same language, were engaged in the same tasks, and had the same goals. They shared meals and partied together in their downtime. These drinking and bonding experiences at Edwards AFB in particular, and socializing with their wives and families back home in Seattle, forged strong life-long bonds. They supported each other, trusted each other, had each other's backs, and made fun of each other's escapades at places like Edwards AFB. Their wives and children were brought into the inner circle, also forming lifelong bonds as they all spent time at each other's homes, water skiing in the summer months, or going on vacation together. For the kids, being around the other Boeing families just reinforced the normality of it all.

31 Dennis Mahan presenting Lew Wallick with a moose head bottle, a joking nod to Moose Milk, a drink consisting of Scotch and milk that my father favored during a trip to Alaska for 737 tests on a gravel runway. The bottle resided in Lew's office until he retired. Photo: Mahan collection.

Some of the pilots and flight test engineers did develop problems with alcohol. I know of DUIs, and in at least one case, Boeing paid for an intervention and treatment for a flight test engineer, which at the time was not a common approach by corporations. As society learned about the pitfalls of excessive drinking, so did the Boeing pilots and flight test engineers. For the most part, through, they monitored themselves, maintaining their professionalism.

I had no idea all this partying was going on when Dad was "out of town" or "at Edwards." His participation in the bonding rituals of Edwards AFB was never discussed in front of us kids. The only vivid reminder of his time at Edwards AFB that I had as a child was the desert tortoise Dad brought home from the Mojave Desert after one stint of testing. It was probably 1961, when I was five years old. Dad came home with a tortoise in a cardboard box.[37] Don Cumming remembers being on the flight that included the tortoise, and remembers some of the other guys bringing home Joshua trees. After my brothers and I got acquainted with our new pet—touching and stroking his scaled forelegs and his remarkably smooth, soft nose, feeding him iceberg lettuce—Dad figured out a way to keep the tortoise safely in our front yard. Reassuring me it wouldn't hurt him—that it was like clipping a fingernail—I watched as Dad used an electric drill to bore a small hole in the tortoise's shell, near the outside edge just above a rear leg. Dad tied one end of a 20-foot cord through the hole and the other end to a water hose bib on the side of our house. The tortoise was free to roam our front yard, keeping it clear of dandelion flowers, which supplemented the greens we provided him. He burrowed into the soft dirt next to the house, protected by shrubs. He didn't move around much—tortoises are slow—but he was a draw for all the neighborhood kids. Every year while in grade school, I took the tortoise to school for show and tell, carrying him in a cardboard box on my lap on the school bus. The tortoise was always a hit with my classmates.[38]

Learning now just how close my father and the rest of the Boeing flight test crews were back in those early days of commercial jet transports makes me smile with envy. Of course they needed to blow off steam; what they were doing on an almost-daily basis was dangerous. I marvel at their luck, not just in terms of overall safety doing such risky work, but also in finding co-workers with whom they could relax, be themselves, and have fun. Such camaraderie and job satisfaction are rare. While Boeing crews still head to Edwards AFB to conduct tests today, I'm told the sense of camaraderie and fun is long gone. The Desert Inn is no longer; new freeways made the location less than desirable, and it became an unkempt and seedy shadow of its former self. Another era, and another icon of that

---

[37] I don't believe it was illegal to remove tortoises from the Mojave at that time; currently, though, they are listed as a threatened species.

[38] Out of habit I refer to the tortoise as male, but several years after arriving in Washington as a special passenger on a 707, our turtle laid an egg. Just one. So "he" was in reality a "she."

era, are gone.

Delivery Flights: Family Invited

Some of my earliest flying memories come from the time when Boeing families were allowed to tag along on delivery flights. Because both of my parents were raised in Kansas and had family living there, if there was a delivery flight to Wichita, we often hitched a ride to visit relatives. I was flying on these delivery flights long before I can remember, our family dressed formally as people used to do when traveling, me just a toddler in my father's arms waiting to board a 707, which he would then pilot.

The first delivery flight I do remember was when I was seven or eight years old, on a 727. Boeing would stock the galleys with box lunches—white cardboard boxes with a sandwich, an apple, chips, and a Hershey's chocolate bar inside. When we reached cruising altitude, Dad came back from the cockpit and convinced me to be the stewardess for the flight, handing out lunches to the other passengers and families onboard. With his help, I tried, starting in first class, but shyness caused me to quickly give up and rush back to my seat in the main cabin. Later, my brothers and I raided the leftover boxes for their candy bars. We ran up and down the aisle of the airplane like it was our personal playground, going up to the cockpit to watch Dad fly, then dashing back through the cabin. We didn't think we were doing anything unusual.

The 737, Also Known as FLUF (Fat Little Ugly Fellow)

By April 1967, the first 737 was ready to fly. This new Boeing jet and the program to test and certify it came after the 727-100 but before the first 727 derivative—the 727-200, which was scheduled for its first flight in July of the same year. For my father, it meant working on the 737 while still flying the 727-100, then being assigned the 727-200 and staying with it until it was certified. Then back to the 737 for additional development work, such as automatic landings, to improve both airplanes. A busy time for all involved.

32 Brien Wygle and Lew Wallick prepare for first flight of the 737. Photo: Boeing Archives.

The first flight of the 737 occurred April 9, 1967. Brien Wygle was pilot, my father was copilot. I know I was there, but only because there's a photo showing me standing next to my mother, not far from Norma Wygle in a group of onlookers, the 737 parked on the ramp. My mother and another woman in the group are wearing rain bonnets, even though the lighting suggests the sun was peeking from behind the clouds. The weather, it seems, was iffy.

My father described the 737's first flight as "fairly routine." There was a delay of a couple hours before taking off because of an electrical problem of some sort, which the mechanics were able to fix. With his usual understatement, Dad said, "We took off and flew our flight. As I recall, it went pretty much the way we had planned it." The one disappointment with that first 737, he told me, was that the thrust reversers were ineffective. The 737 had the same engines and power plant that the 727 had, so they simply used the same 727 thrust reversers. "The difference, unfortunately, was that on the 737, the thrust reverser was underneath the wing, where on the 727, the engines were out in the open on the sides," Dad explained. "The interference between the thrust reverser exhaust and the wing essentially rendered the thrust reverser ineffective. They made a lot of noise but didn't do much." Brien used brakes to slow the 737 after landing, which was of course more than sufficient. The discovery led to a big redesign of the 737 thrust reversers, which ultimately were very effective.

The fact that the 737 was the first of Boeing's commercial jets to have a two-person cockpit led to some noise from the pilots' unions of some airlines. The 737 had a jump seat in the cockpit, but as Dad said, anyone sitting there wouldn't have anything to do; the airplane's controls were all within reach of the pilot and copilot. There was no flight engineer's station, like in the 707 and 727. The issue was eventually resolved; the 737 and most subsequent Boeing airplanes (with the exception of the early 747s) have two-person cockpits, including the 747-400 and 747-8.

My father thoroughly enjoyed flying the 737. I think all the pilots did. "It was just a nice hot airplane to fly," Dad told me. "It's kind of like a sports car—you put it on and wear it. It's smaller, lighter weight, more maneuverable, and has snappy acceleration. It had great performance." Being a twin-engine airplane, it had to be designed to fly on one engine in an emergency, for example, if the other engine suddenly lost power. All commercial airplanes, to be certified, have to demonstrate an ability to fly with one engine out, including during takeoff and landing. On a twin-engine airplane, with one engine out you lose half your thrust; on a triple-engine 727, you lose one third thrust; on a four-engine airplane like the 747, you lose one quarter thrust. In either the 727 or 747, losing an engine doesn't affect performance as dramatically as in a twin-engine airplane like the 737. Conversely, when both 737 engines are operating, there is "excess" thrust, so the pilot gets the feeling of higher performance and more acceleration compared to the three- or four-engine airplanes coming back after an engine out.

Dad also noted that the 737, being smaller, was easier to move on the ground and had a shorter turning radius for taxi turns. "It's like comparing a sports car to a sedan, or a sedan to a pickup truck. The 737 is the sports car; the 727 is a deluxe sedan. The 707 and 747 were nice big airplanes, but were more like a truck or a big deluxe bus as far as taxiing was concerned, because they took a lot more room to turn and maneuver. Even though they flew very nicely, they didn't give you that feeling of being right with you, like the 737 and 727 did."

Dennis Mahan was onboard one day when my father had some fun demonstrating just how maneuverable the 737 was. Remember, Dad had already gotten lots of practice backing up other airplanes, like that 707 at Edwards AFB when he purposefully got it nose-to-nose to the Douglas DC-8, then backed out of its way with fanfare as a way of showing the Air Force general onboard the DC-8 that Boeing had working thrust reversers when Douglas didn't.

"Backing up airplanes was one of your dad's things," Dennis told me. "We came back to Boeing from a test mission of some sort in a 737. The normal procedure is to stop just past and 90 degrees to the parking stall and have a tug push the airplane back into the stall. For some reason the tug didn't show up. Your Dad got that twinkle in his eye and communicated to the ground crew that he would just back the airplane in. And he did, with some hand-signal directions from the guys outside. It involved backing up while making a 90-degree turn with the nose swinging left. Your Dad enjoyed it immensely. Actually, I did too. That's not exactly an approved procedure, since there's a big risk of ingesting things into the front of the engine if the ramp isn't clean."

My father considered the 737 a fun airplane to demonstrate to potential customers because it was easy to fly. He said he could put someone who'd never flown one in the pilot's seat and with very little instruction, just kind of talking them through taxiing out and takeoff, within that first flight they could fly the airplane like they'd been in it a month.

Astronaut Neil Armstrong was one of the celebrities Dad took up in a 737 for a demonstration flight. Pro golfer Arnold Palmer was another, who was given the demo because, according to Dad, there were a lot of Boeing executives who were avid golfers. They figured offering him an airplane ride was a good way to get him to come spend two or three days in Seattle and go golfing with them. Palmer was an easy target, though. He loved to fly. He was once quoted as saying, "Had I not become a professional golfer, I think I would have pursued some type of career in aviation."

Because the 737 was designed for short- and medium-range routes with fewer passengers, it was marketed to airlines using unimproved airports, or that frequently had to fly in dicey weather. In fact, when certified by the FAA in December 1967, the 737 was the first airplane whose initial certification included automatic approaches in bad weather (100-foot ceilings and 1,200-foot runway visual range). A versatile airplane, to be sure. Several derivatives soon followed.

My father and the other pilots involved in certifying and later "proving" the 737 took it to all sorts of unusual airports, landing on a variety of surfaces: gravel, compact snow, grass, even coral. Once such airport is in Hope, British Columbia, Canada; it's a grass runway. I've driven through Hope many times on my way to a dude ranch near 100 Mile House in the South Cariboo region of British Columbia. There are dramatic, steep, tree-covered mountains all around Hope. Its airport is used primarily by gliders and small private airplanes. In a picture taken after landing the 737 at Hope, my father stands in the grass in front of the airplane, talking to a group of youngsters who had come out to see the 737 at their local airport. It's my father in his element—sharing his love of flying and airplanes with the next generation of enthusiasts.

The 737 series is the best-selling jet airliner in aviation history, and has been continuously manufactured since 1967. Derivatives still being produced by Boeing include the -600, -700, -800, and -900ER, with plans to for the new 737 MAX to debut in the next few years.

Meanwhile, Back on the Home Front

My brothers and I had absolutely no clue, as kids, that our father's job was dangerous. He never let on to that fact at home, didn't discuss it in front of us, nor did our mother. The only evidence of his job in our house were the old flight helmets and oxygen masks that had become our toys, the paper airplanes and airplane models we made with his encouragement, and the professional models of various Boeing airplanes adorning our fireplace mantel and living-room end tables. Otherwise, we were busy being a middle-class family enjoying life in Bellevue.

As a family, we liked playing in the mountain snow during wintertime. Early home movies show us sledding at Snoqualmie Pass, or just romping in the snow, tossing snowballs. Very quickly, the winter focus turned to downhill skiing. I remember my father helping me learn to snow ski. It was the winter I turned seven. To help me get up the bunny hill, he'd have me stand next to the rope tow and hand him my ski poles. Standing right behind me, his skis to the outside of mine so I could loop my arms back around his legs, he grasped the rope tow, letting it pull us gently up the barely perceptible slope. On the way back down, he'd demonstrate snowplow turns for me to imitate in his wake.

We had leather ski boots that tied with sturdy red laces and nestled into cable bindings on our wood skis. Our poles were bamboo or metal with plastic grips and leather straps on top, huge baskets of metal and leather straps on the bottom. We wore stretch ski pants with stirrups that tucked into our boots, wool socks and hats, leather gloves or mittens, and insulated nylon ski jackets. GORE-TEX hadn't been invented; all of the clothing was easily soaked by falling snow or rain, or too many falls, despite spray-on waterproofing products. Did we care? Hardly. We were having a blast.

As my father was teaching me, my brothers were already good enough to be off skiing on the steeper Poma, T-bar, and chair-lift runs. Mom sometimes came along and sat in the lodge reading while we skied. She tried downhill skiing soon after we moved to Seattle, but fell during her first lesson and broke her leg.[39] Mom decided skiing wasn't for her.

Eventually my brothers and I were enrolled in ski school. Sam and Rick took lessons with the Bellevue Ski School, sponsored by our school district for junior-high and high-school students. Kids rode up to Snoqualmie Pass on yellow school buses most Saturdays between December and March; parents would deliver the kids to their school in the morning and pick them up by 5:00 pm. But Tim and I were still in elementary school, too young for the school-sponsored ski school, so we enrolled in Fiorini Ski School, started in 1947 by local Seattle adventurer Buzz Fiorini. Credited with creating the second-largest private ski school in the country, second only to Sun Valley's, Fiorini is said to have taught much of the Pacific Northwest how to ski, including students such as Bill Gates and the Nordstrom and McCaw kids. In my day, students were transported to Snoqualmie Summit on Greyhound-like buses, which was luxurious compared to the school district's ski school. Mom would pack our lunches—sandwich, potato chips, apple, beef jerky—along with something hot in a thermos, usually chicken noodle soup or hot chocolate. Often those lunches were ignored until the trip home because we were having too much fun on the slopes to stop and trudge back to the bus in the parking lot for lunch.

I started at Fiorini when I was in fourth grade. By this time, I had already skied quite a bit with Dad. My instructor that first

---

[39] Her consolation prize: a dozen roses sent to her hospital room by radio and TV star Arthur Godfrey, who heard of her condition while being given a demonstration ride on the Dash 80 by my father.

year was a young skier from Czechoslovakia; handsome and dashing with an accent and a wonderful sense of fun, he was my first unattainable crush. I remember hearing something about him having "escaped from Czechoslovakia," but I didn't understand what that meant. I just loved that he taught us skills like the stem-Christie technique and how to do parallel turns. At the end of the season, he made a jump for anyone brave enough to try doing spread eagles. Having such an instructor pushed my skill level forward, fast. This continued in fifth and sixth grades.

The quality of instructors at Fiorini was high, and we learned a lot. So much so that by the time I was in seventh grade and started with the Bellevue Ski School, I enrolled in *racing.* In addition to learning how to set and run slalom courses, I was taught how to ski the moguls and ice that were the pox of Snoqualmie Pass skiing in those days before regular grooming. Tough conditions made for tough, versatile skiers. Our skills were helped tremendously by improved equipment, in particular Lange buckle ski boots and Head metal skis. Good thing my father had nerves of steel; I can only imagine what it cost him to outfit four constantly growing kids in such state-of-the-art skiing gear. But as a test pilot used to the advantages of the best and latest innovations in airplanes, he knew the importance of having the right equipment for the task.

Dad's skiing improved along with ours. Often he'd take all of us up on Sundays, or we'd go on ski vacations as a family. There came a time, when I was in junior high, when Dad could no longer keep up even with me. Still, I loved skiing with Dad so much that I'd hang with him most of the day, riding up the chair lift with him and waiting for him at the bottom before the next ride up.

Conditions in the mountains of the Pacific Northwest can be challenging for any skier. In winter, the temperatures tend to hover just below freezing; when it does snow, the flakes are often big, wet and heavy, creating a base of what we locals fondly refer to as Cascade Cement. As kids, we loved skiing so much that even a cold rain rarely deterred us from staying on the slopes. We always wanted to be at the head of the chair lift line when it opened for the first ride up, and stayed on the slopes until the lifts closed in the afternoon, trying to be the last off the mountain, skipping lunch if the conditions were good.

When it did get too cold for me—when my fingers or toes got so numb they were painful—Dad would take me into the lodge and get me situated at a table. He'd go to the cafeteria and buy us both a hot chocolate while I sat waiting, shivering and miserable. Bringing the hot drinks back to the table, he'd take off his coat, sit across the aisle from me and rub my hands between his until the blood started circulating again. Then, as I sipped my hot chocolate, he's take off my ski boots, have me put one socked foot between his knees for warmth while he rubbed the other with his hands until they, too, returned to normal circulation. Once restored to warmth, he'd smile at me and say, "Ready to go out again?"

When we weren't snow skiing or water skiing, my brothers and I spent many Saturdays at the John Danz Theatre in downtown Bellevue, watching the kids' matinee. The theatre was next door to the bowling alley, where we also enjoyed spending time but not nearly as much time as watching movies. Tickets to the matinees were free. Management knew we'd spend enough on popcorn, candy, and pop to make up for it.

I remember the thrill of watching movies in a huge theatre with two seating levels. The balcony section had loge seats, spacious cushioned chairs with bottoms that would slide forward a bit for comfort, and ashtrays in the armrests (this was a time when smoking was common and allowed in public places). The main level seats were standard smaller seats, still plenty roomy for kids. Behind the balcony seats was the projection room, big reels of film moving through the camera visible behind a window, a giant's version of our home movie projector.

It was a rite of passage to be deemed mature enough to sit in the loge seats on a Saturday afternoon without a parent. But mostly we kids stayed on the main level while transfixed by the Lone Ranger, John Wayne, or some other western hero, the feature always following two or three full-length cartoons (Bugs Bunny or some other Disney character) and previews of coming attractions. Commercials had yet to tarnish the theatre-going experience.

Those Saturday matinees for kids were free babysitting for the local parents. Drop the kids off at noon; they'll buy popcorn and find a seat, watch several cartoons and previews followed by one or two feature movies suitable for children; pick them up at 3:00 pm. Everyone's happy.

CHAPTER FIVE: PUSHING THE ENVELOPE

Aviation is the branch of engineering that is least forgiving of mistakes.

—Freeman Dyson, theoretical physicist and mathematician

A Typical Test Program for Certifying a New Jet

The first flight of any new commercial aircraft is also the start of an extensive test program, the ultimate goal being certification by the FAA for airline service. Most travelers have no idea what airplane manufacturers put each new model through to verify that it can and will fly safely in the most extreme conditions. It's actually shocking, the stresses the test pilots put the aircraft through in order to obtain certification. Jim Day's story of the "movie flight" gives just a taste of what a common test flight was like in the days of the 707. I've waited until this point in the book to outline some of the major types of tests done on each new airplane so that the reader is already familiar with the models involved in the stories.

My father said that a typical test program can be imagined by drawing a rectangular box on a piece of paper. The left vertical line, bottom to top, represents low altitude to high altitude; the bottom horizontal line, left to right, represents increasing speeds. Data obtained during the airplane's first flight becomes a few points someplace in the middle of that box. Over the course of the test program, the entire box is eventually filled in with data points that include variations in speed, altitude, loading, gross weight, center of gravity, runway length and surface, and so on. In fact, even before that first flight, Boeing engineers perform "failure mode and effects analysis" on every component and assembly to ensure that the impacts of failures are known. You end up with a very complex set of data that first must satisfy all the Boeing engineers that they got the design right, and then the FAA during certification that the airlines can operate the airplane safely under a whole variety of conditions.

It's a very complicated data collection and analysis process, starting with those few first points and then expanding with a multitude of points in all directions toward the outlines of the box. Not only are the pilots and engineers looking at the airplane's performance and handling characteristics, but also its engines, air conditioning and pressurization, electrical system, fuel system, hydraulic system, autopilot—all of it, everything it takes to make the airplane fly. The entire program is very complex, highly organized, and incredibly intense. Everybody's working hard toward the goal of seeing the word "Certified" stamped over the box full of data points.

On the 727, maybe as many as 150 flight test engineers worked on the project at any one time: writing test plans, working on instrumentation, doing data analysis, and reading and processing information. Perhaps an equal number of technical and support staff were involved. As many as five 727s were flying the tests. "It's a huge undertaking," my father said. "You're trying to do it in less than a year from first flight to certification. You're working seven days a week, three shifts. People are out there twenty-four hours a day. It's expensive, costing a lot of overtime." But if the crews don't push, Boeing ends up with millions of dollars tied up in hardware. There's no return on investment until the airlines take delivery.

"You want to make sure it's done correctly so the airlines *can* accept it," my father said. "Of course, it has to be FAA licensed before they can accept it. Toward the end, it gets really intense. At the last minute, there's always something that comes up. It'll pass, but it's a delay. You think you're going to make a certain date, and all of a sudden you realize it's going to be another week or two, or maybe a month later. You tell the airlines they are going to get their airplane on a certain date and they make plans. They get their schedules all set up, they get their crews trained and in some cases they even get rid of some of their old airplanes that are being replaced. If the new airplanes show up a month late, it's a real problem for the airlines. They let you know about it. And, of course, you pay a penalty to the airline."

No one wants to feel responsible for such a costly delay, but the Boeing employees also want and need to get it right. They take immense pride in their airplanes. Ultimately, passenger safety as well as the viability of The Boeing Company and all its employees rests on doing the job correctly. Each valid data point put into the box gets the airplane closer to certification.

Stalls

Often, the very first flight's test plan includes seeing if the airplane's stall speed and characteristics are as anticipated. A stall is a condition where the airplane's angle of attack increases, causing airflow separation over the wings. As the angle of attack and airflow disruption increases, the airplane may experience buffeting. At a critical angle of attack, the wings lose their ability to create lift. Most aircraft are designed so that the nose drops down naturally as lift decreases, allowing the pilot to increase speed, level out, and regain lift—to resume normal flight.

Stall speed is the most important early point in that box, a point that determines so many others. "There's no point in going any further until you're pretty sure that the airplane's stall characteristics—its flying characteristics—are solid and stall speeds are what you expect," my father said. "All takeoff and landing distances, as well as flying performance, are based on a percentage speed above the stall speed."

It's critical that any airplane, as it approaches stall speed and progresses through buffet, be stable and controllable, enough so that, even in buffet, the pilot can maintain the wings within a 20-degree bank angle. If an airplane isn't flying straight—especially if it is a swept-wing airplane—and one wing skids ahead of the other, the uneven airflow can cause the airplane to roll.

The test pilots put the 727 through its paces, doing stalls with varying configurations of speed, power on, power off, flap settings, gear up, gear down, and weight distribution, until they were satisfied with its handling. When the 727 reached the speed at which it could no longer fly under a set configuration, the nose would pitch down, defining minimum speed, or stall point, for takeoff and approach under those configurations. These stall speeds became the basis for many later tests, including departure and climbing speeds for airports of various surfaces, lengths, and altitudes; climbing performance; and approach and landing speeds. For example, takeoff speed at 35 feet above the runway is 1.2 times the stall speed, and landing speed at 50 feet is 1.3 times the stall speed. If the airplane's stall speeds are high, you'll have problems with landing-field length, weight capability on takeoff, and other issues. So getting stall speeds into the expected range has to be done first. Eventually, that was accomplished to Boeing's satisfaction with the 727.

One day, though, when doing a stall test with an FAA pilot[40] onboard for certification, things did not go according to plan. I didn't hear even a whisper of this story when I was growing up. In 2002, I sat down to interview flight test engineer Dennis Mahan. He asked me, "Did your dad ever tell you the story about the day he nearly died in a deep stall?"

Well, no! As you can imagine, I went back to the source—Dad—and demanded he tell me the story. A version of the story, *The Deep Stall,* was published in *Flight Journal* magazine in October 2008. Here's a shorter version. Hang on to your seat.

It was the autumn of 1963. My father, with the FAA pilot and full crew, was flying the number one 727. My uncle Jesse was one of the flight test engineers onboard. Tom Edmonds was flying alongside the 727 in Boeing's F-86 chase airplane, providing the crew with visual observations and feedback.

The 727's unique design—three engines on the back and a T-

---

[40] My father specifically asked me to not name this pilot. He didn't want him, or his heirs, to suffer any embarrassment. I'm honoring that request, although every former member of Boeing Flight Test that I interviewed who knew of this story knew exactly which FAA pilot was involved.

tail—meant it handled quite differently than the 707. Earlier that year, the crew on a British prototype BAC 111, also a T-tail design commercial jet, entered a deep stall during testing. Unable to recover, the airplane tumbled to the earth, killing all onboard. Understandably, the FAA had concerns about the ability of the T-tail 727 to recover from a similar stall. For certification, the FAA wanted proof that the 727 could recover from a flap-down stall even with the spoilers up, a wing configuration normally used only upon approach for landing.

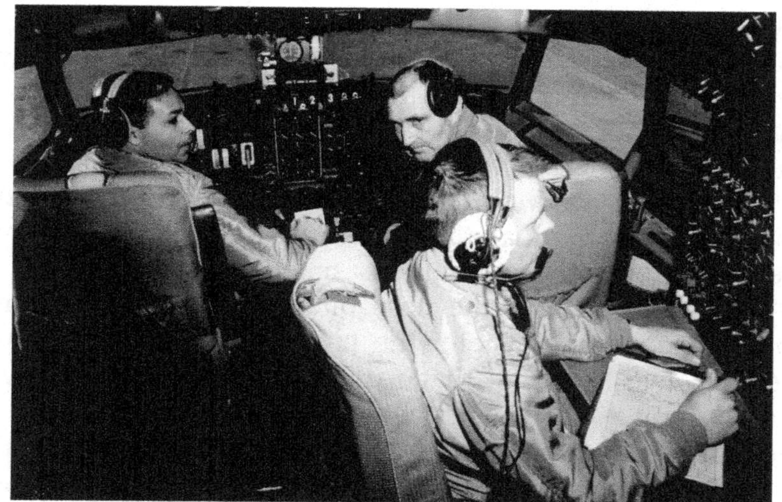

33 The 727 cockpit with its first flight crew: Lew Wallick, Dix Loesch, and M. K. "Shuly" Shulenberger. Photo: Boeing Archives.

Boeing test crews had already successfully completed the stall test using this configuration. All that remained was repeating the test with the FAA pilot at the controls.

Indeed, my father estimated that over the course of testing and certifying the 727, as many as 700 stalls were performed, starting with the inaugural flight when he and Dix flew approaches to a stall. The pilots and engineers became concerned about handling characteristics as the 727 approached a stall; after buffet but before stall speed, the nose had a tendency to pitch up. "We knew from wind-tunnel tests that this would be dicey testing," Dad said. On the second or third flight of the 727—still a minimum-crew flight so only Dad, Dix, and Shuly were onboard—they did a pitch-up maneuver, sort of a prelude to a stall. Dix described the sensation of that maneuver to me in 2004. "It's an awful, sickening feeling, because you just sit there, falling, nothing going on until finally, finally the nose starts coming down." When pressed, Dix said it was probably a good ten seconds before the 727's nose started to go back down. Don Cumming was in the radio room during this flight and said there were several seconds of silence from the crew until he heard my father say, "Well, let's not do that again!"

That tendency to pitch up required an immediate, interim fix while the engineers worked on a permanent one. "We rigged the airplane so that all of the leading-edge slats could be extended at once," Dad said. "We started initial stall tests, and when the airplane pitched up, I'd yell at Dix to put the slats out; he would, and that controlled it." (That switch, that allowed Dix to extend all the slats at once, was later nicknamed "the chicken switch" by Flight Test mechanics.)

A deep stall—when the nose pitches *way* up—is a highly dangerous condition. There's no precise definition. My father described it as, "A stall that reaches an angle of attack well beyond normal stall angle, where the airplane loses all its normal tendency to pitch nose down on its own; a super stall." No pilot would ever intentionally do one, in testing or at any other time, unless they were suicidal. A deep stall is especially dangerous in swept-wing airplanes with a T-tail design where the horizontal stabilizer and elevator are set high on top of the vertical tail fin. As the nose of the airplane rises and the wings' angle of attack increases, air flow over the wings becomes turbulent, causing ever-increasing buffet. That buffet is actually the "significant stall warning" that ideally occurs at a speed 10 percent before stall speed. As the wing begins to stall and lose lift, the turbulence also affects the air flow over the high T-tail, making its control surfaces ineffective. It becomes difficult, if not impossible, to control the pitch of the airplane. A pilot might not be able to bring the nose back down to level by using the elevators—the moveable surfaces on the horizontal stabilizer—because of the disturbed air flow across those surfaces. In the case of the BAC 111, the turbulent air flow likely kept the elevators in the up position, which reinforced the nose-up attitude of the airplane and kept it there as it fell back to earth, killing the crew.

On this particularly memorable test flight, the FAA pilot sat in the right seat, while my father sat in the captain's seat. The 727 cockpit could accommodate five—a pilot, copilot, flight engineer, and two test operations members, and was roomy enough for them to sit comfortably without interfering with one another. Each pilot had access to a full set of controls. There were instrument panels all around them—above their heads, directly in front, above and below the windshield, and slightly behind them on the side walls of the cockpit. Dials, levers, switches, lights, and gauges all fanned about in an amazing number and variety. A band of windows allowed them to see forward as well as to the side and below. On the floor between the pilots sat the aisle stand, which held the engine throttles, fuel controls, flap levers, trim controls, and some radio controls. During testing and certification, special flight test instrumentation was mounted to the top of the glare shield as well as on the instrument and overhead panels. Each item of critical importance was within easy reach of their hands or feet.

Every item, that is, except their parachutes. These were stowed in the main body of the airplane. My father told me that the pilots considered these to be nearly worthless, actually; they'd only use a parachute to exit the airplane if it was stable and flying level—if it were on fire, for example—otherwise, they would be too busy trying to save themselves by controlling the airplane to consider putting on a parachute and jumping. If they did decide to strap on parachutes to escape a flying 727, they'd jettison a cargo door in the belly to jump. Not a pleasing prospect. As Dad said, they'd only be kidding themselves.

Dad and the FAA pilot took the 727 up to about 14,000 feet, flying in clear skies over the less populated areas of western Washington between Port Townsend and Shelton. During each test condition, everyone in the cockpit was all business, calling out air speed and angles of attack, observing and writing down instrument readings. Between test conditions, everyone would relax and chat.

They got to the critical flaps down, spoilers up test. The FAA pilot set up the stall with the desired flap setting and spoilers full up, as required by the test plan. And even though my father had learned from past experience to watch this particular FAA pilot closely because of his tendency to pull back too far on the control column, Dad said he was still taken by surprise when the guy abruptly pulled back so hard that the 727 entered an *extreme* angle of attack—70 degrees rather than the usual maximum of 25 to 30 degrees—what an aerobatics pilot would do to start a snap roll or a spin.

My father immediately took over. "I've got it," he said, forcefully taking the controls of the stalled and falling Boeing 727 from the FAA pilot. Those three words were all the rest of the crew, including the FAA pilot, needed to hear; in that moment, they put their fates in my father's hands. Fueled by seat-of-the-pants instinct and a burst of adrenaline, my father quickly and simultaneously lowered the spoilers and pushed the control column all the way forward to the instrument panel; raised the flaps to five degrees; alternated right and left rudder and aileron as the airplane's wild gyrations required; and firewalled the throttles.[41] Keeping his eyes on the horizon as the wings dipped to what felt like 45 degrees on each side, Dad did everything he could to return the wings to level as all three engines roared with the added thrust and the airplane rolled and yawed like a crazed mechanical bull trying to go backward.

"It was way beyond flying; it was floating, and falling," Dad said of the airplane's handling. "I was concerned we'd go into an uncontrolled spin, perhaps the hardest maneuver from which to recover. I just reacted; I wasn't even thinking, didn't take time to analyze, just acting on survival instinct and adrenaline." He described his reactions as *ingrained*, based on years of flying at the envelope's edge.

As he fought the controls to stop the airplane's oscillations, the 727 finally responded, and the nose slowly edged back down toward the horizon. After losing nearly 4,000 feet in

---

[41] Pushed the throttles as far forward as possible, actually exceeding normal rated thrust.

altitude, the wings finally regained normal lift and the 727 leveled off. Dad throttled back and took a deep breath. Then he lit a cigarette. Several minutes of complete silence hung like a thick fog in the cockpit before anyone regained enough composure to speak, knowing just how close they had come to total disaster, certain death. The adrenaline in their systems dissipated as their heart rates slowly returned to normal.

Jesse was tasked with manually recording various data during the flight. He had just taken off his seat belt to stand and peer over the pilots' shoulders to obtain specific numbers when the unexpected deep stall began. As the airplane's nose pitched severely upward and he heard my father say, "I've got it," Jesse felt the wings roll at least 30 degrees to one side, then swing the same amount to the other side, then back again, through three such alarming cycles while Dad fought for control. Jesse struggled to stay on his feet, grasping anything he could for balance as the airplane's frame vibrated from the buffeting. "I was worried it would spin," he said. "Then I hoped it *would* spin, so the nose might go down. It was awful quiet in there." Dad described that side-to-side rolling as similar to something he did in training as a World War II Navy cadet, an aerobatic maneuver called "the falling leaf."

Tom Edmonds remembers that test flight vividly. Under normal circumstances, it was difficult for him to fly the F-86 slowly enough to match pace with the 727 when it entered a typical stall test maneuver. On this day, he found himself unable to stay alongside at all as the 727 went into a deep stall and lost all forward momentum. Tom watched the nose of the 727 pitch upward at an angle that he knew was way too severe. He flew past, trying to watch over his shoulder as the bigger jet fell back behind him. He didn't get to see the rolling so dramatically felt by those onboard but was able to circle back to witness the recovery.

When the flight test data recordings were later analyzed, the angle of attack trace was off the scale. For seventeen long seconds the elevators were full down (control column full forward) and no air speed data were recorded as the 727 simply fell back and down toward the earth, seconds that felt like an eternity to those onboard.

My father didn't tell the tower about the near disaster as he returned to Boeing Field, knowing that the radio frequency could be monitored by anyone, including Boeing's competitors. This was not the sort of test flight Boeing wanted publicized.

Don Cumming, flight test engineer and supervisor of the 727's aerodynamics and flight controls groups, also remembers that day. "We could tell, as the guys walked in, that something had happened. That was a serious postflight conference. We knew we were in trouble, certification-wise." Don also recalls that the angle of attack was so severe during that deep stall that turbulence coming off the 727's wings and two side engines "blanked out" the T-tail (disrupted the flow of air over the tail's control surfaces).[42] Don Archer also remembers the severity of that stall, describing it as "a very close encounter."

When describing that flight to me, my father joked that he plastered the elevator control column so hard against the instrument panel that it made a dent. He could joke easily afterward, of course, having survived. Dad felt that they did survive because the 727's hydraulic elevator control system gave him just enough control to ease the nose downward; the BAC 111 that crashed didn't have hydraulics to that critical control surface. I think that explanation is another example of my father's legendary modesty, which wouldn't allow him to credit his own extraordinary flying skills and calm under pressure for the recovery.

The FAA pilot responsible for putting the 727 into that deep stall, nearly killing himself, my father, my uncle, and the rest of the crew, never discussed the incident with my father or anyone else. He neither apologized nor accepted responsibility for the near disaster. To his credit, he didn't fight my father for the controls during the critical recovery. All concerned—Boeing and the FAA—agreed that a warning horn should be installed so that a pilot would never inadvertently deploy the spoilers with the flaps down while in flight, potentially causing a deep stall condition. There was simply no practical way to train

---

[42] For an illustration of this condition, see http://en.wikipedia.org/wiki/File:Deep_stall.svg#file.

commercial pilots how to recover from a deep stall, so better to do everything possible to ensure they never got into such a maneuver in the first place.

After much testing and analysis of various configurations of leading-edge slats and fences, the 727 ended up with a small fence on the inboard slat, which seemed to solve the early pitch-up problem. "It took a lot of flights and a lot of stalls, trying out different configurations," Dad said. "It's the sort of thing that's more art than science, because the fence is a small device, relatively speaking, to the size of the airplane. When you try to do it on a wind-tunnel model, it's hard to sort out what's going on. When you put it on a real airplane, full scale, then you can sort it out. I don't remember how many configurations we went through, but probably a dozen."

Another result of such dicey stall-test experiences was to install what's known as the "stick shaker" on customer 727s. All commercial airplanes, most private jets, and military aircraft now have a warning system that causes the steering column to violently and noisily shake as the airplane nears stall conditions. In some airplanes there is a natural buffet, or vibration, of the entire airplane body that occurs near stall and warns the pilots, but in those airplanes without such natural buffet, the stick shaker provides a very visceral alert. What starts as a distinctive, strong pulsation at near-stall conditions becomes a tooth-rattling, arms-shaking vibration as the plane enters a stall; no pilot could fail to notice or heed such a warning.

Because of the British BAC 111 accident, the FAA remained dubious of the 727 T-tail design's safety if it entered a stall. It was Dix's task to convince the FAA it was safe. "I don't know how many trips I made to New York and other places to try and convince everybody that the 727 would not lock in [to a deep stall]," Dix told me. The FAA had the data from both of my father's dramatic flights—the first one with Dix onboard when the 727 pitched up severely and the subsequent deep stall with the FAA pilot onboard. "We finally did convince everybody that it would recover," Dix continued. "But frankly, I think it's possible that you could get it into a situation where you couldn't recover. I always felt the way to get around it was to install a tiny sign in the airplane that said, 'Don't stall this airplane—it will kill you!'"

As I gathered the details of this story and realized just how close I came to not having a father at the age of six, I wondered why I'd never heard anything about it until I was in my forties. I'd already interviewed my father extensively about his flying career, and he had never mentioned it. Ultimately, it was Tom Edmonds who provided some insight into why I'd been kept in the dark. As he said, "You don't come home for dinner and say to your wife, 'Hi honey; I almost died today.'" While all the pilots knew of these close calls, the wives didn't always, and the children almost certainly were never told. In retrospect, I think that was the right approach.

Eventually I asked Dad if he'd had other close calls doing stalls. He shared the story of an earlier incident in the number one 707-300, with a younger Boeing pilot, Fred Spofforth, flying copilot. There were a few other crewmembers onboard, including Don Cumming. Fred was new to the commercial program, having earlier flown B-52s and the F-86 chase plane. This may have been his first time flying the 707. They were cruising over eastern Washington. The last test condition of the day was stalls, to test a new horizontal stabilizer designed for this model of the 707 to improve its maneuvering. To read static air pressure away from the airplane, the 707 had a trailing bomb[43] below it.

Dad told me that he always insisted they start stall maneuvers when they were at least 10,000 feet up, especially if someone else was doing the stall. This day, Dad agreed to let

[43] The trailing bomb was a 100-lb device that looked like a torpedo bomb, thus the name. It had a probe to sense static pressure outside the influence of the airplane. The bomb trailed below the airplane, connected by a 125-ft cable surrounded by a pneumatic hose that transferred pressure to transducers located inside the airplane. Occasionally, if a test airplane shed its trailing bomb during testing, a Boeing test engineer had to travel to the test site on a commercial flight, a new trailing bomb in his baggage. Originally, the travel box the trailing bomb was packed into was labeled "Trailing bomb." This did not go over well with the airlines, so the trailing bomb was renamed "Trailing static device," which didn't alarm anyone.

the young pilot try a couple stalls. The first stall was fine. In the second one, however, the airplane started to roll to the left at or near initial buffet, and Fred used the wheel as well as a lot of right rudder to control it. Fred, holding right rudder, made the 707 roll rapidly to the right, and they entered into a spin. That's when Dad said, "I've got it," and took over. Don remembers Dad quickly following that with, "The first thing we got to do is get that rudder out of there." Dad stopped the turn to the right by turning a half turn to the left. The nose started coming down, and by then Dad had enough control to return to normal flight. Don remembers that recovery turn to the left by Dad being nearly as violent as the initial entry into the spin by Fred. Then suddenly, the wheel was nearly jerked from my father's hands as some part of the trailing bomb system hit the 707's tail, either the elevator or the tab.

After the airplane returned to level flight, another engineer, who had been in the cabin monitoring airspeed at the trailing bomb, came rushing up to the cockpit. "He informed us that he had seen the bomb pass very near by a cabin window," Don recalled. "By this time Lew had discovered there was a problem with the elevator-control system; the elevators would stick when moved and had to be forced to trim. We had visions of the bomb stuck in the middle of our new, one-of-a-kind stabilizer. Upon landing, we were pleased to find this was not the case. There was, however, considerable damage to the left elevator, tab, and anti-balance tab." The trailing bomb's hose and cable had hit those control surfaces and jammed between the fuselage and elevator. My father said that after recovering from the stall and realizing that he no longer had full elevator control, "I flew home very carefully."

Don later ordered the data from that flight, curious to see all the control movements, attitudes, and other parameters. Everything was normal until the sharp roll began. "That caused the instrumentation gyros to tumble as we rolled past 90 degrees," Don said. "From a subjective standpoint, I remember that all I could see was the ground in the front cockpit and eyebrow windows. As we returned to level flight, I believe someone in the cockpit had pooped their pants during the maneuver because of the smell that ensued. I only know it wasn't me." Later, Don discussed the spin entry and recovery with my father, asking him why he didn't just let the airplane go on around and complete one turn of the spin. "He first said facetiously, 'I like to take things out the way they go in' but admitted that his real concern was that the nose would get so low we wouldn't have enough altitude to recover."

Flutter

Next, in terms of adding data points into the box, come tests of the high speed/high altitude handling characteristics of the airplane—the upper portion of the box. The flight test crews need to determine the handling characteristics and structural capabilities of the airplane under extreme speeds and weights, and that requires a fair amount of flying, taking the airplane to the very edge of its envelope. The crews call it *high-speed flutter clearance*—in other words, they are proving that the airplane doesn't have aerodynamic flutter, or vibration, at high speeds and/or high altitudes, and that it will maintain its structural integrity under those extreme conditions.

Flutter. It sounds so innocuous, doesn't it? One thinks of a butterfly, a falling leaf, an eyelash tickling a cheek; something gentle and soft. But in the world of test flying, *flutter* means vibration, and uncontrolled vibration is one of the most dangerous events that can happen during flight. Flutter is anything but innocuous.

Galloping Gertie (the first Tacoma Narrows Bridge) in Washington State is a well-known and dramatic example of resonance (or vibration) and its consequences. Completed in 1940, the bridge earned its nickname when workers building it noticed a bounce, or ripple effect, that had them chewing on lemons to counteract motion sickness. On November 7, 1940, just four months after opening to traffic, wind gusts of up to 42 mph funneled through the Narrows, hitting the bridge. It was designed to withstand winds of up to 120 mph, but on this fateful day, the wind hit it *just so*. The bridge began to oscillate dangerously up and down—to resonate—until ultimately the oscillations increased so dramatically that the bridge broke apart and fell in huge pieces into the waterway far below, all of it caught on film.

When pilots talk about flutter, they're referring to the vibration induced on an airplane's wings, tail, or control surfaces by the force of airflow during flight. The amount of vibration depends upon the airplane's structural characteristics (its flexibility and stiffness) as well as its altitude, airspeed, and Mach number.[44]

If flutter is present, it usually increases with increased airspeed. In well-designed airplanes, any flutter will damp out on its own within a reasonable time. If damping doesn't occur or is insufficient, however, resonance occurs, dramatically increasing the vibration and potentially leading to catastrophic structural failure—a wing, or the tail, could break and the airplane could crash. During a six-month span in late 1959–early 1960, two Lockheed L-188 Electras disintegrated in midair, killing all crew and passengers onboard.[45] Beyond ascertaining that something originating in the left wing caused the first accident, investigators were stymied. After the second, nearly identical incident, the Civil Aeronautics Board determined that harmonic coupling between the wing and the rotating propeller caused of both disasters.

In new aircraft, where the aerodynamics and mechanical properties can't be fully known until it flies, stall characteristics and flutter—and flutter clearance—can only be determined through flight testing. These early stall and flutter clearance tests are what Boeing refers to as "minimum crew" flights because of their danger. (First and early flights of any new airplane are also minimum crew.) In the case of the 727, only the pilot, copilot, and flight engineer were onboard; in the 737 with its two-person cockpit, just the pilot and copilot. They

---

[44] Mach number is the ratio of the true airspeed of the airplane to the speed of sound; e.g., Mach 0.9 is 90% of the speed of sound. Mach number can apply to an airplane, bullet, missile, or any object moving through the atmosphere.

[45] Braniff Airways flights 542 on September 29, 1959; Northwest Airlines flight 710 on March 17, 1960.

were given extra pay because of the increased danger. The test engineers remained on the ground, data transmitted to them by telemetry (radio signals). Data were also being recorded onboard the airplane, in more detail than the telemetry showed, but wasn't analyzed until the flight was completed.

Flutter clearance testing is especially interesting for the crew in the cockpit. Remember, the tests are meant to prove that the airplane won't experience vibrations that don't quickly damp out, under various configurations and at various speeds and altitudes. Each new configuration—a certain speed, altitude, gross weight, center of gravity loading—becomes a new data point within the certification box, and initially there's a lot of blank space to fill with flutter-clearance points. The pilots are carefully feeling their way as they push the airplane's speed envelope to obtain each data point. Each new push of the envelope means taking the airplane to a new extreme.

There are two methods the pilots use to test for flutter clearance: sending impulses to mechanical vanes[46] on the wing tips and tail to excite a vibration, and manually putting impulses to the flight controls to cause a part of the airplane to vibrate.

Imagine a rubber band, or a violin string. When tight, if you tweak it, it has a frequency, or vibration. Tighten it more, and the frequency changes, causing a change in pitch. An aerodynamic vane, attached to a wing tip, and in some cases to the tip of the horizontal stabilizer on the tail, acts in a similar way—tweak it and it vibrates. Like the violin string, the vane also has a range of frequencies. It's controlled with an ON/OFF switch installed in the cockpit. Flipping the switch

---

[46] A mechanical vane is a flat metal plate or blade attached to a surface. A common example is a weather vane, which helps determine wind direction, or vanes (fins) on a missile or projectile used for guidance and stabilization. For flutter-clearance testing on aircraft, the vane is attached to the tips of wings, fins, or stabilizers and can rotate at the point of attachment. An analogy: Imagine your arm, extended out the window of a moving vehicle, as air airplane wing; your flattened hand, fingers together pointing out, palm down, is the vane. By rotating your hand at the wrist, you change its angle of attack, changing airflow over your hand, which is transmitted up your arm as a vibration.

causes the vane to cycle through a preset frequency range, which changes the angle of attack of the vane, which in turn excites (or vibrates) the structure it's attached to because of air flow over the vane.

When the pilot flips the ON/OFF switch to excite the vane, its movement starts out slow, then becomes faster and faster until the airplane structurally responds with its own movement—a vibration on the wing that should quickly damp out on its own. This movement is all recorded, both onboard and transmitted by telemetry to the engineers on the ground. If the engineers on the ground see vibration that isn't damping as expected, they can tell the crew onboard to immediately stop the input.

The other method involves the pilot using the controls to manually input impulses to the airplane's wings and other control surfaces. My father described it this way. "You can up an elevator on the tail real sharp to make the airplane bounce and pitch, while you input an aileron real hard, which makes the wings flex up and down. Or you hit the rudder [push against a rudder pedal], which makes the fuselage and engines go sideways. The instrumentation records how rapidly these vibrations or oscillations damp out. If they start to diverge, you are in trouble, and if you don't back out pretty quickly, you're in *real* trouble." The pilots rely heavily on the engineers on the ground, especially the flutter experts and structural engineers; if they see a problem in the telemetry, they tell the pilots to knock it off pronto.

Flutter-clearance flying can be a really bumpy ride for the pilots. According to my father, "Often you call it off before the engineers do, because you feel it *right now* but they have to wait and see it, to look at it." Even though the engineers see the traces almost instantaneously, their reaction time may not be quite as fast as the pilot feeling it in real time.

Dix shared an early flutter-clearance testing story that involved the KC-135. Tex Johnston and Dix made the first flight on August 31, 1956. Dix noted there was no extra pay offered the pilots for that first flight. "It was so close to the Dash 80 in terms of flying qualities, nobody thought it was necessary to pay extra," Dix said. "Yet it's the one model of the whole bunch we ever built that got into serious trouble in the first three flights."

Soon after, on the KC-135's third flight, Dix and Ray McPherson were doing flutter-clearance tests. They were taking the airplane to very high speeds—way above its operational limit—at high altitude, exciting a vibration by kicking the rudder real hard, or quickly jabbing the aileron, testing through all three axes.[47] After one particularly hard input that started a vibration, it didn't damp out as expected. In fact, it amplified until the KC-135 lost part of its tail.

"I thought the airplane was just going to come completely apart," Dix told me. "I wouldn't have given a plug nickel for it. The chase pilot thought so, too. He could see the airplane was beginning to come apart. There wasn't much of the tail left, aerodynamically; it was just hanging there. Then the big decision was where to try to land it. I finally decided I could control it well enough with the engines to land at Boeing Field if I could keep it straight and not excite it. I had to be careful; it was awful goosey."

I was surprised he was allowed to bring it in to land over a populated area like Boeing Field. "In hindsight, yeah," Dix said. "But at the time I thought, first off, it would be a lot of bad publicity if we land anywhere else, and secondly, it seemed as if it was safe enough to control. I practiced at higher altitude, coming down to the right approach speed, to be sure I could feel good about it."

Dix brought the airplane in safely, a testament to his skill as a pilot. The engineers immediately went to work to fix the problem. "The flutter guys are sort of the black magic guys," said Dix.

As Dix's story illustrates, the most critical factor in flutter-clearance testing is speed. At low speeds, the oscillations damp out fairly quickly; at higher speeds, the oscillations are faster

---

[47] The three axes are (1) yaw, which moves the tail and cockpit left and right; (2) pitch, which moves the tail and cockpit up and down; and (3) roll, which moves the wings into a bank left and right.

and continue longer. The high-speed tests are done at high, medium, and low altitudes because air pressure changes with altitude, causing differences in air flow and aerodynamic loading on the structure of the airplane. The pilots must demonstrate that the airplane is clear of flutter at all altitudes at high speed.

I was curious just how fast the high-speed tests were. Dad said that in the 727, the design dive speed is Mach .95 (approximately 550 knots, or 650 mph; Mach 1 is the speed of sound, which ranges from 659.8 to 761.1 mph, depending on altitude). "Real fast," he said. To get to that speed at high altitudes, the pilot had to put the 727 into a steep dive; at lower altitudes, you could get there in level flight. These speeds are *much* faster than an airline would ever be flying passengers; typical cruise speed for the 727 is 540 mph.

It can take a while to run through all the high-speed conditions. It takes the engineers in the telemetry room some time to go over their data and say okay, time for the next condition. "Of course," said Dad, "if you're pretty confident, you're already sitting there at the next speed, waiting, having already accelerated." It can take several flights to get through the entire flutter-clearance series of tests, adding all the necessary points into the certification box.

My father said that the ride in the cockpit gets interesting as the vane goes through its sweep. The vane starts at a low frequency, perhaps one cycle per second, and gradually increases to the desired maximum frequency, say twenty cycles per second. At the beginning, there is little or no motion in the cockpit. As the frequency gradually increases, but while still fairly low, the airplane structure responds with a pronounced "bounce" in the cockpit. At higher frequencies, the motion in the cockpit may change to a lateral motion, and eventually it may feel like the airplane is trying to do a jig but the cockpit can't quite respond to the more rapid tune.

"Flying a new airplane to its maximum speeds the first time is similar to walking to the edge of a cliff in the fog," my father explained. "You don't want to step over the edge, but you can't see the edge; it isn't clearly defined. You approach cautiously.

You increase airspeed increment by increment, until you make the final increment and you haven't fallen over the edge. While conducting these flights, the pilots' senses are all very tuned, listening for changes in sounds, aware of changes in the airplane's feel, and relying on instinct and intuition based on experience in other airplanes and similar test conditions." With each successful test, the pilots believe they can safely go to that speed again and so are more relaxed. But they never relax completely.

According to my father, because flutter-clearance testing is the first time the new airplane is flown at very high speeds, something invariably comes loose—maybe an access panel on an engine strut or a door underneath the airplane opens, or a fairing blows completely off. Engineers are unable to measure air flow loads in the wind tunnel accurately enough to prevent these "mishaps." Early in his career, Dix was testing B-52s. He remembered one incident when they were climbing up to about 20,000 feet when one of the pressure doors blew off. "Boy, that is a real sensation, a horrible *kaPOW!* You don't know what it is. It's very stunning." It was just a minor door, however, so losing it didn't affect flying qualities, Dix assured me.

My father remembered doing flutter-clearance tests on the 707. The NTSB was in charge of documenting and investigating accidents. The rules back then required the filing of a report in any incident that resulted in a certain dollar amount of damage to an airplane, say $250. As you can imagine, building and replacing a panel on a 707 only a foot square in size that blows off would cost way more than $250. "I was flying these flutter flights and almost every flight, I'd lose something," Dad recalled. "They came off with a bang, like a twelve-gauge shotgun. I was dutifully filing these reports to the NTSB, probably two or three a month, maybe two or three a week in some cases. This guy finally called me up one day and said, 'Hey, will you quit filing these darn reports. I'll let you know if I want you to file one.' It was a lot of work that he didn't want."

The 727 was no different. For example, access doors on the belly of the airplane were sucking open at high speeds. The doors had latches on them. The temporary "fix" was to put nut plates in, drill holes and install bolts to hold the doors closed until the tests were done, after which the engineers could design stronger doors and latches.

In case you're wondering the same thing I was when I heard these stories, these high-speed flights were usually conducted out over the Olympic Mountains or other minimally populated areas. I've often fantasized about hiking in the forest on the Olympic Peninsula and coming upon a 707 or 727 access door half buried in the ground like a meteor. They're out there somewhere.

Dad said that the 727 landing gear doors were also problematic. "We wanted them to come open at high speed, to extend the gear to increase drag so you can make a rapid descent from altitude. If you're up at 39,000 feet and you have a sudden loss of cabin pressure, you want to get down very rapidly to 12,000 feet or lower. You use the landing gear and spoilers for drag to help get down." The doors weren't able to open at high speeds, so they had to put in a bigger actuator. As Dad said, there's always something like that that comes along in any test program. They'd discover something doesn't work like it's supposed to, figure out a way to make it better, and go test it again.

Early in 727 flutter-clearance testing, my father was very interested in what the airplane's cruise performance was going to be. "I had a pretty good idea," he said, "having been involved in the program all through the design phase. So while we're sitting there [waiting for the engineers in the telemetry room to give the okay for the next test] I'd set up a performance data point, very rudimentary, take a look at the data and manually record it. It quickly became apparent to me that the airplane was going quite a bit faster than what we'd predicted. I didn't say anything on the radio because everybody else in those early days of the test program—Douglas, Convair—monitored our frequencies. When we got back after the flight, in postflight, I mentioned to the aero guys what I had observed and they got really excited. It was apparent that the airplane was substantially better at high-altitude cruise than what we had advertised and guaranteed to the airlines, which was great." After some problems in the 707 days, where optimism ruled and guarantees were made to airlines that went unfulfilled, everyone was cautious about overselling the 727. Luckily, Boeing didn't have much competition for this particular model—only the de Havilland Trident was similar—so caution was okay. The airlines were pleasantly surprised with what the 727 delivered.

Early in the Boeing 737 certification program, test pilots Brien Wygle and Ralph Cokely, flying a minimum-crew flutter test, experienced an extraordinary loss of control while in a steep high-speed dive, an event that almost resulted in the loss of the airplane. While the cause of the near disaster ironically wasn't flutter, the incident occurred during the final and most critical (and most dangerous) stage of the flutter-clearance-test program. It was a flight Brien will never forget.

Brien was project pilot for the 737 certification program. With my father as his copilot, Brien made the first flight of the 737 on April 9, 1967, an event he later described with typical understatement as "pretty straightforward."

By that summer, Brien and the other test pilots were putting the 737 through flutter-clearance tests. The 737 had progressed satisfactorily through the bulk of its flutter tests. Now, they reached the maximum-speed point in the series of tests. Once the speed required for a test condition exceeds what can be achieved in level flight, the desired speed is obtained by putting the airplane into a dive with maximum engine thrust. As faster speeds are required, steeper dives are needed. To minimize the time in the dive as well as the altitude lost, the pilots try to make the control kicks as close together as the damping permits, but only in one direction. One kick must damp out before the next kick is made.

The pilots are especially alert for changes in the sounds, vibrations, and "feel" of the airplane as the airspeed and Mach number increase. The conditions that are usually of most concern to the flight crew are the medium-altitude conditions where the airplane is flown so that maximum airspeed and maximum Mach number are reached simultaneously. At that point, Dad explained, the airplane feels tight and buzzes like a string on a banjo. The air noises around the cockpit are at their loudest, and every nerve in the pilot's body is waiting for some indication that something is not quite right.

If an access panel or door does blow off the airplane, it makes a sudden loud bang and change in sound in the cockpit, along with some buffeting. This always gets a quick response from the pilots: initially pulling back the power to idle until reaching a decreased airspeed in the medium range of about 250 knots. Chase-plane pilots are an important part of high-speed testing, flying alongside the test airplane where they can do a quick visual in-flight inspection and advise the pilots as to the condition of the test airplane. If the test airplane *has* lost an access panel or door, testing is finished for that flight and the airplane returns home. Once the engineers have designed a "fix" for the missing part and the new part is installed by the mechanics, the tests can continue.

In the final and most critical flutter test, the airplane is put at a high Mach number and a high indicated airspeed at medium altitude. The 737 had high drag at high Mach numbers, so getting to the desired test speeds required a steep dive of 5,000–6,000 feet using maximum thrust so that the airplane would reach Mach 0.9 and an indicated airspeed of around 420–450 knots (approximately 520 mph), far beyond the red line that is eventually established.[48] As Brien said, "flutter testing is always a little nerve-wracking, because the consequences of flutter are devastating, frequently resulting in loss of the airplane and crew right on the spot, or taking severe damage yet managing to get home. It's a difficult point to reach, because you have to do it just right, and the consequences of being wrong are very severe."

---

[48] All airplanes have a red line on the airspeed indicator. This is referred to by pilots as the airplane's "red line" and is $V_{MO}/_{MO}$ (maximum operating limit speed for the airplane in "clean" configuration of landing gear retracted and flaps up) for all operations. However, the airplane structure is designed to withstand a much higher speed, V_D/M_D (the design diving speed).This higher speed is intended to provide a substantial structural margin for normal airline operations. Flutter testing requires the test pilots to fly the airplane at V_D/M_D and demonstrate that the airplane is free from flutter even at that extreme speed.

On their fateful flutter-clearance flight that summer of 1967, Brien and Ralph proceeded to set up the test conditions over the Cascade Mountains and the foothills of western Washington. They were shadowed by Tom Edmonds in the F-86 chase plane. Earlier in the flight, the radio link to the F-86 failed; Brien was unable to communicate directly with Tom. Brien elected to continue, as he still had radio contact with the flight test station on the ground.

Brien put the airplane into the steep dive needed to attain the required high Mach number and airspeed, engines at full thrust, when suddenly, "All hell broke loose!" as he put it. The airplane "pitched up, and then down, and yawed wildly in both directions, and rolled. I seemed to have no control at all." First one engine surged, and then the other, something Brien had never encountered at such high speeds. His brain racing, Brien tried to understand what was causing the complete loss of control.

Because it was a flutter test, his first thought was that he'd lost the empennage (the rear part of the airplane, comprising the stabilizer, elevator, vertical fin and rudder). If that were true, there was no way he and Ralph were going to survive. "I remember looking out ahead with Mount Rainier right in front of me and thinking, that's the end of my career, right there," Brien said. "Not a life-flashing-in-front-of-my-eyes sort of thing, but a darting thought that after years of test flying, this was how it might all end for me."

As Brien wrestled with the 737, Ralph came on the radio linked to the ground crew with one terse sentence: "We're out of control, but we're recovering slowly." Close to a minute later—a minute when the ground crew must have held their collective breath—Brien came on the radio: "Okay. There was a terrible incident here. We've got it back under control. We see what it is. Our leading-edge flaps have come down and there is a great deal of slat damage.... The airplane was, as far as I was concerned, totally out of control in all axes for a while. We got the power back, but there were engine surges, enormous yaws, pitches. We'll be planning on coming in flaps down. We're nicely under control again now. In good shape." You can sense

Brien calming himself down as he provided the ground crew this information.

Brien managed the recovery by grabbing the throttles, bringing the power to idle, pulling back on the control column to bring the nose up, and carefully slowing the airplane while easing it out of the steep dive, all the while testing his ability to fly with the damaged flaps. Barely a word passed between Brien and Ralph for that long minute-and-a-half recovery. When it was clear they could fly and make it back to Boeing Field, they exchanged looks of relief. They'd survived.

Continuing to assess the handling characteristics of the airplane—Brien reported on the radio that he was "holding considerable left roll"—they alerted the ground crew that they'd be landing at a faster speed than normal.

Fire crews would have to be ready because Brien couldn't tell if the flap damage had affected the wings' fuel cells. Carefully, they flew toward Boeing Field while giving the ground crew descriptions of what they could see of the damaged flaps as well as the instrument readings. Noticing a loss of hydraulics in their A-system, they shut it down. When the airplane's speed reduced to 230, then 220 knots, Brien reported they were "nicely back in trim. I don't anticipate any landing problems, incidentally."

The ground crew advised Brien that he would have to do a manual extension of the gear because of the hydraulic issue. Normally, Tom in the chase plane would do a visual verification that the gear was down. "Okay, Tommy, we're going to head for the barn, and we're going to call Air Traffic for our letdown," Brien said on radio, knowing Tom could hear him in the F-86 but couldn't reply to the 737. "If you want to fly in on us, if you have got enough fuel, fine. But if you wish to break off, why do so. You will stay with us? [Tom gave Brien hand signals while flying in formation with the 737 so that Brien knew he would stay with them.] Okay. Good deal. Tommy, I think we'll take the gear right here at 215 [knots]. Okay, nose gear is apparently coming down. We've got a green on the nose gear."

Brien made an instrument approach, landing at 160 knots—

normal landing speed would be 130 knots at their weight—with 10 degrees of trailing-edge flaps. Not using reversers, Brien pulled up the speed brakes slowly to make sure there wasn't an asymmetric effect, and applied brakes steadily until they could taxi off the runway. Brien and Ralph deplaned and, with shock and amazement, surveyed the damage, finally grasping the true severity of their earlier situation.

The next day at the postflight meeting, Brien and Ralph went over what they saw and felt during those tense moments. Getting technical details on the record, Brien said, "There was heavy buffet, and I guess this yaw was the worst thing. But the feeling was that it was doing it without any—perhaps without anything from me, it was doing this on its own. That may have been what gave me the feeling of being out of control." Ralph added, "And there was noise associated with it, too. There were sounds like metal breaking up and that sort of thing." Brien noted that when they landed, they discovered lots of paper and other items strewn all over the cockpit, including up against the rudder pedal area, adding, "We probably took some longitudinal *g*'s there."

"When the incident itself occurred, I thought I saw some debris pass me outside the airplane on my side, and there was other debris inside," Ralph said. "For approximately three to five seconds, I also had the same impression that Brien did, that the airplane was completely out of control. The sensation that went through my mind was that having been in on so many discussions of incidents where data were not available or nobody said anything over the radio, I was going to try to give a rundown on what was occurring as long as I could. But then in about three to five seconds, it appeared that there was some hope that we would recover."

Engineers later determined that the slats had come out almost randomly, which accounted for the crazy pitching, yawing, rolling, and engine surging. Some of them had broken their fittings because the placard speed[49] for them was normally

[49] The flap placard speed is the design speed for flap operation and extension, similar in concept to the red line speed, or V_{MO} (the maximum operating speed), but for flaps rather than the entire airplane.

about 230 knots, yet they had been flying at double that speed. Some of the slats had been left hanging and broken, some of them had retracted, and some had remained deployed.

It turned out that the combination of high Mach, high indicated air speed, air pressure on the leading edge of the wings, and aerodynamic forces caused the leading-edge devices (slats) to extend out of the front edges of the wings. It was something that happened only that one time, during that particular test condition, a condition that couldn't have been worse in terms of the resulting loss of control.

"The yaw was so severe—and remember, this was all happening at very high speeds—that the engines surged wildly," Brien said. "Normally, you never get engine surges at high speed, you get them at low speed or at a high angle of attack or stall, but here these things were surging, both of them, one of them off, then on, the airplane rolling and pitching. I think we went to a negative half *g*, and up to a couple of *g* positive, but when you realize this is all done without any input from me, and at high speed... the feeling...," Brien recalled, his voice trailing off to a whisper, at a loss of words to describe it. "What I wanted to do was get the nose up. I think my one instinct was that. Anytime you're doing flutter testing, the first thing you do is get the nose up if you want the speed to come back down."

Don Archer was in the radio room that day. He remembers that incident as a very tense time. "My most vivid memory," Don said, "is that the pilots had very little to say when it happened. I'm sure they had other things on their minds, like trying to save their lives."

Brien acknowledged that he and Ralph said little to each other during the initial incident. "I don't think we said a word," Brien said, "other than a quick 'We're out of control.' I think it was so startling and sudden, we didn't talk. You often find that pilots, just before they die, or even before, when they know they're in serious trouble, they don't talk to the tower. People often wonder why they didn't say something further. You're just so wrapped up in what you're involved in." Such as saving your life.

Ben Wheat, Seattle Division VP-General Manager for the 707 and 727 programs, attended that postflight meeting. He brought a bottle of Scotch for the pilots.

For the engineers, the result of this incident was a redesign of the leading-edge slats. Even though it was believed that the same thing could happen only at those extreme test conditions, a mechanical lock was put on the slats so that when they were fully retracted, hydraulic pressure moved a mechanical lock into place that could only be removed when the pilot applied hydraulic pressure the other way to extend them. But while waiting for that permanent fix, with pressure to finish flutter testing for certification, they bolted the leading edge up and Brien took off and landed without a leading edge for a short period of time, to keep the test program on track.

I asked Brien if he had any trepidation about doing flutter tests after this close call, even though it wasn't a result of flutter. "No, I don't think I had any lasting effects from it," he replied. "I've never experienced the feeling that I don't want to be a test pilot anymore because I had a very bad experience. I'm sure Lew didn't either, or Jim Gannett or Jack Waddell. But there were pilots who had some pretty hair-raising experiences and chose not to do flight test work anymore. You rarely hear of it, but I'm sure it happens. Some people may have quit and not said that was the reason, with all the macho posturing." In hindsight, Brien felt his narrow escape in the B-47 aft center-of-gravity test in Wichita was the worst of his career. Of the flutter incident, he summed up, "In the end it wasn't such a close call."

Good test pilots, like Brien, my father, and many others at Boeing, have sharp instincts that kick in when the going gets tough. Brien said, "I think I probably had my share of those instincts, and Lew certainly had them. And so did Tex Johnston. Tex had a very great survival instinct, he survived a lot of things; I think he was very good at really not knowing why he was doing something but instinctively doing it. Jim Gannett had that same trait. Jim was a very good test pilot, a very skillful pilot. Jim and Lew were very smooth, two very smooth pilots. Lew had such good hands."

Performance Tests

The next sets of data points filling the test and certification box include what my father described as "the fun stuff." Well, actually he said it was *all* fun, but some of it was *more* interesting and fun. He included in that category takeoff and landing performance tests, which he referred to as "the pilot's skill part of it."

One of the more challenging maneuvers for any test pilot is referred to as "minimum unstick" or V_{MU} tests.[50] Flight test engineer Dennis Mahan described minimum unstick tests this way: "It's dragging the tail on the runway to determine the slowest speed the airplane will fly. It's done for all takeoff flap settings and the complete weight range of the airplane. It's a basic parameter used to determine the normal takeoff speeds."[51]

In most airplane models, when the airplane is moving very slowly down the runway and the nose rotates up for takeoff, the tail drags along the runway surface for some distance until the rear landing gear finally lift off and the airplane flies. That tail dragging throws a shower of sparks from the tail's skin. Knowing this, in preparation for V_{MU} tests, engineers designed and ground crews attached a skid to the airplane's tail to protect it from damage. Except for the 727, which had a production skid of metal, skids were made of oak or ash (leading some to refer to "Lew's hot ash" when he was doing V_{MU} tests).

My father described the challenge of flying minimum unstick tests this way: "You climb out very shallow. You're just threading the needle there. You're flying it very tenderly because if you pull the nose up too much, you are going to slow down even more; if you let the nose down too much, you are going to have too long a distance. If you get way too slow, it goes into a stall." A stall at that point, so soon after takeoff, and so close to the ground, would be nearly impossible to recover

---

[50] V_{MU} stands for "velocity minimum unstick" and refers to the slowest speed at which an airplane of a certain weight and configuration can take off without stalling and continue to climb.

[51] Generally, takeoff speed for commercial airline use is ten-percent faster than the speeds determined during V_{MU} tests.

from; the airplane—all lift gone and unable to fly—would simply slam back down onto the runway or just past the runway's end. Clearly, pilot skill is required to fly these tests successfully. And lots of runway, which is why most V_{MU} tests were done at Edwards AFB. "It's not that unusual to use nearly all of that 15,000 foot runway for maximum weight V_{MU}'s," Dennis told me.

The following story involves a 707, and while the test being flown wasn't a V_{MU} but rather a performance takeoff test, it illustrates just how dicey this sort of flying can be and how precisely the airplane must be flown under extreme conditions—especially when you add into the mix an FAA pilot who makes a mistake at a critical point.

In 1960, Brien Wygle was at Edwards AFB doing certification tests in a BOAC 707-420, the first 707 with Rolls Royce engines. An FAA pilot—the same one who later put the 727 into its deep stall during certification with my father, and who shall remain nameless here as well at Brien's request—was in the copilot's seat. Flight test engineer Don Archer was onboard, sitting right behind Brien. Boeing was trying to prove that this 707 could take off at high weight and early rotation, with one engine out; succeeding would shorten the certified takeoff length for airline operations, increasing the number of airports from which the airplane could operate. "We had to do the takeoff at maximum weight and cut an engine at V_1—the minimum speed at which the aircraft could tolerate an engine failure and still complete the takeoff," Brien explained. "I was then to wait until we reached V_R—the speed at which to rotate the nose up—and complete the takeoff."

"It was hotter than hell," said Don. "We engineers had miscalculated and given Brien the wrong speed for rotation."

The FAA pilot had been briefed to retard the throttle of the number 4 engine (far right engine) at V_1, simulating an engine out. He did, and Brien rotated at the reduced V_R speed given to him. "The airplane took off," Brien said, "but it was soon apparent to me that the speed was too slow, and the drag too high, to continue the flight. [The FAA pilot] had his hand on the number 4 throttle and I knew I needed that engine to come back in to enable us to fly. I said 'bring it up' meaning the throttle, but he thought I meant the gear. He raised the gear, which momentarily increased the drag. I immediately shouted to lower it again, as now we *had* to land. He did, but by then we had used up that entire long runway and had to land on the lake bed, which stretched for miles in front of us. I don't think I got over 100 feet in the air the whole time."

Don Archer watched this potential disaster unfold from his vantage point behind Brien. "I knew Brien meant the throttle," said Don, "because I almost reached up and pushed the throttle. The FAA guy thought he meant the landing gear. So he raised the gear. God lifted us up."

Brien knew military aircraft frequently landed on the dry lake bed, so he wasn't concerned about using it. This is, after all, why so many tests are done at Edwards AFB. In fact, he said he wouldn't have attempted this extreme end of test flying anywhere else. In the brief time before touchdown, the blast from the engines at high power and at a high angle of attack (nose up) sent sand blasting back up against the aft belly skin.

This fiasco did not go unnoticed by a BOAC crew who were also at Edwards AFB. "There's Dexter Field, the BOAC pilot, standing on the side of the runway," said Don. "He sees this takeoff and thinks, 'Blimey them blokes have had it.'" As Don Cumming said, "We were all pleased to see the airplane appear out of the dust, taxiing out of the desert."

When the airplane was later refurbished—including re-skinning that sand-blasted section of the belly—they took the landing gear off and found some bent bolts. The gear apparently didn't have time to fully extend back down before they landed on the dry lake bed.

"That FAA pilot was an average pilot," my father told me when we discussed Brien's experience in the 707, "but unpredictable. He would sit there, in a situation like that, once the throttle was chocked, and put his hand on the gear handle, which just used to scare the livin' daylights out of me. You just knew that sooner or later he was going to do something you didn't want him to do. He was spring-loaded to bring that gear up." Brien actually gives this FAA pilot a higher mark than my father did, saying he liked flying with him more than any of the other FAA pilots he flew with. "He had his faults, as I guess we all do, but he was a good pilot. We didn't always agree with him, but he was never unreasonable." Brien added that he never had a chance to fly with Walt Haldeman, the FAA pilot my father so enjoyed working and flying with.

Like Brien, my father certainly didn't consider this FAA pilot the worst the Boeing pilots had to work with. "There was another FAA pilot who was always screwing up," Dad continued. "The Boeing pilots complained and got the FAA to quit assigning him. He simply lacked good judgment." Dad heard later that that FAA pilot taught his son to fly small airplanes and let him fly without a license, in bad weather. The kid crashed and died.

High-altitude performance takeoffs were often done in Albuquerque, New Mexico; the airport sits at 5,355 feet. Don Archer recalls a day when my father's practical side allowed them to kill two 707 test birds with one stone. They did all the required takeoff tests in the early morning, when winds were minimal. Later that day they were preparing to return to Seattle when Dad noticed the wind picking up significantly, blowing directly across the runway. "Lew had everyone get off the airplane and said we'll do our crosswind takeoff and landing tests," Don recalled. "Since our wind equipment was already loaded on the airplane, I went to the airport tower to record the wind speed and direction on their equipment. A CAA flight test engineer was with me to verify the readings. The winds weren't too high, but high enough to use for initial certification. That was the only time I can remember doing performance takeoffs and crosswinds on the same day at the same airport, thanks to Lew's quick thinking."

My father described landing performance tests as also requiring real pilot skill. The term "landing performance" means making the best landing that the airplane can handle under various configurations. The shortest possible distance from touchdown to stop is usually what the test pilot is after. "The goal back then was to come in on approach at a pretty steep angle, rotate and land, stopping very short, as short as you can," Dad said. The FAA regulations took the stopping distance of these tests and increased it by a substantial amount to derive the field length required for airline operations.

These early performance landings were challenging enough on their own; even more dicey when Mother Nature throws a curve ball at the last minute. Dad remembered flying landing performance tests in the 707 at Edwards AFB with Walt Haldeman as copilot and a guy named Jim Allison on a camp seat behind them. "I didn't have a lot of experience at that time in these types of landings. Haldeman's approach was to fly in on airspeed, then look out and make the landing. At about 175 feet, he'd call out the altitude and I'd look up to make a flare. We were doing this, and all of a sudden, I just sensed that the airplane was really sinking. I had flown the airspeed perfectly. I put full throttle on and started flaring, and hit the ground pretty firmly. My headset fell off. Old Allison, he just reached down, picked it up and put it back over my ears... didn't say a word! We made a touch-and-go out of it, came back around and landed. We figured out we had a wind shear we had no way of predicting."

Because Boeing wanted the airlines to be able to fly the 727 into as many airports as possible, the test pilots really worked to keep the distance short on these performance tests. And unlike the airlines, the Boeing pilots weren't allowed to use their thrust reversers on performance landings. The idea behind the FAA regulation was to give the airlines a big margin for landings. For the Boeing pilots, though, making brakes-only stops in the shortest possible distance often resulted in some drama—as in tires blowing or brakes catching fire from the heat generated by bringing the hulking airplane to a stop. If the brakes couldn't take the stress, the engineers would go back and redesign, leading to more tests.

Similar to landing performance tests are refused takeoff tests, or RTOs. They're pretty much what the name implies: the pilot starts a normal takeoff run down the runway, then at the last moment, as if in an emergency, refuses to takeoff by hitting the brakes. "I hated them," Dad said, "because you're loaded up to a very heavy weight, and go charging down the runway at a very high speed, putting on the brakes and stopping. Invariably the first two or three times you attempt it, something goes wrong—with airplane damage—and you didn't even get to fly! All it is, is taxi tests," he added disdainfully.

"Taxi tests" that often resulted in fire and drama. According to Dix Loesch, "Lew and I were at Edwards on the 707. The whole idea was to come to a braked halt, get off the runway and get the hell out of the airplane as fast as you can because tires are exploding."

34 Dash 80 landing-gear fire suppression. Photo: Boeing Archives.

Don Archer vividly remembers an RTO test at Edwards AFB on the first 707. It was a minimum-crew test with my father and Walt Haldeman in the cockpit. "We loaded the airplane to maximum takeoff weight," Don said. "Lew accelerated down the runway, Walt pulled one throttle to idle, Lew retarded the other throttles and simultaneously applied full brakes and no reversers. The airplane came to a full stop on the runway. Lew taxied about three miles back to the parking ramp, followed by the base fire trucks. After stopping, the wheels and tires began exploding with pieces flying everywhere.

Those of us on the ground ran for cover. One wheel damaged an engine nacelle, and other pieces damaged the underside of a wing. The windshield of one of the fire trucks was blown out." There's a picture of my father standing next to the gaping hole in the engine, inspecting the damage Don describes. The ragged, mangled hole is big enough for a man to crawl through.

The result of these exploding tire incidents was the design of fuse plugs for the landing gear tires so that during high-energy stops—those generating very extreme temperatures—the plugs melt, letting air out of the tires, avoiding explosions. The wheels sink down into the rubber of the deflating tires. Those plugs became standard on all future Boeing airplanes.

35 Lew Wallick next to 707 damaged by exploding gear. Photo: Boeing Archives.

To pass the RTO test, the airplane has to come to a stop and wait five minutes without any outside assistance to extinguish any fire—presumably long enough to get fire engines to the airplane and to evacuate passengers in a real emergency. There's Boeing film of a 747 RTO test at Edwards AFB in the 1970s; in fact, it was the first 747 Air Force Command Post, prior to delivery. In that particular test, the brakes couldn't handle the RTO conditions and the tires caught fire and exploded, creating a blaze in the landing gear area and a real hazard to ground crews as tire parts flew through the air. Boeing's ground crew let things burn for about three and a half minutes—even though clearly the test was a failure—before calling in the base fire crew waiting nearby to put it out. Still, there wasn't any structural damage to the airplane; they simply replaced the burned gear and flaps. The airplane was flown back to Seattle a week later.

Dennis Mahan recalls a 727 RTO test with my father. "We had an instrumentation engineer onboard by the name of Fred Quealey. He really didn't like RTOs because of some bad experiences," Dennis told me. "Part of your Dad's pre-test briefing was to tell us to exit the airplane immediately through the aft airstair and run away down the airplane centerline [because hot wheels explode sideways]. 'When you encounter Fred Quealey, you have run far enough.'" Pretty sound advice.

Clearly, Dad wasn't kidding about airplanes frequently being damaged when doing RTO tests. This was one reason these tests—and the V_{MU} tests, with sparks flying off the tail—were done at Edwards AFB, where there was plenty of runway as well as fire crews used to putting out fires. Since it wasn't uncommon for tires to explode or catch fire during maximum weight RTOs, airplanes could end up disabled on the runway; all the wheels, tires, and brakes would have to be changed there. A commercial airport couldn't tolerate losing a runway for such significant periods of time. In fact, the Air Force allowed those tests to be done at Edwards AFB only on weekends when other traffic was light.

Another reason to use Edwards AFB: one wouldn't want future airline passengers to be alarmed by witnessing the exploding tires and fires, or sparks from tails skidding against the runway. In fact, in early 727 V_{MU} tests at Boeing Field, sparks from the tail's metal skid set grass along the edges of the runway afire. But even before that, Bill Allen had seen through his own office window sparks flying off the tail of a 707 during V_{MU} tests at Boeing Field. After the grass fire, Allen decreed thenceforth such tests should occur at Edwards AFB or Moses Lake—away from the public's eye.

Crosswind landings are another type of performance test. While landing in a crosswind requires pilot skill, Dad said the bigger challenge was finding a place with sufficient crosswind to do the tests, getting there before the wind goes away. "You look at the weather sequence and reports, and they're saying Great Falls, Montana, is going to have a good crosswind today," he explained. "Maybe it's 7:00 am here, 8:00 am there; by the time you get organized and get going, it's going to be mid-day over there. You get there, and the wind has either changed direction or has quieted down. That's as big a challenge as actually flying the condition." Dad insisted that Boeing's airplanes have so much margin that one could hardly find a crosswind that's limiting. With the 707, however, they found a crosswind that came close: 60 knots [roughly 70 mph] straight across the runway. Surprised at hearing this, I asked Dad if they actually tried landing. He assured me they did: Jim Gannett took off *and* landed in that crosswind, with an FAA pilot in the copilot's seat. Dad said the strongest crosswind he landed in was 40 to 45 knots. He added that in such crosswinds, the pilot approaches the runway a little bit sideways—they call it crabbing—nose into the wind, then straightening down the runway as soon as the wheels touch.

On its own initiative, Boeing tests the landing characteristics of its airplanes in severe crosswinds. FAA regulations set the bar airlines must observe for certain crosswind conditions. Boeing of course wants to demonstrate that its airplanes can handle crosswinds well beyond what the FAA regulations state. Dad, though, felt some frustration that the airlines often saw a certain number in the flight manual as a limit. For example, using the FAA regulations, the flight manual might say the airplane is demonstrated at a crosswind of X velocity. But it's not a limit—the airplane can handle a greater crosswind.

There were some days doing performance takeoffs or landings that it must have seemed that's all they did—no real time in the air, just taking off and landing. My father's pilot log shows days in the early 1970s when he was doing performance tests on the 737-200ADV (Advanced—with improved payload and range, and better short-field performance). On February 23, 1971, he did twelve takeoffs and twelve landings at Roswell, New Mexico, in five hours; the next day, he did fifteen more in just under four hours. A few days later he took a 727-200 to Fresno for noise tests, doing repeated takeoffs and landings there; then for the next two weeks, he was testing that same 727-200 at Edwards AFB. Dad liked to joke that his ability to fly a 737 one day, then a 727 the next meant he was ambidextrous.

Another aspect of performance testing involves taking the airplanes to unusual types of airports—high altitude (including Albuquerque); short runways; gravel, grass, or coral runways. For example, Jack Waddell took the 727 to La Paz, Bolivia, (13,323 feet) to qualify the airplane for extreme high-elevation airports. Similarly, Boeing had to prove to Faucett Airlines of Peru that a 727 could take off, fully loaded with one engine out, from the Cusco Airport (10,860 feet) which is surrounded on three sides by mountains.[52] These performance tests took the pilots and crews all around the world.

The 727 was the first Boeing airplane that tested landings on gravel and turf runways and was certified for such airports. The Boeing crews went to Annette Island, Alaska, for gravel runway tests. The gravel was usually wet, and the airplane took a beating from the gravel if they weren't careful. They extended the flaps a little more than normal for takeoffs and landings to protect the engines from gravel, and put mud flaps between the

---

[52] In May 2000, I flew into Cusco on LAN Airlines. I vividly remember those high mountains and how remote Cusco's airport seemed as the 737-200 circled to land. After several days high in the Andes, including running the Inca Trail to Machu Picchu, I flew back to Cusco on a Russian Mi-17 helicopter, a unique opportunity and perhaps the only aircraft type I flew on that my father never did.

wheels. Because the belly of the airplane took a thrashing from the gravel, they designed a retractable rotating beacon for the airplane's underside to prevent gravel damage.

The 737 was also tested for gravel runways at Annette Island. Dennis Mahan was onboard one day when Tom Edmonds was doing these tests. One landing in particular, on slick wet gravel, stood out. "When the captain says, 'Oh, shit!' it gets my attention and I changed focus from head down, taking notes to what the heck is going on, and I'll write it down later! We nearly ran off the end of the runway into the trees."

My father joked about landing a 737 on a grass field in Africa. The surface was more slippery than expected. When they got out of the airplane and saw lots of centipedes in the grass, Dad commented, "Crushed centipedes are slick!"

In addition to the tests described earlier, Boeing crews also test *all* of the airplane's systems—including electrical, fuel, hydraulics, air conditioning and pressurization, and autopilot. In the case of the 727, the automatic approach and landing systems actually came after the 727 was certified; it was the first airplane where Boeing developed the automatic-landing system as a follow-on program.

The 727 met the goal of certification within its first year. The airlines loved the airplane. The biggest problem encountered in the first two or three years of its operation carrying passengers: too many crashes, involving fatalities. It was a training problem, according to Dad, and Boeing. "The airplane was pretty easy to fly," Dad said. "That was one of the objectives those of us who worked on its design had, that it would be easy to fly. You could fly it with one hand. It required lighter forces and was more responsive. But as a result, it also gave the pilot a high level of confidence." Remember, starting with the 707 and continuing with the 727, a lot of the airline pilots getting checked out had never operated a jet of any kind. For pilots like my father, Brien Wygle, and others at Boeing, who had been flying jets since the early 1950s, it was old stuff. But for many airline pilots, it was much too new.

The fact that the 727 was easy to fly made some of the airline pilots overconfident. They didn't pay close enough attention, and they were crashing on approach and landing, letting the airplane get ahead of them, especially on nighttime visual approaches. "After about the fifth crash," my father said, "the FAA and, of course, Boeing, were quite concerned." The FAA established what they called the Gold Team and sent them out to Seattle to work on the problem. Dad and other Boeing pilots re-flew some of the tests with the FAA pilots to validate that yes, the 727 was doing what it was supposed to do. "Boeing was able to convince the FAA and the airlines that they needed to concentrate on training," Dad said, "emphasizing approach speeds and the control configuration on approach, flying by the numbers published in the flight manual, and not just flying like they had been for the last twenty years in old prop airplanes." This approach was a success, because thereafter the 727 had an excellent safety record.

And, at this point, simulators were starting to be used to train airline personnel. Errors could be made by airline pilots in the simulators without real-life consequences.

Initially, all of the various tests a new airplane is put through are done strictly for Boeing, checking the numbers, and making sure the airplane performs as expected before bringing the FAA pilot out to do the flying for certification. For some aspects of performance certification, for example landings, the FAA insists that its pilot do half of the performance runs. Dad said he and the other pilots would first take the FAA pilots flying in the Boeing jet to make sure they acquired enough experience to do a reasonable job flying. Then, the Boeing pilot might get a competition going with the FAA pilot, to see who does best at the particular type of flying being certified—maybe typical airline (service) conditions, or performance (for example, short runway) conditions.

When I asked if an FAA pilot ever bested him in these informal competitions, Dad initially said no, then reconsidered. "I had one guy who was a really, really terrible pilot," Dad remembered. "We put liquid-cooled brakes on the 727. We were going to re-certify landing distance with those brakes. The FAA said we had to do fifty service-type landings using heavy braking, then a total of twelve performance landings where we measured for actual stopping distance. I decided I'd take this FAA guy and put him in the left seat. I'd flown with him before; he was terrible. I took him out there and I made him do all fifty of those service landings. That got him pretty sharp. Then when we went to do the actual performance landings, he did half of them and I did half, and he beat me. I'd trained him well. It's like anything else—proficiency is a big part of it." It turns out that after all those additional certification tests, Boeing ended up not using liquid-cooled brakes on the 727. But my father's approach to the problem of an FAA pilot lacking skill was one I saw him use in many situations in life. Practice makes perfect, especially when practicing is fun and maybe even a little competitive, in a friendly way.

Scott Linn was a young Boeing Flight Test engineer in the spring of 1982. He was onboard the company 727 as it ferried Boeing people and equipment to Edwards AFB and back, making several round trips in a day. My father and Uncle Jesse were in the cockpit, putting this philosophy of practice-makes-perfect and competition into practice. Dad and Jesse decided to have a contest: who could make the best, or softest, landings. They let Scott and others in the cabin vote without knowing who was doing the flying for any given landing. "They'd then ask, on a scale of one to ten, how was that one?" Scott said. "It made the trips fun because now we're paying attention. I saw three landings. They were all squeakers... *we're not on the ground, we're not on the ground, I think we're on the ground....* They explained they had a bet going. I think it was pretty much a tie."

✈

When the testing and certification box is filled with acceptable data points, the FAA certifies a new airplane, which allows the airlines to operate it. During my father's early career, most of the data points were obtained through flying; wind-tunnel tests could predict only so much. Test crews had to take the airplane up and see whether it performed as the engineers who designed it hoped it would. Today, certifying new commercial jets is far less dramatic and much more routine. Computer modeling has significantly reduced the risks, making test flights more predictable. There's a lot less seat-of-the-pants flying today, something my father would say is a shame, at least for the pilots.

The Closest Calls

There's a pilot's proverb that goes something like, Truly superior pilots are those who use their superior judgment to avoid those situations where they might have to use their superior skills.

Don Archer was involved as a flight test engineer on an incredible number of flights over the years, from 707s through 767s. I asked him to comment on the deep stall story involving my father, as well as Brien's 737 flutter test that went awry. "I do remember the famous stall incident," Don wrote to me in an email. "I can't remember if I was in the radio room, but I do remember going over the data traces. The angle of attack was off the scale, and the air speed trace did show zero, but that could be because the Pitot tube[53] stalled out. It was a very close encounter. Brien's flutter test incident was also a very tense time. I was in the radio room for that one, and my most vivid memory is that the pilots had very little to say when it happened. I'm sure they had other things on their minds, like trying to save their lives. There were numerous other incidents over the years that were also intense, but nothing like those two. We had bad moments with RTO tests, tail drag tests, minimum-control speed tests, etc. But that is what they were paying us to do, and I am sure there has never been a more dedicated group of people working together than our test pilots and flight test engineers. We had tremendous trust in each other, and learned to listen to each other at all times. I never said this to Lew, but he was the one guy that I would feel good

---

[53] A Pitot tube is used on many airplanes to measure air speed. It's a tube with a single hole pointing forward, into the airflow. By comparing air pressure in the Pitot tube to static pressure measured on the side of the airplane, air speed can be determined.

about going on any test with."

That last comment was one I heard often from people involved in Flight Test during my father's tenure. I'm pretty sure they weren't saying it just because I'm Lew Wallick's daughter.

Confidently Competent or Competitively Incompetent

Many of the stories I heard—the overblown egos of some of the military test pilots at Edwards AFB in the 1950s and 1960s, Russ Baum's ego leading to the crash of the Braniff 707 training flight, and others—coupled with how the test pilots felt about those they thought had outsize egos led me to contemplate the subject of *confidence*. Test pilots have it; they can't succeed and survive without a healthy dose of confidence in their own skill. Yet the test pilots I grew up around were very humble. They certainly didn't exhibit overblown egos. What is the distinction between confidence and "ego," as my father and others used that term in a derogatory sense, meaning overconfidence? And how did my father's views on confidence, ego, and competence influence how he raised me?

My father is usually described by his colleagues as a true gentleman, an excellent pilot who was modest about his accomplishments. Whenever I interviewed Dad about his career, he always highlighted the contributions of his Boeing co-workers—those who helped design, build, maintain and test airplanes; those who sold them; and the janitors who cleaned the offices at night—and minimized his own. He lived by a personal code that justified the description "gentleman." He was kind, fair, upbeat, and confident. He was the sort of man that everyone—his kids, relatives, neighbors, colleagues, and co-workers—was proud to call "friend" and sought to emulate. He was comfortable in his own skin.

A successful test pilot must, of course, have confidence in his abilities and his airplane every time he climbs into the cockpit. His life and those of the crew all depend on his skill and his ability to handle whatever may happen during each flight. Psychologists might even say test pilots possess extreme self-confidence. In his book *Eiger Dreams: Ventures Among Men and Mountains,* about climbers and the addiction to risk exhibited by some of them, Jon Krakauer writes, "Most climbers aren't in fact deranged, they're just infected with a particularly virulent strain of the Human Condition." I think the same applies to test pilots and their comfort with taking risks.

Yet there's a fine line in that risk-taking attribute. When it comes to pilots, those who are overconfident, foolish, or simply don't possess sufficient skill wash out at some point in the process of learning to fly or trying to become a test pilot. Those who succeed don't need to prove their ability by talking about it, by bragging. In fact, bragging signals a lack of confidence and skill. Who wants to share the cockpit of a test airplane with such an individual, someone who can't be entirely trusted to do the right thing at the right time?

The confidence possessed by my father and most of the other Boeing test pilots I knew growing up was a quiet, understated sort, acquired over time as their experience grew. I never heard them brag or boast about themselves. In fact, they rarely discussed with their families the day-to-day details of their work, and when pressed, downplayed it. Yet with each year of successful testing, their abilities and confidence in themselves grew. The crews working with them—flight test engineers, mechanics, even Boeing management—were also confident in their abilities. Boeing was, at least during my father's tenure, the only major corporation which flew most of its board members and senior managers on the same airplane to board meetings, a Boeing airplane frequently piloted by my father. That speaks volumes. A crash involving a majority of senior management would have been devastating to the company's viability. (Or, as Dad joked, it would have created a lot of promotion opportunities.) By flying as a group on their own airplanes, Boeing's board and management were making a clear statement to the world about the safety and reliability of their product, and their trust in the skill of their test pilots.

I've often marveled that the flight test engineers who flew on test flights had to have an amazing level of confidence in the test pilots, putting their fate in their hands, because if something went wrong, the engineers are just passengers with no ability to intervene. Yet they assured me they never gave it much thought, so strong was their trust and faith in the pilots with whom they flew, even after some close calls. George Stutsman, a flight test engineer who was my father's colleague and friend, was once asked by a military pilot which of the Boeing pilots he liked best. George replied, "If they put a rocket on a skateboard and Lew Wallick was gonna fly it, I'd go along."

I grew up around that confidence, and believed it to be normal. As a kid, I was infused with a similar confidence, assured by my father that I could do anything I put my mind to. It really seemed that simple. I may stumble as I learned, I might not become the best at a certain task, skill, or sport, but if I tried, and worked hard, I could do anything. That message came through loud and clear. In my father's view, practice made perfect, and we kids were afforded the opportunity to practice anything we showed an interest in. Being a girl wasn't any reason to avoid trying something that society said only boys did, or to refrain from aspiring to some skill or occupation. This lesson was imparted to me as much by words, encouragement, and opportunity as by example. I saw, day in and day out, my father's demeanor, and he always exuded calm competence and confidence.

My brothers and I were encouraged to try all sorts of sports, although the subtle push from my parents was toward individual sports—water and snow skiing, for example—as opposed to team sports. The message was to compete against ourselves and the clock, not against others. My father always told me that comparing myself to others in sports competitions was silly; far better to gauge my progress by competing against myself, taking pride in my own improvement rather than beating someone else.

I was also instructed to *never* brag about myself. Bragging was, my father assured me, truly bad form. No one likes a braggart. Actions always speak louder than words.

My father spent much of his free time helping us learn and enjoy whatever sports we wanted to pursue. He taught us to ride our bicycles; he drove us up to the mountains to snow ski many winter weekends; he drove the boat while we water skied most summer weekends (and sometimes, very early in the morning before he went to work because the lake looked like glass and was just begging for someone to ski it); he shot baskets and played croquet and badminton with us; he helped us build model train and slot car tracks, and marble chutes made by pairing two garden hoses and running them over obstacles in the yard. He seemed to have as much fun as we did. Both homes we lived in when I was growing up were designed with kids in mind; the neighborhoods were kid-friendly and safe. We were blessed with natural athletic ability that Dad's nurturing turned into skill. And with skill came *confidence*.

Often, Dad would take a turn at whatever sport we were doing. He didn't ski nearly as often as my brothers and I did, and we kids eventually became better skiers than Dad, but he always added a twist that made us laugh and admire his skill and confidence—that jump start off the dock with a lit cigarette in his mouth, for example. Sometimes, when we kids were just hanging out on the dock in the summer, Dad would stroll out on the end of the diving board and do his signature half gainer without any warning or hoopla. Just one dive. No amount of pleading would get him to do it again that day.

That same sort of confidence can be seen in certain amateur and professional athletes, from Olympic skaters to professional baseball and football players. The way they walk and hold themselves says it all. They don't need to *tell* us they're good; they *show* us. As I look back on the test pilots and flight test engineers I knew growing up, they were all fit, with natural athleticism. They stood tall and straight yet relaxed, broad-shouldered and smiling, their body language saying: *You can trust me.*

I didn't realize I possessed confidence until I was well into adulthood and friends started to remark upon it, because deep inside, I always felt shy and awkward. But apparently I walk and hold myself in a way that says *confident*. I have my father to thank for that.

I did have to learn the hard way that just because someone

says they have a skill or speaks confidently about their abilities doesn't mean it's true. Growing up around very skilled pilots who never bragged about themselves, I became a young adult who assumed that if someone *did* brag about something, well, they must *really* be good. It was hard for me to grasp that there are far too many people who lack skill and experience, and rather than admit it, try to fool others with verbal bluster to cover up their inadequacies. Big talkers can get you hurt or killed. You don't want to find yourself on the other end of a climbing rope with someone who exaggerated their actual experience and ability, or who panics in a crisis.

With experience—some of it negative—I learned to sift out those whose confidence is based on experience and true ability from the braggarts who wish they had a skill but can compete only with words and bluffing. I think my father, in telling me to never brag, was trying to help me understand the difference between those who are confidently competent and those who are competitively incompetent. All too often, it is the latter who bristle at the quietly confident and seem compelled to try to take them down with snide or cruel comments; their narcissism and inflated egos can't stand the thought that someone else can actually do what they only wish they could.

As I grew into adulthood, I found myself drawn to sports that required individual skill and mental competence, where I could test myself against nature. I gravitated toward climbing, white-water kayaking, and eventually ultra-distance trail running. I realize now this was a natural result of my upbringing. Trail running ended up being the perfect fit for me, the test pilot's daughter raised to be independent and to challenge herself and her skills—mental as well as physical—against the clock and the elements.

Over time, I've become adept at recognizing the competitively incompetent as I encounter them in life. They come in all shapes, sizes, occupations, and backgrounds. I've learned there's nothing one can say or do to quash their need to prove that they're better than others. It's best to simply walk away.

Walking away and disengaging is exactly what my father

always advised me to do. He knew, as a test pilot, that there was no room in experimental test flying for an outsized ego or a braggart whose skill didn't match his words. He wanted me to learn to avoid similar people in my own life. By teaching me to rely on and have confidence in myself, he gave me the skills to do just that. It just took me a while to figure it all out. My father taught me that I can control only myself and how I choose to react to a situation or to those around me. Sometimes that means having the confidence to say, "No, I'm not going to do that or go there with you. But hey—you go ahead."

Stalling a Simulator

In 2004, to help me better understand the concept of a stall, my father called in a favor at Boeing. He was eighty years old and hadn't flown a Boeing jet in twenty years, although he was still flying his amphibious Cessna 185, enjoying occasional fishing trips to remote lakes in British Columbia. Dad contacted Rod Richardson, one of Boeing's pilots and a simulator instructor. Rod and Dad worked together years earlier, and both flew private airplanes for fun. Dad asked if I could be given a demonstration of how simulators work and what a stall feels like. Rod readily agreed, and a weekend day was arranged.

We met at Boeing's training facility south of Seattle, where thoroughbred horse racing used to occur at Longacres Racetrack. The facility is called Boeing Longacres Industrial Park. Outside, it looks like any other mundane suburban two-story office park. Rod ushered Dad and I into a big open windowless warehouse-like space. Several simulators sat in two rows, looking like large space pods on robotic hydraulic legs. As we entered, I could see at least one of the simulators rocking slightly and hear the sound of its legs pumping. Someone was inside it, flying.

Dad and I followed Rod as he climbed a ladder to a 737 simulator's door. We ducked inside. It was dark, the only light coming from a vast array of electronic instruments on the cockpit's dashboard. It felt claustrophobic. Where cockpit windows would be, computer screens displayed a very realistic daytime airport runway scene: Boeing Field. I anticipated simply watching as my father and Rod did the flying, but both insisted I sit in the pilot's seat on the left. Stepping over the center console consisting of throttles and other instruments, I gingerly made it into my seat. Rod took the copilot's seat. Dad made himself comfortable in a jump seat behind us.

To my surprise, I felt incredibly nervous, as if mistakes I made would cause a real crash. I've spent countless hours in small airplanes, mostly in the copilot's seat next to my father, and a few times in the pilot's seat when I was sixteen and taking flying lessons from him. As copilot, I would often take over the control column when we were aloft, Dad showing me how to scan the horizon, visually set a course, watch the altimeter and other instruments to gauge air speed, direction, altitude, and so on. I'm familiar with airplane cockpits and basic instruments. But this simulator was so realistic, I actually felt like I was being asked to fly a modern 737, with its daunting array of digital instruments and displays, without any experience. Patiently, Rod explained the basics and got us ready to go.

We started accelerating down the runway to take off, the sound inside the simulator just what one would expect in terms of engine noise. The scene of the airport displayed on the simulator screen was exactly what one would see if taking off from Boeing Field in the real world: stripes and numbers painted on the runway flashing underneath the airplane's nose as buildings rush by on each side. Gaining speed and lifting off, the ground and buildings diminished in size as we climbed out. Once "in the air" we flew around the Puget Sound area, the screen showing us the major landmarks—city skyscrapers, lakes, Puget Sound, the San Juan Islands, and Mount Rainier. It felt so *real.* I held the control column and followed Rod's instructions to turn right or left, climb or dive. Depending on the input I gave, the simulator might lean one direction or another, rise up, or dip down, while the scene on the screen changed as expected. I was shy and tentative at the controls, but felt incredibly lucky to have this opportunity.

The primary reason for the simulator flight was to allow me to experience a deep stall like the one my father recovered from during the 727 certification program. For this, I let Rod do all the flying. He set up the stall condition. The 737's nose started pitching up and I felt and heard some buffeting, like the rumbling jarring of a car driving over railroad tracks. As the angle of attack increased, so did the buffeting, until the simulator was bouncing and shaking, making a huge racket inside the cockpit. It felt like the simulator capsule would disintegrate or tumble off its hydraulic legs. The noise created by a deep stall is *loud*, the sensation visceral: my heart rate increased and my brain screamed *danger.*

I was relieved when Rod brought the airplane's nose back down and we resumed normal flight.

Demonstration completed, we were ready to return to Boeing Field and land. Rod asked if I wanted to try a landing. I declined. I didn't want to experience a crash, even a fake one.

Rod took over the controls and we turned toward Seattle and Boeing Field. Looking over his shoulder toward my father, Rod asked, "Hey Lew; did Tex come in over Seafair from the west?" Dad responded that yes, he thought he did. On the simulator screen, I watched as we flew over Puget Sound, approaching Seattle from the west. After flying low over downtown Seattle and Capitol Hill, Lake Washington came into view. Rod dropped us down to about 300 feet. Just as we flew over the lake—where the Seafair hydroplane races are held—Rod executed a roll, exactly as Tex did in the Dash 80 some fifty years earlier.

The simulator didn't roll, of course, but the scene on the screen did. It was amazing. I held my breath while smiling broadly. We rolled a 737! When I looked at Dad, he was smiling, too. "Excellent roll, Rod," Dad said.

I'm pretty sure Rod had no idea how often my father had actually rolled Boeing's jets, including the 737.

Selling the Newly Certified Airplanes

Clearly test pilots and flight test crews play a critical role in proving the handling characteristics of, and certifying, a new airplane. But that's only half the equation. Once the airplane flies and is certified, it also has to *sell.* In the early days of commercial jets, the test pilots actually played a big role in helping sell a new airplane: taking airline pilots and VIPs on demonstration flights to show them in a clear and direct way why they should buy Boeing jets for their routes, delivering newly purchased airplanes to the airline's base, wherever in the world that might be, and sometimes taking celebrities for a spin for a little good publicity.

In November 1960, my father was involved in delivering three 720s (a shorter version of the 707) to Irish airline Aer Lingus. These 720s would be that airline's first commercial jets. What Dad remembered most about this interaction with the Irish was how cleverly they created their long-distance routes.

The 720 had a shorter range than the 707. Still, Aer Lingus was going to fly them nonstop from Dublin to Boston and New York. "That's a long way for that airplane," Dad said, "but they had it all figured out. Of course, going eastbound with a tail wind, no problem. But when they were coming westbound, on days when they had a pretty strong head wind they couldn't make it nonstop comfortably, so they would land in Bangor, Maine. They'd put on fuel without letting the passengers off, then takeoff and complete the flight to their destination." Dad explained that on those westbound flights, knowing they'd have to land to refuel, they'd cruise at high speed so their scheduled arrival time wasn't too far off a nonstop flight. "Pretty clever back then," Dad continued. "They were competing with Pan Am, British Airways, and other airlines with their larger, longer-range airplanes. Their 720 was faster than a 707."

My mother went along with Dad on this trip. She always spoke fondly of Ireland. While Dad was busy flying with the Irish crews back and forth between Dublin and New York, Mom stayed in Dublin and did some sightseeing and shopping, and was entertained by the wives of the Irish pilots. My brother Rick remembers a wool sweater Mom brought him from Ireland. "When I put it on, I imagined the smell of the wool to be the smell of Irish heather." I have memories of a very soft, sky-blue wool shawl from Ireland, something I used more like a blanket than a garment.

In 1964, my father was part of a Boeing crew that delivered 727s to Australia's two airlines, Ansett and Trans-Australia Airways. Both airlines had already sent their own chief pilots, check pilots, and instructor pilots to Seattle for training. (Actually, most of the training occurred in Tucson because there was less air traffic there.) After completing training in the United States, Dad flew one of the 727s with an Ansett crew to Australia. Dad remembered at least three Boeing crews for each airline went with these deliveries, which included the airline's own crews as well as a representative of Australia's equivalent of the FAA. They left the West Coast on October 13th, and over the course of three days, landed in Hawaii, Canton Island Airport in the middle of the Pacific (on Kanton Island, in the Republic of Kiribati), Nadi Island in Fiji, and finally Melbourne, Australia. Once in Australia, Dad and the Boeing crews immediately started doing more training and some route-proving flights. Additional training was required because Australian regulations required that anyone who flew the line as pilot in command had to have fifty hours of supervision. The Boeing pilots were training and riding as supervision pilots. My father flew the local airline routes in Australia nearly daily until finally returning home in early December.

During his time in Australia, my father had a chance to put his practical problem-solving skills to good use. The Australians wanted higher capacity brakes on their 727s. Boeing added an extra set of rotors to the 727's disc-type brakes. When they starting flying routes in Australia and the brakes started wearing a bit, they gave some chatter when applied. (If you've ever had the rotors on your car wear so that when the brakes are applied the whole car vibrates, you know what chatter is.) The airplane was designed to automatically apply the brakes when the landing gear started retracting after takeoff so the wheels would stop spinning before they came up into the wheel well. "It would make the whole airplane shake," Dad said. "This is disturbing to the passengers, who were first experiencing a jet. So I, being the project pilot, took more authority than I really had. I told the people at Ansett to just try manually applying the brakes very lightly right after lift-off but before retracting the gear, slow it down maybe two seconds… and it worked." He told the pilots at Trans-Australia Airlines about it as well, then called Boeing in Seattle to report what he'd suggested. Boeing thought it was a good interim step while they went to work with the brake manufacturer to solve the problem.

During that month in Australia, Dad and the others were so busy training or flying the line as supervising pilots that they didn't get much time to sight-see. Dad did remember one day off when he was able to go water skiing. The Boeing crews were spending most nights in Melbourne, which is on the southern coast not far from the sea, so when time allowed, they would visit the beaches, which my father described as really beautiful. One of the Australian pilots Dad worked with and befriended during this time went by the name Dusty Lane, a name I found hilarious. Dusty visited our house on Lake Sammamish at least once when I was a kid, and I remember being charmed by his personality and his accent.

When Dad returned from Australia, he brought my brothers and me lots of great gifts—boomerangs, clapsticks, kangaroo and sheepskin rugs, bush hats, and a toy koala bear for me. Whenever Dad came home from an overseas trip, it was like Christmas, but better, because the gifts were unique to the country he'd visited.

As with the Australians, airlines purchasing Boeing's early jets would send their pilots to Seattle for training. On occasion, my parents would take some out to dinner, or invite them home for socializing. One particular time stands out in my memory. It was 1965, and some Japanese pilots were in town for training. My father brought them home for dinner. I was eager to meet them. When they arrived, my father made introductions. When he introduced me, the Japanese men looked very surprised, said something to each other in Japanese and started laughing! Already shy, this was more attention than I could stand, and I ran to hide in my room. I refused to join them for dinner. The pilots felt awful, and insisted on returning the next day to apologize and give me a gift. It wasn't until years later than I got the full story: On the way to our house, my father had provided the men with the names and ages of his children. English was challenging for them; the Japanese misunderstood and thought the daughter of the family was eighteen, when in fact I was eight. No wonder they were surprised when they met me!

The DC-8, Convair 880, and the Boeing 707 weren't to fly into some of the smaller airports where the 727 could—Lake Tahoe, for instance, or Astoria, Oregon. A lot of small airlines, such as Piedmont or Pacific Western, had routes at these smaller airports, and Boeing wanted them to buy 727s.

In 1965, Boeing asked my father to take the head of Piedmont, Tom Davis, and the airline's chief pilots on proving flights on the 727. One of the first stops was a small airport where the airline had only used propeller airplanes. "It was raining cats and dogs," Dad said. "It was right at minimums—an ADF approach.[54] We shot the approach, landed on this wet runway, taxied up to the ramp—a very small ramp—and shut down. Opened and closed the door. Then we got the airplane ready to go again, got off the ramp, backed up to turn around, went out and took off. We flew to various airports, quite a few, some in the mountains of Virginia, and finally ended up back at home base."

Boeing's crew on these proving flights included an aerodynamicist and some performance experts; they took data from the flights, including gross weight, speed, and so on, and presented the information to Piedmont in a postflight briefing. Eventually, Piedmont's chief pilot stood up and told the Boeing crew that they were the only airplane to make it into that early airport that day; everybody else overflew it because of the poor weather. Piedmont bought from Boeing, but elected to sign a contract for the purchase of the upcoming 737 instead of the 727, feeling the smaller 737 suited their short and medium range routes better. While waiting over a year for delivery of its 737s, Piedmont leased two 727s and put them into service.

---

[54] ADF = automatic direction finder; inside the airplane, the finder detects a nondirectional radio beacon from the airport when weather makes visual approach impossible.

Another of my father's favorite stories involved a July 24, 1965, sales and proving flight on the 727. I had suggested to my father that he write some of his stories down. He'd already co-authored one book, *Flying the P-12* about finding, restoring, and flying a 1928 Boeing biplane. My father was an excellent storyteller and a good writer. I'll let Dad tell this particular story—one that includes my uncle Jesse and Paul "Pablo" Bennett—as he wrote it for me.

One Long Day

Some days start better than other days. Some days improve when they start poorly and others remain a challenge; but no matter how the day progresses, a day flying is better than a day sitting in meetings.

This day started with a promise of good things. We were in Houston, Texas, with a 727 parked at the FBO's (fixed base operator) ramp at the Houston airport. We had arrived the previous afternoon with a small crew of maintenance technicians, sales department personnel, engineering department specialists, and Boeing VIPs. We were to welcome Frontier Airlines' Board of Directors and executives—who had attended their board meeting in Houston the previous day—onboard for a lengthy demonstration flight. The plan was to depart Houston at 9:00 am. The weather was perfect, clear and sunny with light winds, and I was anticipating a pleasant flight to Albuquerque, our first destination.

The passengers arrived by bus about 8:45 am, and they boarded the airplane while the maintenance crew put their luggage in the baggage compartment. The Frontier cabin attendants welcomed all the passengers—Frontier board members and executives and the Boeing personnel who had breakfasted together at a hotel. The attendants had been checked out on the galley operation by the Boeing people, so the coffee was ready and it gave a pleasant morning aroma to the airplane.

The passengers were seated and all the exterior doors

were secured. After engine start and a report from the crew chief, everything appeared normal and he was instructed to remove the wheel chocks, disconnect the intercom, and come aboard the airplane. The cabin crew informed us in the cockpit they were ready for taxi. Trying to give a smooth ride, I slowly advanced the throttles and the airplane moved forward—about 15 feet—and then suddenly lurched to the right about 10 degrees, wing down, and came to an abrupt stop. In the cockpit we had no clue to what had happened. We asked the crew chief to go outside again and enlighten us if possible. He informed us the right landing gear wheels had broken through the pavement and we were 12 to 16 inches deep into the ramp. He suggested we try high thrust to see if the airplane would move, but it didn't. We had to give up and shut down the engines. Time to regroup. This day had made a sudden change in direction, so a new plan was needed.

The passengers were informed there would be a delay and a bus was being called to take them to the hotel to await developments. All the passengers had an opportunity to see the situation as they were allowed to either deplane then or remain onboard until the bus arrived. By the time the passengers had left for the hotel, preparations to get the airplane out of the hole were underway.

John Stucky, maintenance crew supervisor and the operator of the FBO, managed to get a construction company crew to come to the airplane. With jackhammers and dirt-moving equipment, they removed pavement and dirt from around and in front of the right-hand gear wheels. While this work was going on, a fuel tanker truck arrived to pump all the fuel from the right wing tank to reduce the weight on the right landing gear as much as practical. The maintenance crew had managed to secure two very strong, heavy steel channel beams about 15-feet long and wide enough for the tires to roll up onto and out of the hole—hopefully.

The maintenance crews from the Flight Test maintenance shop and their supervisors never failed to impress me with their ingenuity and resourcefulness. They worked miracles, in a very quick and efficient manner, and with makeshift equipment if necessary.

After the preparations were made and the steel beams were in place, the flight crew and maintenance crew gathered around the temporary incline and discussed how we were going to proceed. There was concern that as the weight of the airplane came up onto the end of the beams in the hole, the forward end of the beams might tip up into the bottom of the wing and punch a hole in the wing. The agreement was to use all of the engines, but just enough thrust to slowly move onto the beams and if it appeared the beams would tip and contact the wing, the man on the ground could warn us in the cockpit to stop. Fortunately, the beams didn't touch the wing (there was about three inches of clearance) and we taxied off the FBO ramp and onto a concrete taxiway, which was plenty strong.

Out of the hole and on thick concrete rather than new blacktop, I was feeling much happier. The ramp at the FBO was new and was supposed to be six to eight inches of pavement (blacktop mix) over compacted base. Where the 727 broke through, the pavement was about three inches thick with a very wet spot underneath. The FBO operator was irate when he saw the situation. I'm sure the contractor who paved the ramp felt some repercussions.

Once the airplane was parked on the taxiway, the fuel tanker was called to reload the fuel into the right wing tank. The hotel was called and the Customer Relations personnel informed that we should be ready for departure in about thirty minutes. The passengers arrived and came aboard. They seemed in good humor, so I assumed they may have had a choice of Bloody Marys or coffee in the hotel. We had deleted the Albuquerque leg because it was originally scheduled to help some board members make an airline connection; we would be much too late to help them, so they had to make other arrangements.

With the passengers onboard and the fuel pumped back into the tank, we were finally ready to go. Or so we thought. The ground crewman said we wouldn't be able to taxi because the fuel truck parked in front of our right wing apparently had a jammed and locked transmission and couldn't move forward or backward. The refueling hose had been disconnected and the refueling panel on the wing was closed and ready for flight—confirmed by the crewman on the ground. I then asked him if the area for 500 feet or so behind the 727 was clear of vehicles and airplanes. He replied it was. I instructed him to monitor engine start, that we would use reverse thrust and back away from the fuel tanker. Jesse and I started the engines, had the ground crewman confirm that chocks and gear-down locks were removed, and had him come aboard. When the aft airstair and door lights were out, I actuated the reverse thrust and backed the airplane away from the stalled tanker. Ground control was watching for us, making sure no one else tried to use the taxiway we were on. After all, the 727 doesn't have rearview mirrors. When we had a comfortable clearance from the fuel tanker, I used forward thrust and made a 180-degree turn on the taxiway while Paul [Bennett; copilot] called for taxi clearance to the departure runway. Upon reaching the takeoff runway we were cleared for takeoff. We were on our way. The day was improving again!

En route to Denver, the Frontier people were invited to visit the cockpit. The Frontier chief pilot was flying in the copilot seat, and he was a good Boeing booster as he explained features of the 727 to the Frontier VIPs. As we approached Denver, a few thunderstorms were visible, but they didn't interfere with our arrival at Denver's Stapleton Airport. After landing, we parked at a Frontier gate at the terminal and deplaned the passengers. Some were making airline connections and some would re-board and continue on the demonstration flight. Several additional Frontier Airlines people joined us—pilots, executives, and managers.

The galley was serviced with food and drinks for the continuing flights, and the airplane was prepared for departure. Our next destination was Grand Junction, Colorado.

Frontier Airlines was very interested in the ability of the 727 to operate from Grand Junction. At this time the airline flew only propeller airplanes, and the pilots and managers had heard all the rumors of how difficult jets were to operate from short runways, especially if the surface was wet. The Grand Junction runway at this time was about 5,500 feet long and 4,800 feet above sea level. As we approached the airport, and as good fortune for me would have it, a rain shower was just at the edge of the airport after having passed across the runway. The runway was very wet from the rain shower. We landed. Using brakes and reverse thrust, we stopped halfway down the runway and exited on the taxiway, which ran from the midpoint of the runway to the terminal building and parking ramp. The passenger cabin erupted with applause and cheers. After shutting down the engines, we lowered the aft airstair and allowed those wishing to do so to deplane, but advised everyone we would leave in about twenty minutes.

The 727 was the first jet transport designed for short-field operations, and it was an excellent airplane for that purpose. Landing at Grand Junction on a wet runway was the perfect opportunity to demonstrate this superior capability and leave no doubt in the minds of the witnesses of the airplane's capabilities.

The departure from Grand Junction was early afternoon, and I believe lunch and refreshments were served to the passengers. In the cockpit, we had Frontier senior pilots and interested observers standing about three deep, observing and talking. Probably at least eight to ten people were inside the cockpit and in the cockpit doorway. By this time Paul had a long extension cord on his headset, and a microphone. He was plugged into the intercom/radio box at the observers station [in the cockpit], but was in the passenger cabin helping with the radio traffic. Jesse [Wallick], at the flight engineer's panel, was also helping monitor the radios.

En route to Salt Lake City, we were asked to contact Frontier's Salt Lake operations on the Frontier radio frequency, and instruct them of a request. The request was for more refreshments—food, liquor, mixes, ice, and cigarettes—and another cabin attendant to be put aboard the 727 after we arrived at the gate in Salt Lake. Apparently a big party was underway in the cabin after the Grand Junction portion of the demonstration.

At Salt Lake, in addition to supplying the cabin, we added fuel. Our itinerary after Salt Lake was to Jackson, Wyoming, (the airport for Jackson Hole); Rapid City, South Dakota; and Denver, Colorado. Paul and some of the other Boeing employees who were riding in the cabin confirmed that a grand party was underway, and would probably get going even better after takeoff. Their predictions were accurate. Arriving at Jackson Hole, we landed and taxied to a Frontier gate and shut down to allow the Frontier guests to deplane and visit with the Jackson Hole people. After about fifteen minutes, we had everyone aboard again. Starting engines, we taxied out for our departure to Rapid City.

Because of our delay in Houston, we were running into darkness en route to Rapid City. That didn't slow the party. Paul was asked to radio Rapid City and order more snacks, liquor, mix, and ice. As we approached Rapid City, we began seeing scattered thunderstorms, especially to the south and west—our direction to Denver. Arriving at a Frontier gate in Rapid City, we again allowed the passengers to deplane with a departure time about twenty minutes later. While on the ground we received a weather briefing from Flight Service and re-filed our flight plan. Flight Service advised of numerous thunderstorms along our route to Denver.

Again, after all the passengers were aboard, we started

engines and taxied out to the runway for takeoff. On each leg, a different senior Frontier pilot occupied the copilot seat. They were all highly experienced pilots; and, though not familiar with the 727, they were familiar with the routes and airports we were flying into and were very helpful in making the demonstration flights a success.

The flight to Denver required numerous deviations to avoid thunderstorms. We were monitoring the weather radar and Denver Center was providing vectors in some cases, approving our requested deviations in other situations. As we threaded our way among the storms, apparently the party in the cabin was still going strong. Fortunately, we were able to avoid most of the storm turbulence and had only light to moderate turbulence. If we spilled a drink, I don't think anyone was overly concerned. As we neared Denver, the storms were more closely spaced, but we did manage to find a reasonable passageway into the Denver airport and landed. After parking at the gate and saying goodbye to all the pilots who had been in the cockpit and the other guests, we were looking forward to fueling and departing for Seattle. It was now about 11:00 pm Mountain Time.

I was informed by a Boeing Sales VP that we had a VIP onboard who we must deliver to Los Angeles. He happened to be the CEO of RKO [Radio Pictures, the movie studio], Frontier Airlines' largest shareholder. Even though we would arrive at Los Angeles after midnight, I had to agree we could do as requested. After leaving Houston that morning, the day had been good, but the night was turning bad. I did not have approach charts for Los Angeles with me. Frontier's VP of Flight Operations loaned a set to me.

Departing Denver, we were cleared as filed to the Los Angeles airport. Once we cleared the mountains west of Denver, the air was smooth, and Paul, Jesse, and I could relax and monitor the autopilot. Arriving at Los Angeles, we were directed to a gate at the terminal by ground control; Frontier Airlines had made arrangements for us while we were en route. It was about 2:00 am, and there was not much activity at the airport, but the airline wanted no publicity. A car was waiting at the gate. We lowered the aft airstair and the car drove to the airplane. The passenger was awakened and helped from the airplane into the car and driven away.

After filing a flight plan to Seattle by radio, we started engines and were directed to taxi to the departure runway. We were cleared for takeoff. Our flight to Seattle was routine, and I don't think any of us in the cockpit felt sleepy—too much adrenaline earlier in the day. We arrived at Boeing Field just before 4:00 am, almost twenty-four hours after starting the day in Houston. It did feel good when I arrived home to have a shower and go to bed.

Boeing Flight Test pilots have many adventures in addition to testing airplanes. Most flight test situations may be more exciting, but they are rarely as humorous or as long-lasting as some sales demonstrations.

A few details Dad neglected to mention in his narrative but offered later: the landing in Lake Tahoe was the first time a commercial jet landed there; Pablo, the official copilot tasked with communicating by radio with airport towers throughout the day, was frequently in the cabin of the airplane while these communications took place (so Frontier pilots and VIPs could be in the cockpit), saying things like, "Roger—we have them in sight," when in fact he couldn't even see out a window; the partying kept getting louder and wilder as the day went on, so that by the time they started their delivery of the RKO Radio Pictures guy to Los Angeles, he'd passed out, requiring the arrangements to arrive at a remote gate where a car would meet them and discreetly whisk the guy away.

In February 1972, my father flew a 737-200ADV to the other side of the world to demonstrate its ability to land on short runways of coral and grass. He left Seattle on February 12th and returned on February 21st. While away, he made stops in the following locations: Honolulu, Hawaii; Wake Island, a coral atoll; Guam; Port Moresby, Papua New Guinea; Sydney, Australia; Norfolk Island, a tiny dot in the ocean between Australia, Fiji, and New Zealand; Sydney; Tamworth (interior Australia, north of Sydney); Sydney; Pago Pago, American Samoa; Honolulu. His pilot's log shows that on one day, he made four landings and takeoffs at Norfolk Island during a flight of an hour and a half; a couple of days later he made five landings and takeoffs at Tamworth. That's what the test pilots did when selling airplanes—fly them into remote locations anywhere in the world, where airports have "local" surfaces, to demonstrate landings and takeoffs with airline pilots and management onboard, convincing them that the airplane was perfect for their unique routes. And if the Boeing crews had time—even if just in local airports—they shopped for unique gifts to bring home to their kids.

The Corporate 727

Boeing made good use of the 727 for its own corporate purposes, even after newer models came into service.

In 1966, there was an airline workers strike, affecting five major airlines. For six weeks during the peak summer travel period, roughly sixty percent of the commercial airlines were grounded when 35,000 workers refused to work. Boeing decided to use a 727 that the company had kept for odd jobs to support company travel. Dad and some of the other pilots were flying it two or three days a week from Seattle to Denver, Wichita, Washington, DC, New York, then back to Seattle, ferrying whoever needed to get from point A to point B.

The fiftieth anniversary of The Boeing Company was on July 15, 1966. Dad flew the company 727 to New York to pick up some VIPs for the celebration. Tom Davis, the President of Piedmont, was one of the passengers, someone Dad remembered from the earlier proving flight as a really nice guy with a good sense of humor. They took off just after sunset and headed west, climbing up to cruise altitude. "There were thunderstorms around; you could see the lightning flashing," Dad said. "From the tops of the clouds it was a pretty sight.

Fortunately, we were above it and managed to stay out of it." Once reaching cruise altitude, Dad went on the public address system and announced they were planning on going nonstop to Seattle. This particular 727 had an extra fuel tank on it, an option Boeing offered, so the cross-country flight was no big deal.

Tom Davis went up to the cockpit and tapped my father on the shoulder.

"Lew," he said, "I thought you told me this was a short-to-medium range airplane."

"Well, it is," my father replied.

"How come you're going nonstop to Seattle?"

"Well, it can do that, too!" my father laughed.

In the 1970s and 1980s, Boeing still used the company 727 in support roles. Dad sometimes flew it as a photo airplane—flying formation with 737s, 747s, 757s, and 767s to get photographs of the airplanes for customers who wanted publicity photos of their new acquisitions, painted with their company logo, with Mount Rainier, the Olympic Mountains, or Puget Sound as a backdrop. This 727 was also used to ferry people and equipment to remote test bases—Edwards AFB, Moses Lake, or Glasgow, Montana. "I liked flying those flights a lot because it was an easy and fun thing to do," Dad told me. "You didn't have a preflight or postflight conference like a regular test flight. You had a brief get-together to discuss what you're going to do, then go do it."

Dad especially enjoyed the photo flights because of the formation flying. He flew the 727 alongside a 747 for a segment of the 1976 IMAX movie *To Fly!* I went to see that movie at the Seattle Science Center when it came out—it was an amazing film, and the IMAX technology, new at that time, made you feel as if you were surrounded by, even *in* the scene. (*To Fly!* is still showing at the Smithsonian.) Dad said the camera, film, and reels used for the IMAX format were *huge*, taking up a lot of space in the 727's cabin.

My father would often fly Boeing VIPs to meetings on the company 727. He fondly remembered one particular flight to the East Coast. He was ferrying several Boeing board members and a crew. One of the board members was George Hunt Weyerhaeuser, then President of Weyerhaeuser Timber Co., which his father and fifteen partners started in 1900 with the acquisition of 900,000 acres of Washington timberland. Also onboard was Mrs. Weyerhaeuser. At some point during the flight, Dad noticed that the center engine surged, then surged again. He opened the bleed valve and there were no more surges. "After landing, the crew told me that Mrs. Weyerhaeuser had gotten up to use the rear lavatory," Dad said. "She had her hand on the door handle when the first surge happened. She jumped back, waited, then tried again just as the second surge occurred. She went back to her seat."

My father's work on the 727 started in 1960, when he was designated project pilot for the 727 program. Its first flight was in 1963. He worked on all the derivatives that were eventually designed and flown. He loved the 727, referring to it as his favorite of all the Boeing commercial jets he flew. Because of his personal involvement in the origination of the airplane, and all of the intricate testing he did, he said the 727 felt like *his* airplane. He continued working on the 727 until he retired from Boeing in 1986, although in his last two years—grounded by Boeing's rule that pilots stop flying at age sixty—he didn't fly it anymore. "I was simply kind of an expert on it," he told me in 2002. Typical understatement on Dad's part. He made 1,845 flights in the 727 series of airplanes; some 3,200 flight hours. I doubt there was another human being on the planet who knew more about the 727 than my father.

The Sound of Airplanes

Living in the Puget Sound area, one becomes used to the sound of airplanes overhead. Boeing's test airplanes, airliners flying in and out of Seattle-Tacoma Airport, and smaller private airplanes keep the skies over western Washington busy.

For me, the singular sound of summer—the one that instantaneously takes me back to my childhood—is the drone of a seaplane engine. The pleasantly deep rumble of a seaplane as it circles, coming in low over a lake, setting up its landing, always flies me back to the halcyon days growing up on Lake Sammamish. For some, it may be a certain smell or melody that starts their childhood flashback. For me, it's that particular engine rumble.

Many summer weekend mornings during the 1960s and early 1970s, I awoke to that unique sound. Crawling out of bed, rubbing my eyes, I'd stumble to my window facing the lake, letting the blind fly upward on its roll with a *whop* and cranking the handle to open the window to the fresh cool air and that wonderful airplane engine buzz. Looking out at the quickly disappearing morning fog still fondling the lake's surface, hearing the robins chirping their first song of the day in the pie cherry tree next to the house while watching the sun rise over the Cascade Mountains beyond the eastern shore of the lake, I'd welcome another summer day with excitement. Water skiing? Playing kick the can with other kids in the neighborhood? Bike riding and swimming? The possibilities were limitless. Sure, Mom might make me pull some weeds before I could go play, to earn my allowance. But every summer day was full of promise.

On really special weekend days, Dad would bring the Widgeon out to our lake, our dock, our beach—and take us for a ride.

The Widgeon—a six seat, twin-engine amphibious seaplane made by Grumman—had its own distinctive rumble, emanating from its two powerful engines, their props cutting the air with authority. I could recognize the Widgeon when it was just a faint whisper on the early morning breeze, no louder than a bee. I could distinguish it from every other seaplane that might fly overheard before landing on our lake—Cessnas on floats, SeaBees, the odd de Havilland Beaver. The sight of the Widgeon overhead, heavy and ungainly, yet beautiful and graceful—more a pelican than a duck—thrilled and excited me because I knew it was unusual and special. I felt lucky because I knew it intimately, like being friends with the coolest kid in the neighborhood. The Widgeon afforded me a status and chic I would not have otherwise enjoyed. Our family co-owned the Widgeon with several other Boeing families.

36 Lew Wallick with the Widgeon, parked on a lake in British Columbia, 1972. Author's collection.

My love of that airplane went beyond the neighborhood kids thinking I was cool. There was something magical about flying in the Widgeon. From infancy, I had been in all sorts of airplanes, from little Cessna 172s to the biggest commercial jets of the day. Flying was old hat. But the Widgeon was *different*, the way a restored and classic Bentley is different than a Ford Pinto: rare, powerful, and solid. Remember "Da plane! Da plane!" from *Fantasy Island*, the 1970s TV show? That was a Widgeon that Tattoo was announcing as it approached the island. The Widgeon is an airplane worthy of fantasy.

Part of the allure is that the Widgeon isn't just a seaplane. It is an *amphibious* airplane—capable of landing on land or sea. For water landings, the gear retracts into a well behind the pilot and copilot seats. Very small windows directly behind those seats allow for visual verification the gear has retracted; landing on water with gear extended would be disastrous. Verification was my job. Dad always asked, "Becky, can you see the wheels? Are they up?" I felt important to be trusted with this vital task.

Water landings were thrilling and just a little scary for me. I'm ashamed to admit the fear, given I'm a test pilot's daughter. Flying low over the lake, Dad would carefully scan the surface, noting all the boats, skiers, and swimmers, along with the wind direction and the amount of surface chop. Selecting a spot, he'd circle and bank steeply, making a final verification that his chosen landing spot was clear. I'd press my cheek against the passenger window, my eyes staring at the tableau of activity on the lake as the boats and people got larger and more distinct. Some boaters waved. Dropping close to the surface, Dad would straighten out, pull back the throttles until the engines barely hummed and glide in a controlled way as we descended toward the surface of the lake on final approach. I'd watch fascinated as the water slowly, steadily got closer until the belly of the Widgeon kissed it with a sudden *swoosh*. Skimming the surface at an impossibly fast rate—faster than our ski boat—I could feel the vibrations of the chop on the Widgeon's belly under my feet, the reassuring sound of water rushing against the hull blending with the hum of the engines. As the airplane slowed and settled into the water, the wing pontoons also kissed the lake surface. The Widgeon became a boat. Gradually coming to a near stop, the water level crept higher up the side of the fuselage until it reached the bottom of the windows. It seemed as though I was sitting *in* the lake. Finally I'd exhale, relieved to have survived another landing. Landing on the airplane's belly somehow made it more immediate, more intense, than landing on wheels in a Cessna.

My view from the Widgeon's window was so close to the lake's surface that it seemed more intimate than riding in the ski boat. I could see the individual prop blades spinning as the engines ran at idle. Eventually Dad would gently push the throttles forward, enough to rev the engines and make the props disappear into the air again, enough to turn our plane into an ungainly sort of boat, plowing its way ponderously through the water as we taxied toward our dock and beach.

Several people living on Lake Sammamish in the 1960s had seaplanes; some kept them tied at their docks in the summer months. One such neighbor was Don Kyte, who now lives in

Florida. In the 1960s, Don lived on the west side of Lake Sammamish, just north of us. He had a Republic Seabee, and was very involved in the world of amphibious airplanes, having formed the Seattle Seabee Club. I recently asked Don what he remembered about the Widgeon my father frequently brought out to the lake. He shared the following story with me.

> I frequently had a number of seaplanes and amphibians park at our beach to visit. One of these amphibians was a G-44 Widgeon with twin 300 hp Lycoming radial engines.
>
> All seaplanes and amphibians are subject to having the leading edge of their propellers pitted by spray during takeoffs, but this Widgeon's props were the worst I had ever seen. All three blades on both engines had been dressed down with a file so much that they would soon have to be replaced.
>
> The owner (whose name I have forgotten) explained that the extra weight of the radial engines and their high thrust-line created more spray than the original Ranger engines or any of the other engine conversions. He took me out for a demonstration ride. When he advanced both engines to takeoff power, water was thrown so high it even blanked out most of the windshield!
>
> One day another round-engine Widgeon landed on our lake and did a number of takeoffs and landings. I watched closely, expecting to see the usual cloud of spray, but none of that happened. The pilot didn't advance the throttles to takeoff power immediately, as normally done. Instead he only went to a fast idle. You could see him watching the small amount of spray created, which didn't rise to the level of the props. As the speed advanced, the spray also moved aft. When the spray pattern had gone behind the props, the pilot THEN applied full takeoff power and was quickly airborne. The props didn't get any spray erosion. What a great idea! He practiced these takeoffs and other maneuvers a bit longer. I was most impressed and vowed to pass this word along to other

Widgeon owners.

It was sometime later that a friend down the lake told me it was Lew Wallick. It didn't surprise me that it was the famous Boeing test pilot. What surprised me was finding out that he was a neighbor!

I love Don's story because it illustrates my father's problem-solving approach, one he passed along to me: experiment, try a new approach, and if it doesn't work, try another; keep at it until you've figured it out. Finesse and a smooth touch trump brute force *and* cause less wear and tear. There are always new and better ways to do things. Strive to improve.

Sometimes when my father brought the Widgeon out to shoot some landings on the lake, he'd bring it to our beach and offer me, my brothers, or maybe even some of our neighborhood friends a quick ride. Since we knew the sound of the Widgeon—Dad would usually do a low flyby over our house or buzz the shore along our section of the lake—we were waiting to watch the spectacle of beaching the Widgeon. We'd wait on a rockery ledge high above the beach, or on the upper deck of our boat house, knowing not to get too close. Dad would bring the Widgeon straight in toward the beach, just south of our dock. As he got near the beach, he'd lower the landing gear so the wheels could hit the lake bottom. At that point, I'd plug my ears, because that's when Dad would push the throttles, gunning the engines while hitting the brake on the right wheel so that the left wheel would continue up the beach, spinning the Widgeon to the right in a tight half circle until it faced out toward the lake. During that turn the engine exhaust would blast sand and pebbles from the beach up toward the rockery; the dry, hard leaves on an old madrona tree growing out over the beach would shudder violently. It was a loud, wild, and exciting maneuver to watch. Once in the position he wanted, Dad would shut down the engines, open the side door behind the passenger seats, and hop onto the beach without getting his feet wet. "Anybody want to go for a ride?" he's ask us, a big grin on his face. Talk about a rhetorical question!

The Widgeon was our family's ticket to fishing vacations on

remote, unspoiled lakes in the interior of British Columbia. Usually our entire family went, since the Widgeon could hold six passengers, so long as we didn't try to take too much gear or bring back too many fish. Other times, my father would take some of his colleagues fishing. One summer, when I was in junior high, I invited my friend and neighbor Kelly to join me, my parents, and my brother Tim on one of those fishing trips. Here's how Kelly remembers that trip, and the Widgeon.

> My first introduction to the Widgeon was when I was about thirteen. Becky's dad landed it on Lake Sammamish and drove it to the beach in front of their house. My dad drove big ships, but Becky's dad landed a plane right in her front yard! How cool is that? The plane was like none other I had ever seen. Living on the lake, we saw floatplanes all the time, but nothing like this. The body of the plane sat on the water, and there were small pontoons at the end of each wing. To my eye it was elegant, but at the same time somewhat homely looking. Aside from that, it was just plain cool.
>
> I think we went for a short flight that day. I don't remember much about the flight, but I do remember the takeoff. Before takeoff, we had to check to be sure the landing gear was retracted—that meant looking through a small window into the wheel well where the gear was stowed. When Mr. Wallick put the "pedal to the metal," it was very loud, and it seemed like it took forever for the plane to take off. It plowed through the water. A lot of water was coming over the windshield of the cockpit and I remember thinking "How can he see where we're going?" Finally it was planing on top of the water, and we took off.
>
> I also had the pleasure of joining the Wallicks on a fishing trip to Canada. We landed on one remote lake that was only accessible by floatplane. It was a beautiful, pristine body of water in the midst of forest and mountains. I remember wondering how in the world Mr. Wallick found this place, not understanding that there are

> road maps for the skies. The Widgeon was beached and an aluminum skiff was retrieved from under the trees near the beach. You mean somebody has been here before us? We caught some nice trout in a very short period of time. The boat was stashed to await the next visitors. We jumped back into the Widgeon and were off. Our next landing was our ultimate destination, another lake where we stayed in a cabin near the water. As I recall, it rained like the dickens most, if not all, of the time we were there. I don't know about the fishing, but we played lots of card games.
>
> Since those days, I've flown in other small amphibious planes, like Otters and Beavers, but none have the special place in my heart that the Widgeon has.

My father's usual patience was always in evidence during those family fishing trips. As Kelly noted, sometimes the weather would be awful, and we'd be stuck in a cabin, or we'd have to stay a day or two longer than planned, waiting for the weather to lift. When the weather was conducive to fishing, my three brothers would leave in one aluminum boat, while Dad, Mom, and I would go in another. My poor father spent most of his time taking fish off my hook, or my mother's, rather than actually fishing. (I was at least willing to put worms on my own hook.) And, despite his showing me how to clean the fish and encouraging me to do so, I preferred to encourage him from the sidelines, standing nearby, talking with him while he squatted near the water's edge to clean the fish Mom and I caught that day. There were years we caught a lot of fish, years we caught a few. If there was time, we'd have some of the fish smoked before returning home. The fresh ones would go into the freezer for future dinners.

Dennis Mahan shared a story my father told him about one of those early Canada fishing trips. "He said that upon arrival, he put you all in a boat and sent you fishing to get you out of the way while he unloaded the airplane and got things set up," Dennis said. "He neglected to mention there are catch limits. You guys came back with an enormous number of fish. They couldn't be thrown back—they were already dead—so he was up for hours, cleaning fish."

One of my father's favorite meals was freshly caught trout cooked over a Canadian campfire. He even ate trout for breakfast on those fishing trips. I don't care much for fish, even less for fresh trout, but I do like smoked trout. After I left home, whenever my father went fishing in Canada and brought back some smoked trout, he'd save at least one for me, giving it to me the next time we saw each other. Smoked trout with saltines—a perfect meal, in both of our opinions.

CHAPTER SIX: THE SEVENTIES

The cockpit was my office. It was a place where I experienced many emotions and learned many lessons. It was a place of work but also a keeper of dreams. It was a place of deadly serious encounters, yet there I discovered much about life.

—Brian Shul, Sled Driver: Flying the World's Fastest Jet *(1992)*

From Boom to Bust

The next new airplane to debut was the 747. My father wasn't onboard on February 9, 1969, when the first 747 took its maiden voyage, but his younger brother Jesse was, as flight engineer. Jack Waddell was pilot and Brien Wygle, who by this time was Assistant Director of Flight Test, was copilot. I remember watching coverage of the 747's first flight on local TV that Sunday, seeing my father offering commentary to TV news reporters, being asked what it was like to have his younger brother onboard. As far as I know, the flight went as planned, but I also know that contrary to what the media is told, there's usually something that goes slightly wrong. Immediately after that inaugural flight, certification work on the 747 began.

As certification testing was still going on, in June 1969 Don Knutson and my father took the number four 747 to the Paris Air Show. They made a very dramatic arrival in Paris. They were supposed to arrive at a specified time. Their route took them across Scotland and England and into French territory, with various air traffic controllers talking to them along the way. Dad was expecting to have trouble understanding the

French controller, but as it happened, they got a guy who spoke very good English. "He just took over and started directing us, taking charge," Dad said. "He knew what we were supposed to be doing, had us all lined up. We told him we wanted to make an approach and a low pass, then come back around for an approach and landing." The weather was a lot worse than they'd been led to believe; the ceiling was down to 400 or 500 feet. "It wasn't down to absolute minimums," Dad continued. "So we came down ILS [instrument landing system] approach and broke out at the base of the clouds, flew along level over the airport for a couple of miles, and then pulled up into the clouds, back around for another approach and full stop landing." The 747 totally wowed the people on the ground who had been alerted by an announcement on the public address system that it was on approach. All of a sudden this monster of an airplane descends from the clouds—an airplane twice as big as any other there, one that appears too massive to fly. With engines throttled back to descend, the 747 quietly drifted down out of the clouds, flew by, and disappeared back into the clouds before returning for a landing. Talk about a dramatic entrance onto the world stage.

That Paris Air Show came early in the 747 program; the first flight had been only four months earlier. Boeing had a lot of trouble with the 747 engines early on and was concerned about Don and Dad getting the 747 to Paris and back without having to change an engine. That would be embarrassing for Boeing as well as Pratt-Whitney, the engine manufacturer. Boeing stashed a spare engine somewhere—Dad couldn't remember if it was on the East Coast or in Europe—so they could get it to Paris quickly if necessary. Luckily, they didn't need it.

Dad had a little extra time for shopping while in Paris. When he returned from this trip, he brought me an elegant bottle of Joy perfume, some soft leather dress gloves, and a beautiful silk scarf.[55]

---

[55] In 2013 I met Kayle Shulenberger, daughter of M. K. "Shuly" Shulenberger who was flight engineer on the first flight of the 727 with my father and Dix Loesch. We shared fond memories of growing up Boeing,

Getting the 747 certified would be a long and stressful process. The 747 was bigger than any commercial airplane Boeing had made. There were issues with the engines, getting the landing gear to pass refused-takeoff tests, and flutter clearance, especially at high speeds. A lot of people worked a lot of hours getting the 747 its certification by December 1969.

The 747 program took a financial toll on Boeing. The company assumed substantial debt to get the 747 into production and testing. In 1969, the company had 83,700 employees, already down about 20,000 from the previous year. By 1971—the year Boeing learned the Senate had refused to fund its SST program—roughly 63,000 employees had been laid off, leaving just 20,750. Those layoffs reverberated throughout the region. It's estimated that for every Boeing employee who lost his or her job, at least one other person in the greater regional economy also lost a job—manufacturing, retail, restaurants, and service jobs were all affected. Everyone felt the hit. Area unemployment rose to 14 percent, the highest in the United States at the time. Housing vacancy rates also rose, from one percent in 1967 to sixteen percent at the height of the economic slump. So many people were leaving Seattle in search of jobs elsewhere, U-Haul dealerships couldn't keep enough trailers in stock. It was during this awful time—the Boeing Bust—that the famous billboard appeared near Seattle-Tacoma Airport: *Will the last person leaving Seattle turn out the lights.* Perhaps the only distraction from all the bad news occurred in November 1971 when D. B. Cooper hijacked a 727, parachuting off the rear airstair with his money, disappearing forever into legend and lore.

I remember talking to Dad about all of this at the time. I was always encouraged to pay attention to current affairs. We had the *Post-Intelligencer* delivered to the house in the morning[56] and the *Seattle Times* in the afternoon; we watched the nightly news

---

and compared notes. When I described these gifts my father brought from Paris, she laughed and said, "Your father had way better taste than mine!"

[56] Like my father, I quickly developed the habit of reading the P-I with my breakfast, so much so that today I can hardly sit down to a meal by myself without something to read.

with Walter Cronkite or David Brinkley on TV. I was very aware of all this bad news. When I asked Dad if he was worried about his job, he admitted that he was, that everyone who was lucky enough to still have a job at Boeing was taking a pay cut. For the first time in my life, Boeing no longer seemed invincible, the safe harbor it always had been. I'm sure that many of us growing up through this time no longer considered Boeing the place we could easily find work as adults. A pall descended over the region. The boom times, when it seemed Boeing and the region had nowhere to go but up, were over. Many of the Boeing employees who were laid off used their downtime well, tinkering and inventing new products in their garages, even starting their own companies. I remember a general sense that the future can't be predicted, that life throws curve balls now and again. I had no clue about the curve ball that would—at the end of 1973—hit me with incredible force, shaking my comfortable and secure world to the core.

The Moroccans

In my eighth grade year, I took French for my foreign language requirement. That summer, 1970, Boeing was hoping to sell some airplanes to the Kingdom of Morocco. The North African nation is home to Casablanca and Marrakesh. Because of its history as a French colony, Moroccan government agencies, the military, and many businesses used French as the primary language, even after gaining independence in the 1950s. I had just one year of junior high French, but apparently that was enough for Dad to work a special arrangement with Boeing, getting me hired as a tour guide.

The family we entertained at our house on Lake Sammamish consisted of a military general, his wife, his two grade school-age children, and their French nanny. The nanny was about twenty years old, didn't speak any English, and very shy. They were invited to enjoy a day at the lake.

The Moroccans were driven to our house in a limo. It was a nice summer day, so most everyone quickly changed into swimsuits and we headed down to the beach. First, Dad taught the general to ski on two skis. I admit, I always got a kick out of watching an adult learn to water ski. No matter how confident or full of themselves they appeared, learning to water ski was the great equalizer—everyone looked tentative and silly on their first few tries. The general succeeded in getting up on the skis and being towed around a big circle on the lake before being brought back to the dock. He was pleased; it may have been the only time I saw him smile.

The general's wife declined an opportunity to try to ski. Next up: the general's son. This boy, who was perhaps eight years old, constantly mimicked his father's tough posture and demeanor and seemed to delight in bossing his older sister and the nanny around. He threw rocks. He banged sticks against things. Because my French was so limited, I rarely understood anything he said. I didn't like him, but I kept my mouth shut; they were our guests.

Using his tried-and-true teaching method—the inner tube—Dad tried to teach the boy to water ski. The boy tried, failed, tried and failed again. He kept falling over before fully standing up on the skis, a common thing when learning. Exhausted, he finally gave up.

Dad then encouraged the general's daughter to try. She was probably ten years old, quiet and reserved. She did try, and... she got up! I whooped and hollered praise from the beach and was secretly proud of her for doing what her show-off brother couldn't.

After lunch, the limo returned. This time, it was for me, the two Moroccan children, and their nanny. Based on Dad's assurance that I spoke some French and could thus translate for the group, Boeing had arranged to hire me to take them all to the Seattle Center Fun Forest for games and rides, to be followed by an early dinner at the Space Needle. I was thrilled, and very nervous. Boeing was going to pay me some outrageous sum (or so it seemed to me; much more than a babysitting gig), so I felt a huge responsibility. I was being trusted with these important people with whom I could barely communicate. I was handed a great deal of cash to purchase tickets for rides and games, and to pay for dinner. Dad instructed me how to tip when paying the dinner tab—I had never paid for a dinner before. The limo would take us to Seattle Center and wait until we were done to drive us back to the house, where all the parents were enjoying their own evening. For those few hours, I was in charge of the children and the nanny. I was just fourteen.

The afternoon went smoothly. At the Fun Forest, the boy wanted to play every game that involved shooting things; he'd make machine gun and explosives noises as he played. The girl was happy to go on the rides and win an occasional stuffed toy at a less violent game. The nanny made sure the kids never got out of sight; she and I communicated primarily through sign language, although I could sometimes grasp the meaning of a few words and from that, get the gist of her comments. I couldn't put into French my own thoughts, however; I was better at reading and interpreting French than speaking it.

The Space Needle was a huge hit with the kids. The ride up the elevator—rising at 10 miles per hour—was exciting for us all. Boeing had made reservations for us. Dinner in the slowly rotating saucer of the restaurant high in the sky was fun, offering a 360-degree view of the city. We all felt a sense of freedom with no adults around to tell us what to order. I assured the children that they could have anything they wanted. Expensive burgers and fries were the choice, followed by fancy desserts. At one point, the boy asked the nanny several questions, and I understood one of them: How many stories high were we? Knowing the restaurant level was 500 feet above ground, I answered him in French, "*Cinquante*"—fifty. His eyes got big; I could see him immediately wondering what else I might have understood. I delighted in making him squirm ever so slightly, keeping his ego in check.

That outing was my first limo ride, and my first paid job other than babysitting. I used to say that I'm the only person in my family who hasn't worked at Boeing or been married to someone who did, but now, reflecting back on the Moroccans, I guess I *was* employed, that one time, by Boeing.

Over the years, Dad and I joked about that boy many times, how militaristic and full of himself he was. Dad wasn't surprised to learn of his penchant for guns and shooting while at the Fun Forest. We both loved that the girl got up on water skis while the boy didn't; we hoped that would dampen his outsized ego a bit, but doubted it.

The Dash 80's Last Hurrah

By 1972, original Dash 80 pilots Tex Johnston and Dix Loesch were no longer flying at Boeing, so it was fitting that my father was asked to be part of the crew taking the Dash 80 to Washington, DC, for a ceremonial donation of the airplane to the Smithsonian Air and Space Museum. He had, after all, spent many hours test flying in the Dash 80 after transferring to Seattle in 1955.

Lots of festivities were planned around this historic event. On May 24, 1972, Dad and Tom Edmonds piloted the Dash 80 from Seattle to New York. My father had been copilot with Tex Johnston fifteen years earlier when they flew the Dash 80 to set a cross-country speed record, Seattle to Baltimore, a highly choreographed event with VIPs and press onboard. A member of the cabin crew on that March 1957 record-setting flight was a woman named Shirlee, a stewardess [this was before they were called flight attendants] for one of the major airlines. In 1965, Shirlee married Henry Fonda; she was his fifth and last wife, and was with him when he died in 1982. Because Shirlee had been onboard the Seattle-to-Baltimore flight, she and another member of the original cabin crew were invited to a dinner Boeing hosted at a club in New York City. The women were also invited to be onboard the next day when Dad flew the Dash 80 from New York to Dulles for the actual donation ceremony. Shirlee and her husband Henry attended the dinner in New York City. The next day, after the flight to Dulles, they arrived at the chalet Boeing set up for the donation ceremony.

"Things were pretty quiet at the dinner," Dad said about the New York City event. "Shirlee comes up to me and asks if I would mind visiting with her husband, Henry. Of course I knew who he was. She said, 'He's pretty shy, but he's interested in airplanes. He used to be a pilot. Please don't say anything about Jane, though.'" (Jane Fonda, a famous actor like her father, was already a well-known and outspoken opponent of the war in Vietnam, which apparently embarrassed her father.)

37 From left: Brien Wygle, unknown former flight attendant, Lew Wallick, and Henry and Shirlee Fonda at Dash 80 donation ceremony, New York City, 1972. Photo: Boeing Archives.

Dad talked with Henry for quite a while. The actor shared that he had learned to fly in the 1930s, before he became a Hollywood star. Several other up-and-coming actors had learned to fly then, including Jimmy Stewart. Henry said they all soloed and got their licenses, but he didn't keep up with it himself. "He was a very pleasant person, very friendly. And like Shirlee said, he was shy. I suppose he learned over the years to be careful around strangers. Celebrities..., people try to take advantage of you."

Brien Wygle was also attending the festivities. He had taken a 737ADV to Dulles for some demonstration flights in conjunction with the Dash 80 donation ceremony.

My father's pilot's log shows that during that trip for the

Dash 80 donation ceremony, he got to spend significant time flying the B & W, a replica of The Boeing Company's very first product. The vintage bi-wing seaplane's name derived from the designers' initials: William Boeing and Navy Lt. Conrad Westervelt. The original B & W, made of wood, linen, and wire, first flew in 1916. Unable to convince the US Navy to buy it, Boeing made its first international sale by selling two to the New Zealand Flying School. A replica of the B & W was built in 1966 for The Boeing Company's fiftieth anniversary. It was disassembled and trucked back to Dulles, where it was reassembled and flown during the Dash 80 donation ceremonies.

My father thoroughly enjoyed flying the B & W replica. He had previously flown it in other air shows, including the Abbotsford Air Show in British Columbia. While in the DC area that summer of 1972, Dad flew the B & W eight days in a row. Most of those flights were two tenths of an hour in duration, at Dulles Airport—likely just a quick takeoff, low flyby or two, and a landing, all part of the show. He wore his old Navy leather bomber jacket, leather flight helmet and goggles, and a white silk scarf. On the last day, he flew the B & W to Andrews Air Force Base, a flight that took an hour. I'm pretty sure that was a thoroughly enjoyable flight for Dad, puttering along—the B & W had a cruise speed of 67 mph—in an open cockpit vintage biplane with huge pontoons over the busy cityscape. What a sight for those who happened to look skyward as he flew by! It's only about 25 miles from Dulles Airport to Andrews AFB, but the view from the vantage point of that B & W cockpit was surely amazing.

My father wore many hats on that Dash 80 donation trip. In addition to flying the Dash 80 to New York City and Washington, DC, for the ceremony, and daily flights of the B & W, he also made a quick flight on the 737ADV from Dulles to Hot Springs, Virginia, and back. Maybe a VIP had to get to Virginia, or perhaps it was a quick demonstration flight. Dad was versatile.

On June 5, 1972, after the donation ceremonies, Dad and Tom flew the Dash 80 to Tucson, Arizona, for storage in the dry desert air; there wasn't space for it at the Smithsonian. Seventeen years later, after a few months of work to get it back into flying shape, the Dash 80 was flown by Pablo Bennett and a crew to Paine Field to be refurbished at the Museum of Flight's Restoration Center. Once refurbished, on July 15, 1991, it made a flyby over all of the Seattle-area Boeing facilities to commemorate the company's seventy-fifth anniversary and the thirty-seventh anniversary of the Dash 80's first flight. Eventually—finally—on August 27, 2003, the Dash 80 made its final flight to Dulles Airport and its new home at the Smithsonian, where it is now on static display.

38 Lew Wallick and the replica B & W, 1972. Photo: Boeing Archives.

The B & W replica my father flew in 1972 now hangs in the Museum of Flight in Seattle, on loan from The Boeing Company. Maybe, someday, it'll fly again.

Gas Lines and the Energy Crisis

I got my learner's permit as soon as I was fifteen and a half, and learned to drive during the summer of 1972. We had a 1964 bronze-colored Buick LaSabre station wagon that I think of as "The Tank," because it was so big and heavy. Solid. It was the family car, used when the entire family went somewhere, for ski trips to Snoqualmie Pass or Stevens Pass, or to haul garbage to the dump. It was also Mom's car, the one she drove for shopping and getting around. For most of my childhood, Dad's car was another Buick, a white two-door convertible. In 1970, after putting sufficient miles on that convertible, he bought a Chevrolet Camaro. The Camaro had a very cramped back seat; it definitely wasn't a family car. It was a sports car. I guess you could say The Tank was a 747, and the Camaro was a 737.

My father taught me to drive in The Tank. We started on a Sunday in the large open parking lot of a nearby Sears. Lots of space with nothing to hit. After learning to accelerate, brake, and turn in the parking lot, Dad had me drive the few miles home. At one point he said with a grin, "You don't have to squeeze the steering wheel so hard, it won't go anywhere." He was so calm, so sure I'd do fine, that I calmed down, too, believing him. He emphasized how to brake evenly, to ease into a curve and accelerate out of it; in short, to drive with smooth hands.

As I got close to our driveway, though, I became nervous about the final portion of my first true driving experience. Our house had a driveway only a test pilot could love. From West Lake Sammamish Parkway, you had to make a 90-degree turn onto the steep, downhill driveway that dropped off from the road. It required a complete leap of faith that the driveway was indeed there; it fell so steeply from the road to our house a couple hundred feet below that you couldn't see it beyond the hood of the car when you initiated the turn. You simply had to aim the car for the water and trust that the front wheels would find the concrete of the driveway. With Dad's encouragement and trust in me—and knowing the driveway well from walking up and down it for several years to wait for the school bus and get the mail—I slowly and carefully made the turn and navigated successfully down the driveway. That was how Dad taught us new things. Go right for the hard stuff; otherwise, you'll work up unnecessary worry and dread, making it far worse in your head. Have confidence in yourself.

Upon turning sixteen and obtaining my driver's license, I was allowed to drive The Tank on my own, especially if there was an errand Mom wanted run. The I-5 freeway through Seattle[57] was new and mostly free of traffic; going the speed limit of 70 mph felt so *fast*. The errand Mom most frequently asked me to run was to get The Tank gassed up. The oil embargo of October 1973 created long lines at all the gas stations. Because it was an excuse to drive—alone—I didn't mind. By 1974, to conserve energy, the national speed limit was reduced to 55 mph, so no more speeding down freeways in The Tank or the Camaro.

My father made a point of explaining that he got that Camaro only after putting as many miles as he could on the Buick convertible. His philosophy about cars was to maintain them well—he did all of the oil changes and routine maintenance himself—and drive them for their entire useful life, ten years or more. Then start again, with another new car. Dad wasn't alone among the Boeing Flight Test group in this approach. Steve Taylor, son of test pilot Dick Taylor, also grew up with this mindset and carries it forward. He refers to it as "mechanical sympathy"—treat the machine well, and it will treat you well. I confess, I have adopted the "drive it 'till it dies" approach, keeping any car I purchase until it has over 200,000 miles on it.

Promotions

In 1970, my father was named Chief Test Pilot, reporting to Brien Wygle as Director of Flight Test. In 1974, Dad was promoted to Director of Flight Test when Brien became VP of Customer Support. When Brien was asked by his boss, E. H. "Tex" Boullioun, who should replace him as Director of Flight Test, he nominated my father. Also in consideration was Jack

---

[57] The final section of I-5, through Seattle, was completed in November 1969.

Waddell. "Jack was a politician and a very impressive person," Brien said. "He had associated himself with Mal Stamper, who was later our president. Jack flew the 747; Stamper was the VP in charge of that program. They became buddies. Jack very much wanted to become Director when I left. He had some support in high levels. I wasn't sure Lew would get it. Lew and Jack were opposites. But Tex Boullioun was my new boss and he asked who I wanted to be Director. I told him I wanted Lew. He asked, 'What about Waddell?' I said Jack would be fine, but I preferred Lew in that job. 'Okay, that's what you want, that's what it'll be.'"

Brien described Jack as a type A personality, smart with a commanding presence about him, very ambitious with a pretty fair-sized ego. "He sometimes had difficulties with the flight test engineers," Brien said, "because he liked to do things his own way. People like Lew and I, Ray McPherson, and nearly all the other test pilots worked closely with the flight test engineers and would rarely overrule them in flight. We accepted them for their jobs and they accepted us. Lew was especially popular. He was smooth, calm, had good hands, and got the information the engineers needed, which they liked. He had an easy, confident way about him, a great way of being a pleasant fellow, a competent person, and impressed people."

There's a photo of Jack taken in the early 747 days. Standing near the airplane, he's posing with his hands pulling open his shirt to display a Superman logo T-shirt underneath.

I had the sense, from comments my father made to me, that Jack may have believed that because he was one of the few pilots in that group with a master's degree, he should have been promoted before others, including my father. Dad always emphasized to me that having a bunch of initials after my name should never be the basis for believing I was better than anyone else, or entitled to job promotions or other benefits.

While we were on the topic of egos, Brien shared a story about his time at Test Pilot School at Edwards AFB in the mid-fifties. I mentioned to Brien that after reading Tom Wolfe's *The Right Stuff,* I had the impression that the military test pilots had very healthy egos and a belief that no matter how far they pushed the envelope, nothing bad would happen to *them,* just to the other guy. Brien agreed, having seen them up close. "Not all of them, but those guys that flew the X airplanes—Yeager, Frank "Pete" Everest, and Crossfield—they all had big egos. They had this devil-may-care attitude. After Norma [Brien's wife] left—she left early because she was pregnant—the last ten days I was there I was 'batching' it. We were in the club bar one night. I said I was going to drive down and have dinner at Pancho's. Frank Everest happened to be in the bar, and asked to go along. Well, Everest was a wild man, and he'd had a few drinks already. I'm driving down, and he didn't like it because I wasn't driving fast enough, I was only 20 or 30 miles over the speed limit. He wanted me to go way faster. He got really irritated; he was a lieutenant colonel by then. He was an abrasive egomaniac, although don't let me take away from his professional career, because all these guys were good professionals. He clamped down on my foot on the accelerator—just clamped down—and I had no option unless I turned off the ignition. It was dangerous as hell. I finally prevailed on him to let up. But that was typical of what they did. There was a lot of ego and a lot of this 'I'm the man' macho stuff. Now, Lew and I were bomber pilots, multi-engine pilots; we'd both been fighter pilots in our pasts, but we weren't in that group at all. They were all separate from us and from most people there. They promoted themselves pretty well. They were all competent pilots, there's no question about that. But at the same time, they were pretty hard to live with."

As Brien and I discussed my father's promotion to Director of Flight Test in 1974, I said that I had a hard time seeing my father as an administrator, that riding herd over budgets and meetings at the expense of flying didn't fit my picture of him. Brien agreed. "I don't think administration was his spark," he said. "He managed Flight Test and that was fine because he delegated a lot to others. Eventually, when I came back as VP of Flight Operations in 1979, Flight Test was a part of Flight Operations—a big part, along with customer support, customer training, simulators, and field service. We were getting into the big test programs on the 757 and 767, overlapping programs with a lot of work to do. I had promoted Don Archer to a key position there; Archer worked for Lew. I said, 'Lew, how about Archer reports to me and administrative guys report to me, and you handle all the pilots, flying, flight operations and the management of all that.' He agreed. I think he actually liked that. He kept the same title."

Brien also let my father know that he wanted to do some of the test flying in the 757 and 767 programs. When Brien left Flight Test to become VP for Customer Support in 1974, he quit flying. He had asthma, something very few people inside Boeing knew about. Brien was taking prednisone, which medically disqualified him from flying. "I didn't tell anyone. I just quit flying," Brien recently told me. The good timing of his promotion to VP—a position that didn't involve flying—was his cover.

When he became VP of Flight Operations five years later and returned to the flight test arena, Brien was using an inhaler to control his asthma. Medically cleared to fly again, he had returned to flying small private airplanes, keeping his instrument rating, things he'd wanted and needed to do. But it had been five years since he'd flown the big airplanes. He was nervous about it, and asked my father to fly with him, knowing Dad would be sensitive to the situation. "I flew badly," Brien shared. "Lew was patient. Eventually I got back to flying test airplanes. I said to Lew, 'You tell me when I fly. You're the boss of flying, I don't want to interfere with that.' And I didn't. When it came to being assigned an airplane, it was his decision. We got along extremely well. That was his happiest time. He didn't have to worry about budgets and things. He was good at managing the pilots. He knew them and how to handle them."

I had a vague sense growing up that among the test pilots my father would mention in his stories, Jack Waddell wasn't his favorite. In fact, he rarely mentioned Jack; that was my biggest clue. I know my parents socialized at parties with the Waddells, because the name was sometimes mentioned in that context. Dad never said anything negative about Jack, but I also sensed that he didn't have the same warmth and sense of camaraderie with Jack that he did with the other pilots. Their "competition" for promotion to Chief Test Pilot and later Director of Flight Test was undoubtedly the cause of the distance. Looking back from my current vantage point, having talked to so many of my father's colleagues about their time in Flight Test, I realize that my father may have had Jack in mind—as well as Russ Baum and maybe those military test pilots from Edwards AFB in the 1950s that Brien described—whenever he warned me about people with big egos.

Don Cumming shared a story illustrating that while my father and Jack got along as professional colleagues, there was perhaps a little strain between them, enough that my father enjoyed tweaking Jack's nose a bit when the opportunity presented itself.

Both men were on a well-attended trip in May 1964, doing 727 demonstration flights in South America. In addition to Jack and my father, there were instrumentation engineers, some sales and marketing people, an FAA pilot and engineer, Don as analysis engineer, and some airline captains. Wanting to keep the crew numbers down, Jack and Dad flipped a coin to see who would do the high-altitude runway tests at La Paz, Bolivia, and who would take the president of Peru, Fernando Belaúnde Terry, on a demonstration flight. Losing the toss, Jack did the high-altitude runway tests, but according to Don, he was fine with that because he wanted to use his downtime in Peru to shop for a silver service, knowing how beautiful Peruvian silverwork was. Don joined Jack on that shopping trip in Lima; someone had arranged a limo and escort for them. "Jack had an idea what he wanted. Our escort took us into the bowels of Lima where the silver pieces were made. He was able to negotiate a good price for what he wanted. Jack was really upset later when Lew told him the president had presented him with a silver service after the demo flight. Lew confessed to me later that he had actually been given a silver tray, not an entire service. I don't know if Jack ever found out the truth."

Don also remembered that the Peruvian president—a pilot himself—wanted a meeting with the Boeing pilot at his palace, or mansion, to discuss the flight plan. When my father got there, the president had aerial maps spread on the floor of his office. Together they got on their hands and knees to look at the maps, the president showing Dad where he wanted to go. I'm sure they communicated easily, not only in the shared language of aviation, but in English; the president had earned his college degree in architecture in the United States. My father readily agreed to the president's desired flight plan, since it involved some fun flying at low altitudes through the rugged Andes Mountains, doing flybys of selected cities. "I'm sure Lew let him do a good bit of flying," Don said. I agree. When he gave demonstration flights, Dad was always happy to let any VIPs who happened to be pilots have a chance at the controls. He did the same for the king of Jordan and Prince Philip of England.

Don also verified my sense that my father didn't enjoy being an administrator when he was promoted to Director of Flight Test. "Lew didn't want it, but he was a good one," Don told me in 2003. "He always backed his engineers. And he always wanted to be debriefed about the pilots' behavior when he wasn't along on a flight." Don remembered one instance where Dad demoted a test pilot to copilot based on a test engineer's report of the pilot's dangerous handling of an airplane. Don said Dad immediately took action and was upset the other pilots hadn't reported the problem to him first. That's just one example of why the engineers favored my father. They knew he listened to and trusted them. "Lew could get away with anything because he was so highly respected," Don said.

While the promotion to Director of Flight Test added administrative duties to my father's job, he was still working in some capacity as a test pilot on all the programs—727, 737, 747, and the early design work of the planned 767. He continued flying as much as he could justify.

My father was an excellent mentor—to me, as well as to the young engineers and pilots working with him in Flight Test. One of those engineers was Alan Mulally, who started at Boeing when in his mid-twenties and worked with my father for twenty years as he rose through Boeing's ranks all the way to President of Commercial Airplanes. Mulally finally left Boeing when he was passed over for CEO, and became CEO of Ford Motor Company in 2006. At my father's retirement party in

1986, Mulally—roughly forty years old—shared an anecdote that illustrated my father's respectful and adroit method of mentoring. Mulally had worked on a particular test plan and presented the data to my father in a preflight meeting. Dad looked over his work, and told Alan it looked like he'd done a good job. "Why don't you go on this test with me tomorrow," my father suggested. Mulally said he stayed up most of that night, checking and rechecking his numbers, because now his life was potentially at risk along with those of the regular crew. What better way to show confidence in the colleague you're mentoring, while also driving home the point how critical it is to do your work to the best of your abilities, to keep *everyone* safe.

As Dennis Mahan said of my father, "He treated everybody, especially the people who worked for him, with a great deal of respect." Treating others with respect was another of the life lessons my father made sure I learned and practiced. Be respectful, and always say "Thank you."

Scott Linn came into the Flight Test division in 1982, after a year working in the Boeing wind tunnel. He stayed another twenty-nine years before retiring. Scott flew with my father several times and had the opportunity to be part of "the good old days" toward the end of my father's career, the days "before things started changing at Boeing," as Scott put it. "When I came in, the process was, you fly, and you don't fly again until you know what you have," Scott said. "We'd process data as fast as we could. It was a very structured approach, as safe as we could make it. We had ultimate faith and trust in Lew and the rest of the pilots because they would stand their ground, say we're not going to do that. They were the final arbiters. They somehow knew the right questions, had the bigger picture. As young guys coming in, we didn't have that yet. It's gotten away from that now, because of schedule pressures."

From Scott's perspective, the test pilots of my father's era were very different than those working today. "They were used to a real cowboy style," he said. "People had more authority, more independence, the ability to just go do something. That's where that trust came in. If someone said something was okay, it was. Tex [Johnston] was that cowboy model. Lew wasn't in that exact mold, but he had some of the characteristics, that 'Let's go see what happens if I do this.' A curiosity tempered with knowledge and experience; let's push the edge a little bit."

China

In December 1973, my father and Tom Edmonds delivered a 707 to the Chinese government, the third of ten ordered. Some historic context: Despite being allies against Japan during World War II, China and the United States parted ways when China's subsequent civil war led to a victory by Mao Zedong's Communist Party. After establishing the People's Republic of China in 1949, Mao rebuffed United States' attempts at formalizing a diplomatic relationship. When the Korean War broke out in 1950, United States and Chinese troops fought each other for the first time since 1900. A dispute over Taiwan began, lasting decades. Relations between China and the United States became extremely chilly with a great deal of mutual mistrust. By 1964, as the United States' involvement in the Vietnam War escalated with troops on the ground supporting South Vietnam, China felt threatened and increased its support for the North Vietnamese. In 1964, China tested its first atomic weapon, emerging as a nuclear power. When tension along the shared border between China and the USSR broke out in 1969, President Nixon declared his intent to improve relations with China and so isolate the Soviet Union. The United States reduced its military presence and assistance in Asia, and announced its reconsideration of earlier attempts to "contain" China. In 1970, ambassadors from both countries met for talks in Warsaw.

During an international table tennis tournament in Japan in 1971, a United States player hitched a ride on the Chinese team bus. Soon thereafter, the United States team was invited to play in Beijing. This was the first semiofficial delegation of Americans to visit China in twenty years. United States-imposed trade and travel restrictions with China were soon eased, and in 1972, the Chinese table tennis team invited the

United States team to visit as reciprocal goodwill.

Cold relations between the two countries thawed. In July 1971, United States National Security Advisor Henry Kissinger made a secret visit to the People's Republic of China, meeting with leaders to pave the way for an official visit by President Nixon. In February 1972, Nixon flew to China on Air Force One, a Boeing 707. That same year, the Civil Aviation Administration of China (CAAC) ordered ten new 707s, a departure from their former practice of purchasing Soviet-built commercial airplanes. A new and enduring relationship between Boeing and China began with that order.[58]

Even before the first commercial 707 was delivered to China in May 1973, some of CAAC's technical staff arrived in Seattle for training. As part of the team that would deliver China's third 707 later that year, my father was involved in the Seattle-based training of Chinese flight and ground crews. Dad said that because of the Chinese government's secrecy and tight control over its people, the Chinese crews stayed in a private building, had their own cooks, and didn't socialize much with their American counterparts while in Seattle. I remember reading at the time about the occasional Chinese scientist or member of the military "escaping" from China, then having the sense that China as a country was very "closed," so it's not surprising that whenever groups of Chinese went abroad on government business, they were accompanied by security to make sure they didn't stray from their intended duties. Chinese citizens weren't allowed to travel freely. Because China wasn't yet integrated into the international banking system, Boeing's airplanes were paid for in cash or gold.

It's not hard to imagine my father's curiosity about Chinese society, and how eager he was to visit this country that had been shrouded so long in mystery .

When Dad and Tom ferried the third of China's 707s to its new home, they carried a Chinese crew that had completed training in Seattle. Boeing's own ground crew also went along.

---

[58] By 1976, the Chinese were ordering 747s. In 1979, diplomatic relations between the two countries were formalized. In 1980, China's first 747 was delivered.

The Chinese government insisted on verifying that the airplane was one-hundred percent as guaranteed after it arrived in China before official acceptance; the Boeing ground crew could address any concerns. A Boeing factory foreman, there for the two previous deliveries, brought added confidence to the Boeing team. The Chinese had even invited him to include his wife on this trip, the only woman aboard.

After departing Seattle, they refueled in Anchorage before proceeding to Shanghai, avoiding South Korean airspace because of the conflict between South Korea and China; instead, they flew through Japanese airspace. Lacking modern navigational aids in that part of the world, Boeing navigator Jim Brown made celestial sights.[59]

As they approached China, Tom, my father, and Jim had no success tuning in to radio frequencies; they weren't getting any response. They asked Jim to visit the cabin and talk to the Chinese navigator. The Chinese were playing cards. When Jim explained the situation through an interpreter (even though the Chinese navigator knew some English), the navigator replied, "I'll be up in a minute." Jim relayed the message to my father and Tom. They were surprised, yet what could they do but keep flying? About an hour later, the Chinese navigator appeared in the cockpit and asked for the radio microphone. The navigator spoke Chinese for a minute, then suddenly, the ADF [automatic direction finder] needle spun and the tower was on the headset. Handing Dad the microphone, the Chinese navigator said, "Okay, now they'll talk to you."

This is why Chinese crews were included on these early delivery flights.

Landing at Shanghai airport, Dad noticed antiaircraft guns scattered liberally around the tarmac. They were met at the

---

[59] Celestial navigation is a technique that has evolved over thousands of years to help sailors cross oceans. Celestial navigators take "sights"—they measure the angles between a celestial body (sun, moon, a planet or star) and the visible horizon, to locate one's position on the globe, either on land or sea. The latitude and longitude of the celestial body at a given time—its geographic position—can be determined from tables in the Nautical or Air Almanac for a particular year. The 707 was the last Boeing airplane model with provisions for a sextant sighting from the cockpit.

airplane by polite airport officials and taken to the Peace Hotel, a unique and imposing hotel built by Sir Victor Sassoon in 1929.

The Boeing crew was installed on one floor of the hotel. They had the entire floor to themselves, even though there were fewer than fifteen in their group. "There were guards on each floor. If you got off on the wrong floor, they would put you right back on the elevator," Dad said. Other groups visiting from other countries were kept to their individual floors.

The Boeing crew was allowed to walk around the vicinity of the hotel without escorts. The first morning, after breakfast in the dining room, my father, Tom, Jim, the flight engineer, and the wife of the factory foreman decided to go for a walk. "It was December; it was cool," Dad said. "The foreman's wife had a long, navy-blue leather coat. She had gray hair down past her shoulders. She was a pretty tall woman, maybe five foot ten. We walked down the street at about eight in the morning. Most of the Chinese were about five foot eight or shorter. We towered above them. The main traffic on the street was bicycles. We heard these bells—ding ding ding—all over the place. We'd walk along, the people on bicycles would see us… I think there were a few collisions!"

The group strolled a couple blocks and saw a large park-like promenade across the street, alongside a river. Locals were there doing their morning stretching exercises. Wanting to see the river, the Boeing group entered the park and leaned against a balustrade, looking at the river below, not paying much attention. "We turned around and there must have been at least two hundred people all around us, just looking at us," Dad remembered. "Talk about feeling weird! Nobody tried to touch us, they weren't threatening, they were just curious. We decided to walk away, and as we turned and started slowly moving, they just opened up and let us through."

For the average Chinese citizen in 1973, visitors from the United States, or indeed most any other country, were a rare sight, something worth staring at. China had been isolated from the rest of the world for some time.

While it was nice to get outside for a bit, that was more

attention than any of the Boeing crew wanted. They returned to the Peace Hotel.

The Chinese officials organized tours for the Americans each day of their stay. Dad never understood the exact protocol or pecking order, but it was clear that the Chinese had decided ahead of time who should travel in each vehicle. Their cars looked like ten-year-old Mercedes, all painted light gray. At the hotel, the Boeing crewmembers were each assigned a car and interpreter, two or three Americans per car. "You didn't go ride with somebody else just because you wanted to," Dad said. "You got in your assigned car. Then they would take off in a convoy." There wasn't much automobile traffic in those days, and few traffic lights; most intersections had uniformed policemen directing traffic. "We would just go sailing down the street like a presidential motorcade. Wherever we went, that was how we traveled."

The Boeing crew was shown a factory where electric motors were made. Dad remembers the workers were hand-winding the motors, very much relying on manual labor. Used to Boeing manufacturing practices, he was shocked. The crew was shown an apartment where people working in the factory lived. "It was very clean," Dad said, "but by our standards crude, just a little gas burner, with concrete floors, walls, and ceilings, [and] a grass mat on the floor." It was cold and everyone wore quilted uniforms; whether they were working indoors or outside, everyone dressed the same. Dad was amazed to see construction workers at work on tall buildings using scaffolding made of bamboo poles lashed together.

The crew visited a jade-carving factory and a rug factory. Dad was very impressed with the jade carvers. "They make some of the most intricate carvings," he said. "Carvings inside a carving. I think some of them must work two or three years on a carving. That was their job. Same with the people making rugs; that was their job. Other people made electric motors. The jade carvers had more artistic ability, obviously, but I doubt they were paid any differently."

One tour stood out in my father's memory. They visited a primary-school class; Dad guessed they were the equivalent of first graders in the United States. Dad was struck by how regimented the children appeared; they stood up and sang songs on cue. He was also impressed with the education they were getting, their ability to read and write. He had the sense they were being indoctrinated, and while he had read about that sort of thing, "I really hadn't appreciated it until I saw it," he told me.

Someone who had been to China on a previous 707 delivery had suggested to my father that he bring some toys for children. "So we had some Frisbees. That's something those kids didn't have. We showed them how to throw them. They were just delighted and quickly caught on." Leave it to my father to help introduce the principles of flight to Chinese first graders in a playful way.

The Boeing crew was in Shanghai for four or five days with little to do, so they appreciated the tours and being treated like VIPs. Toward the end of their stay, the Chinese announced that they were going to fly the Boeing crew to Canton (Guangdong). "We got to the airport and there was a 707!" Dad told me. "They hadn't really started service yet with the 707s, but they were doing what we call 'proving' runs in this country. There were eight or ten other passengers on the airplane—in a cabin that holds one hundred thirty to one hundred forty people. When we were getting ready to go, I opened the cockpit door and looked in. There were at least seven people in the cockpit—two people sitting on the observer's seat, two more sitting on the navigator's seat. I couldn't believe it! They were real proud of taking us down in the 707, which was great. We had a nice flight; they did a good job."

Before leaving the Peace Hotel for Canton, Dad purchased a few presents for my brothers and me. He brought each of us a dark blue Chairman Mao cap, and Mao's *Little Red Book*. He also bought me a very small pair of folding scissors and a tiny sewing kit. I still have the *Little Red Book* and the folding scissors, which after all these years remain sharp and work great for delicate tasks, like cutting mats from behind my dogs' ears.

The Fairy Tale Ends

My father's trip to China ended December 17, 1973; he arrived home on the eve of my seventeenth birthday. I was eagerly awaiting his return, not just because I missed him and he'd been away for nearly two weeks, but because I was looking forward to celebrating my birthday.

I went to bed that night anticipating a great birthday the next day. At some point during the night, I heard the garage door go up and Dad's car drive in. Secure in the knowledge that he was home, I went back to sleep. Sometime later, I was awakened by the sound of the garage door going up again, then down. That was odd, but the house was otherwise quiet, so I went back to sleep.

When I woke the next morning and went upstairs for breakfast—it was a Tuesday, a school day—I didn't see Dad at his usual place for breakfast. I did see my mother, seated in the family room, legs tucked up underneath her and her eyes swollen and red from crying.

"Mom? What's going on?" I whispered, alarmed.

"Your father left last night," she said.

With those words, my world imploded and changed unalterably. Like most teenagers, who tend to see the world revolving around them, I interpreted those words to mean my father had left *me*, didn't want *me*. He didn't even say goodbye. I didn't realize he'd been told to leave. My seventeenth birthday became a day I'll never forget. Wanting nothing more than to run away—from my crying mother, from the awful news, from my own disbelief that the father I adored was *gone*—I ran downstairs and called my boyfriend, asking him to *please* come get me.

Dad never did come home again. My parents separated and eventually divorced. Soon my mother purchased a townhouse where she and I lived during my high school senior year. My father moved back into the lake house for a short time, eventually selling it in 1977, before the real estate market rebounded from the Bust. Losing that house for good pained me, salt in the wound caused by the divorce. The house I loved so much, origin of so many wonderful childhood memories, was gone. So was that Beaver Cleaver childhood I had enjoyed.

Also gone with the lake house was my ability to see Butch, the seal that had been such an integral part of that landscape since my family first started spending summers in the 1960s at our lake cabin.

Butch was *my* seal. Or so I liked to think. His origins, his age—even his true sex and name—remain a mystery. But he was real. He wore that faded red collar, which became painfully tight as he aged, creating a ring of raw angry flesh, like a gruesome necklace he couldn't unclasp. My own childishly romantic theory defined him as a traveling circus escapee, now safely living near our dock.

Butch was beautiful, plump yet sleek, his dark form gliding effortlessly and phantom-like just under the lake's surface. I would watch, transfixed and jealous: his head gently breaking the surface, nostrils exploding with exhaled breath, dark round eyes scanning my world before silently slipping back to his own. To be so weightless and graceful! Heavy and ungainly on land, he was elegant and agile in his watery element. As a growing and athletic child who loved to swim, I envied that agility.

My father loved animals. He grew up on a Kansas farm, with cows to milk and mules to help plow the fields, plus an assortment of pets. He felt kids should have animals to care for, so despite my mother's aversion to animals, we always had a dog and usually some fish or gerbils; eventually I adopted my own cat. She was all gray, a dark steel-blue color with green eyes. Dad helped in naming her Blue, after the character played by Jane Fonda in the movie *Cat Ballou* (1965), also starring Lee Marvin, an actor who was one of our favorites, especially after we saw him in *Paint Your Wagon* (1969).

Growing up, I was a typical horse-crazy girl, each birthday wish consistently centered on that yearning for a horse of my own, even long after I knew I'd never have that wish granted. Our family focused on the lake and boats; a horse didn't fit in the picture. Still, Dad made sure I got the chance to learn to ride at nearby stables that rented horses by the hour, or by going to the Gannetts' house in Redmond, where I could ride their horses with Laurie Gannett. During this period, I got to know the Gannett family better. Jim Gannett—my father's colleague and fellow test pilot, the copilot with Tex Johnston during the famous barrel roll over Seafair in 1955—always impressed me with his quiet, calm demeanor. Kind and helpful around us kids, he seemed very much like my own father. He thrived on outdoor chores, always working in or around their barn—they had two horses and a pony—or on their property, hunting dogs by his side. Their acreage, back in the 1960s before Redmond boomed with Microsoft's growth, seemed very rural and remote. Several times the Gannetts invited my family and others to their home for some skeet shooting, where I first experienced shooting a rifle. I decided I didn't like the kick or the noise.[60]

Dad had a way with animals. He was gentle, quiet, and careful, and they trusted him. I remember Dad using the hose of our vacuum cleaner to groom our beagle-mix, Trinket: with calm reassurance, he got her used to the sound and feel of the suction as he used the hose to pull the loose fur off of her, minimizing shedding in the house. Trinket loved being vacuumed, mostly because she thrived on attention from my father. Dad taught Trinket several tricks, using bits of carrot as reward. Today, I suppose Dad would be called an animal whisperer, he was so good with them. He passed that love of all animals on to me, along with the gentle approach, something that has consistently enriched my life.

Dad and I watched *Mutual of Omaha's Wild Kingdom* with Marlin Perkins most Sunday nights, or *The Wonderful World of Disney*. Sometimes Dad could add his own stories about seeing interesting animals—like kangaroos—during his travels for

---

[60]The Gannetts eventually sold their land to Rocket Research (in the late 1970s or early 1980s), long before Microsoft created their huge Redmond campus not far away. While I was sad, thinking of the Gannett property being commercially developed, it was somehow apropos that they sold to Rocket Research, a company founded by ex-Boeing engineers in 1959 and which now—after being purchased by Aerojet in 2002—designs and builds engines for military and commercial satellites and spacecraft. That's the sort of technology Jim Gannett loved.

Boeing. I regularly watched shows like *Sea Hunt*, *Flipper*, re-runs of *My Friend Flicka*, and anything else animal-themed. A love of animals and observing them in their natural habitats created a special bond between Dad and me. It's no surprise that Dad taught me how to observe Butch quietly, from a distance, so he wouldn't be spooked and swim away.

Dogs were as crucial to Butch's well-being as the lake fish on which he dined. Dogs were his playmates. Butch's local favorites were Spot and Tar, large mongrels with simple names that aptly described their appearance: one shaggy white with occasional black spots, the other all black.

I loved watching all three interact. The dogs would pace back and forth on our dock, signaling and waiting. Spying them, Butch stealthily swam under the dock, under the waiting dogs, setting up his moment. With an explosion of speed, he'd break the surface, inches below them, surprising and titillating them into paroxysms of spinning and barking, lingering just beyond the reach of their mouths before he slipped back under. Spot and Tar maintained a frenzied focus, leaning perilously over the edge of the dock, tails wagging furiously in circles for balance while barking excitedly as Butch teased them from below, literally brushing their noses with his, diving back down for several seconds to increase the tension, then breaching like a SeaWorld performer, slapping his hind flippers against the water's surface with a resounding *whop!!* that drenched both dogs and dock, leaving us all breathless! Over and over, this sequence went on, with little variation, for as long as thirty minutes per session.

They played regularly, to the obvious delight of all involved, especially me. It was almost as though they *knew* when it was playtime, because the dogs were rarely stood up. From a distance I would watch, with intense stillness, for as soon as a human approached too close, the show ended with Butch swimming away silently. Over the years, Butch allowed me to observe from an ever-closer vantage point, rewarding my patience and gentleness, my respect for him. I considered this his supreme compliment. He trusted me.

If a dog fell into the water during the game, Butch would

gently grab its hind leg and briefly pull it under before releasing it to swim to shore. Butch never hurt a dog. I always believed he just wanted them to swim with him, be like him, learn to play like a seal in the water. Butch surely was lonely, the only seal in the lake. I often felt like an outsider, too, the only girl in a household and neighborhood full of boys. In my mind, Butch and I were kindred spirits.

39 Spot and Tar on the Wallick's dock, playing with Butch the harbor seal. Photo: Author's collection.

Having observed this play from the age of five, I imagined—even feared a little—that Butch would come up underneath *me* while I swam, grabbing *my* ankle. The fact that no one knew of any negative encounters between Butch and humans didn't stop my wild imagination. In reality, I had only two close encounters with him, the first during a lazy summer afternoon. Snorkeling, alone, focused on crawdads near a snag, I made an abrupt turn, coming face to face with an equally surprised Butch. I'm not sure which of us coughed more air bubbles or whose nostrils flared widest; we both beat a hasty retreat. The second involved our family dog, Trinket. Barking furiously at Butch alongside Spot and Tar one summer day, she became so excited she slipped and fell in. Butch started treating her like a beach ball. Fearing she would drown, I dashed down to the beach and across the dock and without thinking jumped in to rescue her, my foot grazing Butch's torso as I plunged into the water. Butch raced away. I'll never forget the adrenaline rush of fear I felt for Trinket—who was unscathed—coupled with the thrill of actually *touching* Butch. Later, I was mortified to think I likely scared him even more than he scared me. I worried that he would fear me and no longer allow me to watch him play with Spot and Tar. But he did. He forgave me. He continued to trust me, as he did the dogs.

I never tired of watching Butch and the dogs. His trust of Spot and Tar grew to the point that he would beach himself while playing, exposing an almost lover-like vulnerability to them. He chose well, because while they'd bark at him from mere inches away, they never harmed him; they played with him in ways they all agreed upon.

Somehow I knew I had to record this relationship. In the year after my parents split, while my mother and I still lived at the lake house, I took some photos of Butch as he beached himself while playing with Spot and Tar. How else to prove the reality of this unique part of my childhood?[61]

Butch met an untimely and unworthy end not long after we sold our family lake home. Spot and Tar, his trusted playmates, had by then died of old age. Clearly lonely, Butch was observed trying to play with a dog on the far side of the lake, where no one knew he existed. Animal Control was called. Deciding that a saltwater harbor seal did not belong in a suburban freshwater lake, threatening people's pets, they shot him with tranquilizers with the idea of removing him. He died at the scene, the stress too much for his system. Who knows how old he was by that time? He had been a known resident of the lake at least twenty years. I was sad, and furious. I felt like someone had killed my beloved pet, a member of my family, for that's how much I had bonded with Butch over those many years.

A necropsy revealed several BBs and pellets embedded in Butch's skin. His distrust of humans was well-founded.

---

[61] Viewing old family movies, I found a few seconds of film my father took of Butch playing with Spot and Tar at our dock. The photo used here is a screen shot taken from that film.

I learned so much by watching Butch over the years—about how different species can learn to trust and play, about bonds forged outside traditional boundaries, about patience rewarded. I'm grateful Butch and the dogs allowed me into their transcendent world of play. While I've never since been blessed with the friendship of a seal, I've always had the unconditional love of one or more dogs in my life, a gift whose value was first shown to me by my father.

747SP: Special Performance

On July 4, 1975, Dad was copilot on the first flight of the 747SP, with Jack Waddell as pilot and Ken Storms as flight engineer. Paul Bennett flew the F-86 chase plane. The SP was designed for "long and thin" airline routes—those long hops that might not need the passenger capacity of the original 747. Pan Am, the motivating customer, agreed to buy ten 747SPs, helping keep the program alive. As far as I know, the first flight was "uneventful," to use typical test pilot jargon. At least, in all my interviews with my father, nothing about this first flight came to mind as worth sharing.

My father did, however, have one funny memory of the 747SP. To demonstrate the 747SP's capabilities, Dad participated in an around-the-world trip, flying the second part. The crew change occurred in Mexico City. From there, they flew nonstop to Belgrade, then Athens, Ivory Coast, Kenya... I don't know where all, until finally returning to Seattle. During the Ivory Coast stop, they were to take some government officials on a demonstration flight. "Somebody had the bright idea that we might as well take some of the people standing around for an airplane ride," Dad said. "So they announced it—anybody wanting to go for an airplane ride could just get onboard and go. I'm sitting up in the cockpit and suddenly realize there's a line of people half a mile long, four abreast! There was no way we had that many seats. I thought, we'll have a riot on our hands. I got hold of somebody and said, 'Hey, you get somebody down there and you shut this off; when the seats are full, that's okay, but don't let anybody else onboard because we don't want to have to put anyone off.' They managed it somehow, even though most everyone there spoke French, not English. We flew, and all these people got about an hour's airplane ride. I'm sure a lot of them had never been on an airplane."

40 The 747 SP first-flight crew: Lew Wallick, Ken Storms, and Jack Waddell. Paul "Pablo" Bennett, right, flew the F-86 chase airplane. Photo: Boeing Archives.

Even by 1975, a Boeing 747 was an amazing thing to see, let

alone fly on. As Dad pointed out, it wouldn't have mattered where they were—the Paris Air Show, anywhere in the United States—you make an announcement that anyone who wants a ride can get on and go for free, you'd get a stampede.

The 747 was nicknamed "The Jumbo Jet," and "Queen of the Skies." Still today, it is the world's most recognizable commercial aircraft.

When Dad returned from that trip, he brought me two necklaces made of beautiful polished African stones. His choice of gift was based on our shared fascination with the natural world. Today, those polished stones necklaces decorate door handles inside my house.

In 1990, two modified 747-200s became Air Force One, replacing the earlier 707s in that important role. NASA would modify two 747-100s into Shuttle Carrier Aircraft to ferry the space shuttle between Edwards AFB in California and Kennedy Space Center in Florida. Both uses of the 747 ensured its status as a true icon of American ingenuity and power.

Getting Married, Getting Rescued

That 747SP first flight occurred the summer after I graduated from high school. I remember my father giving me some mementos—a silk scarf with a Boeing logo; a brass medallion commemorating the around-the-world flight. My parents had separated eighteen months earlier; I didn't see my father very often. I was no longer privy to all the stories I'd heard growing up when asking Dad at dinner, "What happened at work today?" After the separation, Dad and I would talk occasionally on the phone, but those were brief and awkward conversations between a father and a daughter whose relationship had been abruptly interrupted. I did visit his office once. I think it was around my eighteenth birthday. I remember thinking that his office—reached after walking through a large open space divided into cubicles full of engineers' desks, where it seemed like everyone was staring at me—wasn't all that nice for a man whose job title included the word "director."

Stilted communication between both of my parents and me

after their shocking separation left me feeling abandoned and adrift. My three older brothers were already living away from home; I didn't have them to talk to. It was just Mom and me. Rather than planning for college like my brothers had as seniors in high school, I was planning to get married to the boyfriend I had called so desperately to come pick me up the day I learned my parents had separated. Looking back, I can't believe I thought this was a good thing to do, but at the time, I felt it was my only option. All I knew was that I wanted to escape the pain, and I didn't want to be a burden (in my imagination at least) to either of my parents. Neither parent voiced an objection to my plans. In fact, my mother seemed excited to help plan the wedding. Her friend Marilyn McPherson, wife of Boeing test pilot Ray McPherson, hosted a wedding shower that included other Boeing test pilots' wives, such as Wilma Edmonds and Norma Wygle. I interpreted all of this to mean everyone was happy with my decision. Neither parent sat me down and said, *Wait a minute, what about college?* I had always been a straight-A student. I had the aptitude, and the desire. But with my parents' separation, I assumed that any wish on their part to put me through college went up in smoke along with their marriage, and I didn't know how to do it on my own. It was a very difficult time. Getting married would allow me to run away from all the pain at home.

I got married in August 1975. I was eighteen years old. My father walked me down the aisle. He was worrying coins in his tuxedo pants pocket like I'd never heard him do before.[62] At one point, I put my hand on his arm to make him stop, it was so loud. The jingling in his pocket was the only outward sign of his anxiety over the wedding. He put on a happy face for me, but later I realized he didn't approve. He just didn't know how to talk to me about it. We all seemed to be wandering in a fog,

---

[62] Jingling the coins in his pants pocket was the only reliable sign that my father was upset, or nervous, or anxious, since he never yelled or lost his temper. He worried coins when giving talks, or when he was faced with a difficult decision. Those who knew him well at some point had occasion to hear him worrying the spare change in his pocket. I always considered it ironic that after a trip to the Middle East, he brought home a string of worry beads as a souvenir. I'm sure he understood their value!

our lives having taken a swerve off course that none of us anticipated.

In the weeks before the ceremony, Dad went shopping for my wedding present: a used car. Dad may have secretly disapproved of my decision to marry, but he was going to make sure I at least had safe transportation. Hearing about some of the clunkers my fiancé was considering on his limited savings, Dad didn't want me driving a car that was likely to break down, so he took action in his quiet, assured way. He found a used, bright-red 1972 Chevrolet Vega hatchback. He then arranged to have it modified, knowing that the biggest issue with that particular car was overheating because of a small radiator, which could cause the aluminum alloy engine block to melt. A larger radiator was installed, and Dad made sure I knew how to check and maintain the radiator's water level and all other engine fluids. Dad paid $2000 for that Vega.

Grateful for such a generous gift, I was beginning then to understand that when my father couldn't find words to say how he felt, he demonstrated his love and concern by ensuring my safety, welfare, or comfort.

A marriage started at such a young age and for all the wrong reasons wasn't destined to last. I knew almost immediately I'd made a mistake, but I felt trapped and unsure what to do. I lived in Ellensburg, where my husband attended Central Washington State College (now Central Washington University) on a basketball scholarship. I quickly found a full-time job to help support us while my husband attended classes. Dad visited soon after I moved, probably to satisfy himself that my living conditions were safe. Then, late in 1975, Dad started sending me occasional checks in the mail. He suggested I use the money to enroll in night classes.

I did. Even though I never took the SAT in high school—I was getting married, not going to college, so why take it?—Central allowed me to enroll in night classes. My father knew me well. He knew that once I got a taste of college classes, I'd want more. I started the winter quarter of 1976, and with Dad's financial assistance, I kept taking more classes over the next year while still working full-time. I earned excellent grades. I was most interested in criminal justice and began to imagine perhaps eventually attending law school. This didn't fit well with my husband's plan for us, that of starting a family as soon as he graduated and found a teaching job.

I grew increasingly unhappy in my marriage. There was nothing bad going on; I just knew my future did not include this marriage. By the end of 1976, I had started spending some weekends with my mother in Bellevue, to get away from the strain of being unhappy with my life in Ellensburg. I tried talking to her about my discontent, about wanting something… more, and while she listened, she always ended the conversation with something akin to, "You've made your bed, now you have to lie in it." She'd send me back after each of these visits admonished to make it work. But I couldn't. My unhappiness increased. Attending classes was the only thing I enjoyed.

By the spring of 1977, I reached my wit's end. I came to stay at my mother's one weekend. When I suggested that maybe I could leave my husband and come live with her, she put her foot down. "You know I love you, but you can't stay here." I was devastated, and felt I had no options. I was preparing to return to Ellensburg—where else could I go?—when the phone rang. Mom answered and handed the phone to me, saying, "It's your father." I hadn't talked to Dad about my unhappiness, the state of my marriage; he and I really didn't talk much about serious matters.

I picked up the phone. Dad said, "I hear you're having some trouble." I instantly started crying because I could hear the compassion in his voice. I was too distraught to respond. Dad filled the silence with, "You know, there's a simple solution. You can stay with me."

Dad threw me the lifeline I so desperately wanted and needed. He came to my rescue.

I learned later that my mother had called him and asked him to talk to me, to bolster her arguments and convince me to make my marriage work. Happily for me, he chose a different approach.

I returned to Ellensburg, but only long enough to talk to my husband, tell him I was leaving, and pack some of my things. I then moved in with my father. With Dad's encouragement and the credits he'd already helped me obtain at Central, I completed the entrance requirements for the University of Washington and transferred there as a sophomore in the fall of 1977. I continued living with Dad for several months. I drove the Vega to classes. When I got a steady part-time job on campus, I moved into an apartment I could afford just north of campus. Dad paid tuition and books while I paid rent and living expenses. Dad paid for my uncontested divorce, which was finalized in November 1977, slightly two years after I was married.

My life was back on track.

Dad did all this for me soon after going through his own divorce. Having sold the house on Lake Sammamish during the depths of the Boeing Bust and recession, just before the recovery began, he worried about his financial health as the recession lingered. He was involved in restoring a 1928 Boeing P-12 biplane, a very costly labor of love. He even took on some side work for a former colleague, James Raisbeck, one of those Boeing engineers who had left Boeing during the economic downturn, eventually starting his own firm, The Raisbeck Group. Dad was their project pilot on the North American Sabreliner redesign, helping his friend while earning some extra income.[63]

According to James, when Boeing management began to question my father's outside work, Dad suggested that James

---

[63] Raisbeck joined Boeing in 1961 as a research aerodynamicist. He and my father worked together, starting with the Dash 80. Raisbeck left Boeing in 1969 to work with companies designing improvements for small aircraft, and by 1973 created his own company, The Raisbeck Group. By the mid-70s, the company was designing wings for Rockwell's Saberliner airplanes; it was during that time that my father did some test flying for his friend and former colleague, helping test and certify the first supercritical wing. In 2007, Raisbeck was awarded the prestigious Pathfinders Award by Seattle's Museum of Flight. In 2013, the Raisbeck Aviation High School opened next door to the Museum of Flight, an aviation- and aerospace-themed school for roughly 400 high school students made possible in large part by a donation from the Raisbeck Foundation, created by James and Sherry Raisbeck.

schedule his test flights on weekends, in the early mornings, during long lunch hours or after 4:00 pm on workdays. "This we did," James said, "and we all got a chuckle over it." Somehow, Dad kept afloat financially.

In June 1980, I graduated from the University of Washington with a degree in history; shortly after, the University of Puget Sound accepted my application to law school. Dad was there to see me get my diploma. He was also there with his checkbook, once again, to pay for my law school education. This time we discussed it ahead of time, and he made it clear he wanted to assist me with my education. I would no longer make poor choices based on misunderstandings or lack of communication between us.

It was during these years, when Dad rescued me from an unhappy marriage and we lived together off and on, that we re-established that close bond I had thrived on while growing up. I continued driving the Vega (fondly referred to as the Vegamatic) through law school. It never did overheat on me, but then, I always checked the radiator and oil like Dad taught me. Dad would do oil changes and minor repairs for me. Every time I'd visit him at his Bellevue house, he'd walk me out to the Vega, give me a bear hug goodbye, open the driver's door for me, close it after I got in, then wipe off the headlights with a rag or his shirt sleeve before waving me off. I finally sold that car in 1984 after landing my first full-time job. I was living in eastern Washington, where it snowed substantially. I upgraded to a four-wheel drive Subaru station wagon, a reliable car my father approved of, although he complained it wasn't nearly as easy to work on as the Vega, that his hands were too big for the compact Japanese engine. He continued wiping the headlights of each car I owned as I prepared to drive away after a visit, a gesture that said, "I love you, be safe."

I came to value my father's "simple solution" approach to problems. He appreciated the popular saying of the time, "Keep it simple, stupid" (usually abbreviated to KISS), embracing the sentiment behind it. Life is complicated enough; there's no need to add to its complexity if you can avoid it.

Opening the Door for Women

Another reason my father eagerly rescued me from my poor decision to marry and encouraged me to continue with my education was that he truly believed that I—and women in general—should have opportunities at the same professions and jobs men traditionally held and enjoyed.

Growing up, Dad would sometimes talk about his sister, Eva, who was a year older. He thought she made a poor marriage, resulting in a life marked by poverty and too much hard work to survive. He occasionally helped her financially. I gathered that the lesson I should take away from that was to always have a skill, a way to support myself, so I would never be dependent upon a man. That meant getting a good education and pursuing whatever occupation I wanted.

Both my father and fellow test pilot Brien Wygle helped advance women in nontraditional roles within Boeing when they made decisions regarding whom to hire as pilots. In 1983, during my last year of law school, my father hired the first female pilot, Rose Loper, who had flown helicopters in the military. She became Boeing's corporate helicopter pilot and later a test pilot. In 1985, Brien hired Suzanna Darcy-Hennemann to become Boeing's first female production test pilot. Brien said Suzanna faced a lot of chauvinism when she started, "But she overcame it."

I imagine having such esteemed test pilots in your corner helped. Having competent and ambitious daughters—Brien has four—both Brien and my father realized the unfairness of gender preventing any woman from obtaining the job she desires and for which she has the skill and aptitude. They walked the talk: equal access to jobs. And in my family, my father put his money where his mouth was by offering to pay college expenses for my brothers and me without any conditions other than passing grades. He expected us to work summers and part time during the school year to help pay our living expenses, but he covered tuition and books and any shortfall. It was important to him that we exit college debt free. We could study whatever we wanted, even when it might not have been what he preferred. An incredibly generous gift.

Yet, like most people, my father was full of contradictions. While he urged me to pursue an education, enter any profession I wanted and be independent, he also insisted that any man I dated who didn't open car and building doors for me, didn't hold my chair as I took a seat, or otherwise show basic manners, wasn't worth my time. He embraced some ideals of feminism while dismissing others. And I was fine with that. My father's bottom line was that I was worthy of respect and shouldn't settle for anything less. Every man I dated, I would ask myself, *What would Dad think of this guy?* There weren't many men I was willing to introduce to my father. In all honesty, I'm glad Dad is my barometer of who is acceptable. Taking that approach has helped me avoid most, but not all, dating mistakes.

The P-12

In the late 1970s, my father found, purchased (with a co-owner) and restored a vintage single cockpit biplane, a 1928 Boeing P-12. He was at the pinnacle of his career, and this "toy" was his reward to himself for a job well done.

A wonderful and very talented airplane mechanic, O. W. Tosch (Orville Wilbur—how perfect is that?), known by everyone simply as Tosch, did the bulk of the restoration work. Test pilot Dick Taylor's son Steve was working for Tosch when the P-12 arrived in pieces at Tosch's hangar and repair shop at Boeing Field. Steve, now in his early fifties, also became a Boeing test pilot and is currently president of Boeing Business Jets.

"My first job was sweeping the floors in Tosch's hangar," Steve told me. "I worked for Tosch every summer and weekends after school from the time I was sixteen until I went off to college. I got my mechanic's license working for Tosch. I've got ten years of college, but I learned more working for Tosch than I did in all the years of formal education. He taught me more valuable life lessons working with machines and working with people than you'll ever get any other way. Tosch did great work, and you learned to work hard and do it right. 'If you don't have time to do it right, then when in the hell are you going to find time to go back and fix it?' he'd say. I owe him an incredible debt, more so than to any other one individual."

I, too, loved Tosch. He was a former Alaskan bush pilot. His very gruff exterior—big beefy body, severe crew cut and sturdy black square-framed glasses—masked his heart of gold. Tosch was a big softy who was also a whiz with a wrench. My father admired him immensely and trusted him completely.

The restored P-12 made its first flight on Monday, September 19, 1977. I was living with Dad at the time, so we drove to Boeing Field together. The P-12 had been painted in Army colors from the 1920s: an olive drab body and bright yellow wings, with the "kicking mule" insignia of the 95th Pursuit Squadron on its sides. Dad and I were both a bit nervous about the rainy weather. Due to low clouds, the inaugural flight consisted of a takeoff (requiring only 200 feet of runway, and even then, Dad said later he hadn't come close to reaching full takeoff power), two quick flybys, and an elegant three-point landing. Dad then taxied back to Tosch's hangar.

41 Lew Wallick celebrating a successful first flight of his Boeing P-12 with his son Tim and daughter, Becky. Photo: Author's collection.

We celebrated afterward at a downtown Seattle restaurant whose name I can't remember. What I do remember is that the aviation stories really flew, a preview of what I would hear and learn at my father's retirement party years later. The mood was happy. I laughed out loud while inwardly I was in awe, my appetite for such stories now whetted.

Steve got to know my father well while the P-12 was being restored at Tosch's. "Your dad had a huge influence on my life. Probably part of the story you wouldn't have anticipated," Steve told me. "He was flying the P-12 when I was learning to fly. He was going to air shows in the P-12 and I was going to the same air shows in my Piper Cub. Very early on, he figured out it was easier to follow me in the Cub, because I could open a map and navigate, and he had a hard time opening a map in the [open-cockpit] P-12, so we literally went all around the country to air shows, me flying my Piper Cub and the chief pilot of Boeing following me around in the P-12. I was sixteen, seventeen, eighteen years old, which is a remarkable story in and of itself."

Steve considered my father a role model. "Of course, you know Mark's Twain's quote about how young boys view their fathers," Steve said with the knowing grin of a man who is now a parent himself. "Twain said, 'When I was a boy of fourteen, my father was so ignorant I could hardly stand to have the old man around. But when I got to be twenty-one, I was astonished at how much the old man had learned in seven years.' When I was sixteen and seventeen, I could hardly stand to be around my father, while Lew was this person who I really respected. I could hang around with Lew, and he helped me come to understand how remarkable my own father really is."

Dad wanted to get aerobatic approval for the P-12. He arranged to fly the P-12 out to the Issaquah Airport[64] and meet

---

[64] The airfield in Issaquah was originally built in 1941 and was called the Seattle Sky Ranch. After World War II, former soldiers took advantage of the GI Bill to go to flight school at the Sky Ranch, which operated until 1951. In 1961, Linn Emrich leased the airfield, named it the Skyport, and founded the Seattle Sky Sports Club, providing training in parachuting, gliding, and ballooning, and hosting weekly air shows. In 1971, when D. B. Cooper hijacked a Boeing 727 and demanded parachutes, they were

an FAA representative there. Once at the airport, they talked about the types of aerobatics Dad would do. "I took off and did my thing over the airport," Dad said. "Then I landed. This was during the lunch hour. As we walked across the field toward the motel at the west side of the airport, we heard applause from people who had seen the impromptu air show."

Dad needed the aerobatic waiver because he would often—but not always—do a short aerial show for the crowd at air shows, a couple of loops, a flyby, a roll or two. I attended several of those shows, at Paine Field and Abbotsford, British Columbia. I'd drive to the airport, meet Dad and Tosch, and we'd all sit on the tarmac next to the P-12 parked on display, making sure nobody harmed it by trying to stand on the wing or climb into the cockpit. Dad would get into character by dressing in his vintage Navy clothing: his leather aviator jacket, leather helmet and goggles, and a white silk scarf. He wore khaki pants and casual shoes, including on occasion some blue suede sneakers. One spectator was aghast when she saw him climb out of the cockpit wearing those; they didn't fit her barnstormer image. Dad said he wore them so his feet wouldn't slide on the rudder pedals; at the time he didn't have any brown shoes with rubber soles.

At one air show, the P-12's rear tire went flat. Tosch and I drove all over the nearest town, looking for some sort of replacement. That's when I got the chance to really talk with Tosch. He tried hard not to swear, me being an impressionable young woman and all, but failed miserably, which was hilarious and only endeared him to me more. Tosch found an inner tube—I think at a lawnmower repair shop—and made the temporary repair to the P-12, allowing Dad to get the airplane safely back to Tosch's hangar after the show.[65]

---

obtained from the Skyport. A late 1970s development boom in Issaquah encroached on the Skyport, as did the widening and increased traffic on Interstate 90. By 1987, the Skyport was no more. I remember as a kid frequently watching parachutists and gliders landing in the grass field there, or watching small airplanes taking off—some with gliders in tow—or coming in to land, low over the road and later the freeway.

[65] The P-12 couldn't be insured; it is a one-of-a-kind airplane. It was worth a lot of money, perhaps $400,000 by the time it was donated to the Museum

My father absolutely loved showing that airplane and talking to people who knew something about vintage aircraft. He even flew the P-12 all the way to the AirVenture show in Oshkosh, Wisconsin, a couple of times. It was there that Dad was approached by a man who said his father had flown P-12s in the Army; could his father perhaps sit in this P-12? My father readily agreed. Dad helped the elderly man onto the airplane's lower wing and into the cockpit, where he happily sat while reliving memories and sharing stories about flying the P-12 long, long ago. I think it's safe to say both men couldn't have been happier.

42 Lew Wallick flying the P-12, Mount Rainier in the background. Photo: Author's collection.

Boeing allowed Dad to park the P-12 on static display in a hangar where some of the jets were parked. One day, Dennis Mahan got a call from my father. "He said there was a local television crew in the hangar to tape some footage of his

---

of Flight in 1988, so my father was *very* careful when he flew it. The P-12 is still on display at the museum, in Seattle.

airplane for a segment on a local kids' show," Dennis said. "He claimed he was busy and asked if I would please go to the airplane and try to answer any questions they might have. Well, not only was he my friend, but he was also the boss, so naturally I said I would be happy to do that. When I arrived at Lew's airplane I found the television crew and J. P. Patches."

Most kids growing up in Seattle in the 1950s and 1960s knew and adored J. P. Patches, the TV clown who was Mayor of the City Dump and who, along with his sidekick girlfriend Gertrude (played by a man in drag) entertained us twice each weekday—before and after school—and every Saturday morning.[66] "There he was, complete with the red nose and big feet," Dennis continued. "J. P. didn't just have some questions; he was there for an on-camera interview, which I had apparently agreed to do. Having done the interview, I can understand why Lew didn't want to do it. I may or may not ever have forgiven him for that little con job."

My brother Rick and others who worked near this hangar at Boeing Field remember watching Dad come out on his lunch hour to take the P-12 for a quick spin. The ground crews would have it pulled out of the hangar and waiting; all Dad had to do was hop in and start the engine. When he was done flying, Dad would taxi right up to the open hangar, turning off the engine at the last moment so that he coasted into the hangar—engines must be off once inside—executed a turn, and parked.

The man had style.

---

[66] J. P. and Gertrude were such Puget Sound area icons, they are immortalized with a statue in the Fremont neighborhood north of downtown Seattle.

CHAPTER SEVEN: NEARING RETIREMENT

If an airplane is still in one piece, don't cheat on it. Ride the bastard down.

—Ernest K. Gann, The Black Watch *(1989)*

The 767 and 757: Wrapping Up a Storied Career

By the late 1970s, design work on both the 757 and 767 was underway. Both would be twin-engine jets. The 757 was designed to replace the 727, retaining a single-aisle layout in the cabin. The 767 was larger, with a two-aisle configuration, designed for longer flights with more passengers.

Tom Edmonds was assigned as project pilot on the 767. My father, Director of Flight Test, would fly copilot on the first flight and was involved in design and testing to the extent that his job title required.

I grew up knowing Tom and Wilma Edmonds and their two boys, Dale and Alan. Both boys were a few years younger than me. The Edmonds family would come out to our place on Lake Sammamish during the summer to enjoy the water. Dad used his well-honed method to teach Dale and Alan how to water ski.[67] When my family upgraded our ski boat to the Purple People Puller, Tom and Wilma purchased our Pacific Mariner 17-foot ski boat with its 75 hp outboard engine to use when they rented a lake-side cabin. Wilma often played bridge with my mother, Norma Wygle, and other Boeing wives, so I saw Wilma more often than the rest of the Edmonds. I liked them all. Wilma especially seemed to always be smiling, laughing, in

---

[67] Tom Edmonds told me that his son Alan went on to teach his own wife and kids how to water-ski using Dad's method.

a good mood.

Tom was the last Boeing test pilot to go through the Air Force Test Pilot School at Edwards AFB at the government's expense. Other Boeing test pilots would go to Edwards AFB, or the Navy's Test Pilot School at Patuxant River, Maryland, but Boeing would pay for it. By the time Tom went to Edwards AFB, the program had been extended from six months to ten, so the Edmonds family spent nearly a year there, where Dale celebrated his first birthday. Just like when Norma Wygle, and then my mother were living at Edwards AFB, the Air Force wives included Wilma in their social circle, once inviting her to a formal tea that couldn't start until the late-arriving base commander's wife appeared. Observing strict protocol never changes.

Graduating in August 1961, Tom won two of three awards given to his class—Chuck Yeager presented them—keeping up the tradition of Boeing test pilots graduating tops in their class at Test Pilot School.

When I interviewed Wilma in 2005, she told me that Tom always preferred having my father with him in the cockpit. My father said the same about Tom, and added that he also preferred having Tom flying the F-86 chase plane because he had a good sense of what to keep an eye on.

Wilma also remembered that when Alan was getting his rating in a Cessna 185, he and Tom invited my father along for the ride. Alan made a landing. Before taking off again, Tom offered my father time in the front seat. According to Wilma, my father declined, saying he didn't want to try to follow Alan's great landing.[68]

After years of professional and personal friendship, the two test pilots would be at the controls when the new 767 took to the sky.

The two-versus-three-person crew cockpit issue that came up with the 737 hadn't been entirely settled with the airline unions as the first 767 was being built, so initially it was designed for a three-person crew. By the time the 767 was actually delivered,

---

[68] This is *so* my father, complimenting and encouraging someone who is learning a new task by using sincere flattery.

the issue was settled (after input from a Presidential Commission) in favor of a two-person crew; the flight engineer's station was removed from airplanes already built and eliminated from the design for all future airplanes. Only one airline in Australia—Ansett, where the pilots' union was especially strong—bought and operated a modified cockpit in which a small flight engineer's panel was configured. Following liquidation of the airline, those airplanes were either scrapped or sold in a refurbished two-person crew configuration.

With all the other airlines agreed on a two-person crew, Boeing decided that the 767 and 757 cockpits should have a common design and layout, although the physical dimensions were slightly different between the two. Cockpits in both airplanes would have electronic flight decks—video displays—much different from earlier Boeing models. This was a very radical change in the look and feel of the cockpit, especially for pilots like my father, who were used to the array of dials, gauges, and switches of the older airplanes.

The 757 would debut less than a year after the 767, so they were being developed almost side by side. As far as airline pilots were concerned, the cockpits were the same—becoming qualified in one airplane meant qualification in the other. Well, the cockpits were the same *except* for how one entered and exited. "In one case you step down from the passenger cabin into the cockpit and the other one you stepped up," Dad said. "We always laughed because the airline pilots would have trouble, forgetting whether they were supposed to step up or down depending on which airplane they're in and they'd fall into the cockpit!" Beyond the unintended pratfalls, the benefit of a common cockpit was that one simulator could now train pilots for either airplane.[69]

---

[69] As 757 flight deck chief engineer, Peter Morton was the point guy on designing the cockpit step lighting and markings so there would be no tripping. "We were actually quite worried about that, more worried about the flight attendants than the pilots. When I retired in 2000, I contacted Boeing's legal firm and asked if there had ever been a suit brought forward due to tripping into the 757 cockpit. To my relief, there was no record of any legal action."

The other controversy regarding the 767 design was that it had only two engines, yet was designed for long-range routes, such as over the Atlantic. FAA rules originally required that any two-engine passenger airplane, if flying over open water, had to always be within one hour of a suitable airport. This rule was referred to as ETOPs—Extended range Twin Operations. (My father and others at Boeing turned that into the joke Engines Turn or Passengers Swim.) When the three-engine 727 came along, the rule was waived. That one-hour restriction was gradually loosened to two hours in 1985, after the 767 had been in service a few years, when some airlines wanted to start operations over the Atlantic. Boeing—led by Dick Taylor—was able to convince the FAA that its 767 and 757 had reliable engines as well as reliable electrical, fire suppression, and air pressurization systems, *and* could operate safely on one engine in an emergency. By 1988, virtually all twin-engine jets qualified for the even less-stringent three-hour limit, opening up nearly the entire planet to twin-engine jet routes, while ringing the death knell for previous three-engine jet designs. Two-engine airliners are much more efficient to operate and maintain.

43 Lew Wallick poses with the P-12, 767, and 757 at Boeing Field, 1982. Photo: Boeing Archives.

The first flight of the 767 occurred on September 26, 1981. Tom Edmonds was pilot, Dad was copilot, and John Britt was flight engineer. Dale Ranz flew the F-86 chase plane.

"So, Dad, tell me about the first flight of the 767," I asked him in 2002. Ask my father an open-ended question and usually he'd answer with typical test pilot understatement coupled with his funniest memory. In all fairness, by this point in his career, first flights probably seemed a little old hat to him.

"It was a typical first flight," Dad said in response to my question. "You get out there, get everything ready to go, everybody's there getting cranked up to get going and everything's going along fine. We go, take off, go through our checks of the airplane in flight. Everything seems to be working pretty good." I gave him a look to say, *Come on, give me something interesting to work with here*. After a pause, he continued, but this time with a twinkle in his eye. "We had two very interesting things happen. This airplane had a new vacuum-toilet system instead of a liquid system that flushed the toilet. During the flight, I got out of the seat and went back and used the toilet. I noticed that there was quite a POP! when I flushed it. It was *noisy*. I came back to the cockpit and I didn't say anything. Pretty soon, Edmonds got up and went back to the toilet. When he came back, his eyes were *big*, and he said, 'Boy, that thing is noisy. I thought we had a structure problem!'"

The other "interesting thing" was much less humorous and could have been a real problem. During each first flight, Boeing wants photos commemorating the historic event. They also want the gear retracted for these photos so the airplane is shown flying in a clean configuration. Preparing for the 767's first-flight photo shoot meant rendezvousing with the photo airplane and retracting the gear for the first time in flight. Not only must the gear retract properly, but it must also extend again properly; the best way to verify that everything is working properly is to have the F-86 pilot visually observe. Dad got on the radio with Dale in the chase plane and told him that on the count of three he'd start retracting gear. The nimble F-86 can fly *very* close to the 767—right underneath, off to the sides, whatever's required—and give visual feedback to the pilots in the cockpit. In this case, Dale was probably within 50 feet of the nose of the airplane to visually monitor and verify the movement of the gear.

Dad started retracting the gear. "As soon as the gear comes up, Dale reports on the radio that we have a fluid leak in the nose wheel," Dad said. "I immediately put the gear handle back in the down position, and fortunately, we had enough hydraulic fluid to put the gear down and lock it." This meant that all of the 767 first flight photographs show the gear extended.[70]

This is another example of a test pilot's quick reactions, making the correct move instantly, without the need for analysis or discussion when something goes wrong. Making the 767's first landing without nose gear fully extended would not have made for happy headlines. This is also an excellent illustration of why the chase plane is an integral part of most test flights—first or subsequent. Had Dale not been there to notice the hydraulic fluid leak, Dad wouldn't have tried to put the gear back down until they were close to completing their flight, and by then, there likely would not have been any hydraulic fluid left to allow the gear to lower. They would have had to rely on a backup system.

My father explained that the hydraulic fluid leak in the nose wheel during that first flight was a good example what can happen in a big company when everyone's in a rush to meet a deadline. As the 767 was being assembled and going through preflight checks, they ran gear-retraction tests with the airplane jacked up. According to my father, there was a fiberglass cover over some of the mechanisms in the nose wheel well that interfered with the hydraulic line on the nose gear strut when the gear was retracted. They observed this and wrote an order to remove it for the first flight. That "order" is a piece of paper that goes into the system, the huge system that keeps track of every little piece that is part of designing, building and flying these enormous airplanes. The amount of paperwork required

---

[70] They rescheduled the photographers to get in-flight photos with the gear up.

by Boeing as well as the FAA is mind boggling. "Maybe a week or two after that order goes into the system," Dad said, "the airplane's being prepped for the first flight. Some really conscientious inspector was going over all the drawings and he noticed this part of our shield missing. All of his paperwork said it was supposed to be there. The removal order hadn't got all the way into the system, so they put the shield back on." Of course, when they went to retract the gear during the first flight, the cover interfered with the hydraulic line and broke it, causing the hydraulic fluid loss. "We had a backup system," Dad said, "but we had the gear down and locked, which is the important thing."

I was waiting at Paine Field for that 767 first flight to land. I was a stressed-out first-year law student, having started classes in late August in Tacoma—40 miles south of Seattle—so I was happy the event was scheduled for a Saturday.

Boeing provided a room for VIPs, family, and a few employees to await the 767's arrival. I remember being able to hear some of the radio communication from the cockpit. While I don't remember what was said, I do remember smiling and laughing at some of my father's flip comments, thinking *Wow, he's so calm and relaxed, cracking jokes!* Maybe it was the toilet incident. Whatever the chitchat, this was the first time I felt like I was *participating* in a first flight, even if just listening in remotely.

After they landed, taxied, and deplaned, there was a quick celebration on the ramp beside the airplane. Tom's wife, Wilma, had brought a bottle of champagne—despite alcohol being forbidden by company regulations—and poured a glass for each crew member. After toasting their successful first flight, Dad offered his glass to me for a sip. I was so proud of him, so proud to be part of this, to be a Wallick. I was even wearing a souvenir Boeing 767 silk scarf around my neck, tied on the side with a knot, a style I normally abhorred. It was a good day.

The 767's second flight from Paine Field was, as far as I know, uneventful.

44 The 767 crew toast their successful first flight with champagne, the author looking on. Photo: Boeing Archives.

Not so the third flight. In fact, when I talk to people like Don Archer, Don Cumming, Dennis Mahan, Brien Wygle, or pretty much anyone who worked within Flight Test from the 1950s through 1980s, they rank the 767's third flight right up there with the 727 deep stall and the 737 flutter test as the most tense test flights in the company's modern history. When my father told me about that flight, in 2002, he didn't make it sound like a big deal, but then, he never did make things sound as bad as they truly were. Here's his version.

> We took off and were starting our climb out. We retracted the gear. I was talking on the radio, trying to give some data back to the ground station. Tom reached over and moved the flap handle to the up position, which is normal. We were at a little higher speed, I think, than when we retracted the flaps on previous flights. The leading edge on the right-hand side came up and over… raised up instead of retracting normally. It floated up, and something broke. We had a real control problem, because it acted like a big spoiler on that right wing. Fortunately, we had enough lateral control that we could keep the wings level. We kind of flew a big wide pattern while

> deciding what we could do. John Britt, the flight engineer, got up and went back to took a look. He came back and reported what he saw. There obviously wasn't anything we could do about it. The only choice we had was to come in and land. Tom got lined up about 10 or 15 miles out with the runway at Paine. We told the control tower what was going on so we had priority to land. Tom did a good job. He flew the airplane in, holding basically full control. He made a good landing and taxied in.

Doesn't sound so bad, right? What Dad didn't mention, what I learned from others, is that for a brief time they considered ditching the airplane in Puget Sound before they realized Tom was able to fly it well enough to attempt a landing, although even that was enormously risky. The broken slats were hanging nearly perpendicular with the wing surface (slats vertical to the horizontal wing). With the leading edge slats broken and sticking up on the right side only, Tom had to exert all his muscle on the control wheel just to keep the airplane level; the airplane wanted to turn sharply to the right and roll, as that flap malfunction created enormous drag on that side only. To maintain control, they'd have to come in much faster than normal on approach for the tricky landing.

And just to spice things up, there was someone on the ground, part of Boeing's Acoustics team, using the same radio frequency as Tom to communicate with the Flight Test ground crew and the F-86 chase plane pilot about what was happening as they worked to keep the airplane flying. They didn't want to say too much, of course; anyone could be listening, and this was only the third flight of the new airplane. Because they didn't yet have ten hours on the 767, they had already planned to land at Paine Field. But now it was an emergency, although they didn't call it than when talking on the radio. Within minutes of takeoff Tom communicated their need for priority landing at Paine. Boeing's Fire Department was already on standby.

Unaware of the intense drama occurring in the air, the Acoustics guy on the ground kept chattering away on the radio frequency, causing Tom to politely tell him to get off the radio, then repeating a second time with force, "Could you get off the air, Acoustics!"

Scott Linn, a flight test engineer, heard the radio communication on the ground in real time. "We were in the telemetry room in the old 235 Building, long since torn down. The word went out: There's a problem. We're listening to it. It was almost like *Houston, we've got a problem.* What else can you do? That's part of the culture. There's nothing to be gained from panicking. Anybody could listen on this public VHF frequency. Around the room, people are looking at these recordings, strip charts and data channels that are showing the stresses or positions of things. Saying 'We see that on the ground' is about all we can say."

Scott described the mood in the room as very tense. "It was the kind of thing, if it's not done just right, you can lose the airplane and the crew. They fussed with it a little while, then, 'We'll bring it back.' They had to be real test pilots." Tom and my father had only had a few precious hours in the 767 when this happened. They were still learning how the airplane handled under normal conditions when suddenly they were dealing with a highly unusual and extremely dangerous condition.

The postflight meeting after that near-disaster third flight was also tense. Scott remembers a particular exchange involving my father as if it were yesterday.

> Lew and Tom are coming back to the MIC room (Management Information Center, in the Flight Test building) for the postflight. Some of us had stuck around to be flies on the wall in the back of the room. Guys like the designers of the flaps, the aero guys, were there. People were wondering, why did this happen? They wanted an answer. It's not atypical for the designers or somebody whose job is to pay attention to a particular part to go on and on, and this guy was trying to explain what had happened. "Well, we'll have to look at the data; we haven't looked at that yet. We think these are

> probably structurally sound, we just need to look at the data." This wasn't the right answer. Lew turned around, matter-of-factly, didn't raise his voice or anything, and said, "Well, you better figure it out because I'm getting too goddamn old for this shit." Lew was a gentleman, he was very smooth, he rarely swore. The guy went white—*the Chief Test Pilot's reaming me… I better figure it out*. That ended that meeting.

That day, Scott and others saw something very rare: my father angry. Dad rarely swore, and he never yelled. I don't think he even knew how. He didn't yell at home at his family, and he didn't yell at the office. He almost never even raised his voice. Normally, at work and at home, Dad was a happy guy, always smiling, cracking jokes, or talking airplanes. He always found the humor in things. But if he wasn't smiling, if his face got long and held a stern look, you instantly knew he wasn't happy and quickly did an internal check to see if it was because of something you'd done. He was the sort of guy you didn't want to disappoint, because his respect and friendship were so valuable, so affirming.

Scott gave me a copy of a photo of the damaged right wing from that 767 test flight. My father autographed the photo with one word above his name: "Whew!"

Not long after the 767's first flight and its more dramatic third flight, my father was once again participating in another first flight: the 757's. This time, John Armstrong was pilot and Dad was in the right seat.

This moment in aviation history took place on February 19, 1982, less than five months after the 767's first flight. There is video of the event on YouTube.[71] It includes some of the radio communication between the cockpit and the tower. I notice two things when I listen: the air traffic controller in Renton is female—a nice trend—and my father maintains his high standard of politeness when, just after lifting off the runway and the controller acknowledges their departure and wishes them "Good day" my father replies, "Thank you very much. We'll

[71] Go to http://www.youtube.com/watch?v=DRar2YONKfk.

be talking to you again soon." Then, when the video switches to show the airplane on approach at Paine Field, you hear John Armstrong talking to the tower, confirming coordinates for "757 Experimental" to land. The airplane, gear down and descending toward the airport, is rocking and bouncing quite a bit; clearly there's turbulence. My father is then heard saying to John, "Windy day, isn't it!" Once safely on the ground, the tower controller says, "Looks like you might have had a little bit of bumpiness there." To which my father replied, "Well, a little bit, it was, uh, different than sometimes." So like my father to joke to lessen the tension and to make such an understatement. And while others may not detect it, I hear the joy in my father's voice.

45 Damaged leading edge of right wing after 767's third flight. Original photo: Boeing Archives, autographed by Lew Wallick and part of the author's collection.

As usual after a first flight, John tells the media that the airplane is wonderful, a dream to fly, blah blah blah. He says everything went according to plan, that he couldn't have written a better script for a first flight.

Well, not quite true.

46 Lew Wallick and John Armstrong, 757 first flight publicity photo. Photo: Boeing Archives.

It turns out the wind was an issue for takeoff as well as landing. They had already delayed the first flight a couple of days because of weather—it was February in Seattle, after all. They were required to take off to the north from Renton Airport, as with all first flights because that put them over the water of Lake Washington right after leaving the runway; if something disastrous happened just after takeoff, they'd crash into the lake rather than buildings. But that also meant waiting for the right wind conditions. Then, on the morning of February 19th, the weather started changing. "That morning, probably 5:00 am, I was getting ready to go to work," Dad said. "I'm in the bathroom and all of a sudden there's a big flash of lightning and a clap of thunder. I thought, *Oh boy, this is it. We are going to go today!* That's a sure sign that a storm is moving out—a front going through—and the weather is going to change."

Lifelong pilots get to know weather patterns pretty well. Dad drove to the office at Boeing Field and talked to John and the rest of the crew, saying he was optimistic. Even though the weather still didn't look good, he convinced them to go over to Renton, where the airplane was waiting. They watched as the weather improved, but the wind was out of the southwest, not what they wanted for takeoff to the north. "Finally we started the engines and taxied out," Dad continued. "We have a wind station we're in contact with, plus the Renton tower has wind reporting. The wind is up and down, kind of gusty. John and I were sitting in the cockpit discussing it. I said, 'Well, we can just wait. Pretty soon the wind will drop down. It may not stay down for very long but we don't need very long. It will take us about a minute to make it down the runway.' Sure enough, the wind died down and off they went.

My father, in telling me about this 757 first flight, noted that they didn't have any problems getting the gear up, as with the 767. Indeed, the video and photos of the first flight show a very sleek, clean-configured 757. They proceeded to go through their typical first flight tests. "Someplace during the sequence of tests, we're doing some engine checks," Dad explained. "One of the engines, when we throttled it back, it kind of hung up. We couldn't accelerate it, so we just shut it down and then restarted it, which was no big deal from our standpoint. We didn't say anything on the radio about it." Nor did John mention that slight glitch to the media after they landed at Paine Field. Who knows what the media would have made of that tidbit had they known?

A funny thing happened after they landed and taxied in. They parked on the ramp, shut off the engines but left the APU (auxiliary power unit) running. The cheering, happy crowd gathered before the airplane stair, waiting to greet the pilots as they descended. Because there was no flight engineer, John waved out the window of the cockpit to the crowd below while Dad got up from his seat to open the door. Dad struggled with the door, which wouldn't budge.

"Open the door!" John yelled back from the cockpit.

"Keep waving!" Dad replied.

As my father knew from experience, on every first flight something goes wrong. "I kept pulling on the door handle, and suddenly it dawns on me that the cabin is pressurized. The outflow valve didn't open when we landed, as it should have. So I returned to the cockpit and turned off the air conditioning and opened the copilot's window, which let all the pressurized air out of the cabin."

"Keep waving, John!" Dad repeated as he went back and got the door opened.

It's always something.

On April Fool's Day 1982, my father was preparing to take the number two 757 for its first flight, again as copilot. Dennis Mahan was onboard as Test Director, and believes the pilot was Bob Galliart, who was project pilot for that airplane. "As we prepared for flight, all the displays on the right side of the 'glass cockpit' (that was the term at the time) went dark. I think it happened twice. Your dad leaned back in his seat, turned to me and announced, 'I'm the copilot, and I have a right to know where I am and where I'm going!' Obviously, we weren't going anywhere without those displays, but his approach was humorous and cut the tension."

British Airways placed an order for some 757s with Rolls-Royce engines. Prince Philip, the Duke of Edinburgh and husband of Queen Elizabeth, arrived in Seattle on April 18, 1982, to inspect the first aircraft in that order. A demonstration flight for the prince was arranged. After arriving at Boeing Field at 9:00 am, the prince had a brief meeting with Brien Wygle, who was then VP of Customer Relations. The two men walked out to the 757 and met Dad, who had been preparing the airplane for the demo flight.

"The three of us climbed onboard the aircraft for what I expected to be a flying demonstration," Prince Philip wrote to me on October 2, 2013. "To my considerable surprise, I was invited to take the left-hand pilot's seat, and told that I was going to fly the aircraft. While the engines were being started, I did my best to figure out the unfamiliar layout of the flight instruments.

"I had several hours in my log book, but I had never flown

such a large jet-powered aircraft before. However, following your father's instructions, we taxied to the runway threshold, took off, and headed over the Cascade Mountains to the airfield at Moses Lake. I succeeded in completing two 'touch-and-go' landings there before flying on toward Mount St. Helens. We then returned and landed at Seattle after a total flight time of 1 hour and 32 minutes. I can only say that it was an exhilarating, although a somewhat nerve-wracking, experience."

47 Prince Philip and Lew Wallick flying a 757, April 1982. Photo: Boeing Archives.

The prince was the first non-Boeing pilot to fly the 757, which was still undergoing certification when the demo flight took place. Upon returning to Boeing Field, some press and several Boeing employees greeted the crew. Scott Linn was among them. According to Scott, a reporter asked the prince what he thought of the airplane with its Rolls-Royce engines. "Oh, they seem to push it along nicely," Prince Philip replied.

My father said he really enjoyed flying with Prince Philip. Dad, Brien, the prince, and a handful of Boeing customer relations personnel were the only people onboard the 757. There was more opportunity for talking during this flight than was typical with other VIPs on demo flights. Dad and Brien both said they appreciated getting to know the prince, who was friendly and comfortable in the cockpit, a good pilot.

BUCKINGHAM PALACE.

9 October 2013

Dear Ms Wallick,

Thank you for your letter of 28 August. I am afraid that this reply has been somewhat delayed as I had to delve into the archives for the details of my visit to the Boeing Company in Seattle. It turns out that the visit took place on 18 April, 1982. The purpose was to inspect the first aircraft of an order by British Airways for a number of 757 aircraft, which were to be powered by Rolls-Royce engines.

I arrived at Boeing Field at 0900 where I was met by Mr B F Wygle – Vice President Flight Operations - and by your father, who was then Director of Flight Test (Chief Test Pilot). The three of us climbed onboard the aircraft for what I expected to be a flying demonstration. To my considerable surprise, I was invited to take the left-hand pilot's seat, and told that I was going to fly the aircraft. While the engines were being started, I did my best to figure out the unfamiliar layout of the flight instruments.

I had several hours in my logbook, but I had never flown such a large jet powered aircraft before. However, following your father's instructions, we taxied to the runway threshold, took off and headed over the Cascade Mountains to the airfield at Moses Lake. I succeeded in completing two 'touch-an-go' landings there before flying on towards Mt St Helens. We then returned and landed at Seattle after a total flight time of 1 hour and 32 minutes. I can only say that it was an exhilarating, although a somewhat nerve-wracking, experience.

I am afraid that this is all there was to it. However, I seem to remember that the Seattle press covered the event, and you may be able to find some further details if you can get a look at their back numbers.

Yours sincerely

Philip

48 Letter from Prince Philip received by the author via certified mail on October 18, 2013.

After the flight, Boeing arranged to take the prince on a luncheon cruise, and Dad and Brien were invited to go along. Dad said they continued talking about airplanes a bit more on the cruise, but there were at least twenty people aboard, and everyone wanted to talk to the prince.[72]

I'm sure they flew by Mount St. Helens, because just two years earlier, on May 18, 1980, it had erupted. It was a truly cataclysmic event—blowing down or scorching 230 acres of forest, sending ice and rock rushing down its flanks and into nearby Spirit Lake. The lake quickly breached its enclosing ridge and a mix of water, mud, and trees rushed down 14 miles of the Toutle River, obliterating more forest, roads, bridges, and homes on its mad rush toward the coast. An ash plume, rising some 12 to 16 miles above sea level before drifting with the wind, turned day into night over great swaths of eastern Washington and into Idaho, the dark, thick ash blocking the sun. By the next morning, ash was found as far east as Edmonton, Alberta, Canada, nearly 1,000 miles away.

I remember the eruption vividly. It occurred on a Sunday morning. I was at my father's house in Bellevue. Despite Washington state being full of volcanoes—Mount Rainier, Mount Adams, Glacier Peak, Mount Baker, and Mount St. Helens, all part of the Cascade Range, a volcanic arc that stretches from British Columbia to northern California—none had experienced even a small eruption since the mid-1800s.[73] Mount St. Helens, though, had begun rumbling and had had a major earthquake earlier in May, followed by several tremors. As a precaution, Washington's governor had ordered the evacuation of a huge area around the mountain. Dad and I noticed what appeared to be huge thunderheads far to the south, which was very odd, since the weather was otherwise fine. We soon heard on the radio that the mountain had

[72] Don Archer remembers meeting Prince Philip in 1969. Don was part of the crew that took the first 747 to the Paris Air Show. Don said the prince arrived, unescorted, for a tour of the airplane's interior, which Don provided. I like to think that the prince enjoyed these moments when he could be just another pilot seeing Boeing's latest jets up close without fussy protocol, or media and an entourage hovering around.

[73] Mount Baker did have a steam eruption in 1975.

erupted. Eventually, the Seattle area received a light dusting of ash, but nothing like what the eastern part of the state experienced. Even two years post-eruption, the change in the landscape on and around Mount St. Helens was extraordinary, best seen from the air among the other volcanoes.

A year after that demo flight, Queen Elizabeth and Prince Philip made an official visit to Seattle. On March 7, 1983, they arrived at Boeing Field in the presidential 707 once used by John F. Kennedy, having spent the previous weekend at Yosemite National Park. Because Dad had flown with Prince Philip a year earlier, he and Brien Wygle both received an invitation to a reception being held for the royal couple. When Dad was introduced to the queen in the receiving line, she said, "Oh, yes, I know who you are." Clearly, she knew my father had flown with her husband. Dad modestly figured that the queen had simply been thoroughly briefed before the reception. I think she knew who my father was because Prince Philip spoke highly of him after the previous year's demonstration flight.

In early September 1982, Boeing took both the 767 and 757 to the Farnborough Air Show in England, near London. Dad and Tom Edmonds flew the 767 and took Boeing's Board of Directors, or—as Dad remembered it—if not all of them, then most of them, and their wives. A few of the directors may have flown on the 757 piloted by John Armstrong and Buzz Nelson. The Boeing airplanes initially landed at a different, nearby airport to allow their passengers off; the crews would then ferry the airplanes to Farnborough for the air show. The pilots got together and decided it would be show-worthy to arrive at Farnborough in a two-plane formation.

"We asked about the possibilities," Dad said. "They said they didn't think we could get approval for it. So we just took off and joined up in formation, came across the Farnborough airport in formation, stood up, and landed. Nobody said a word."

Damn Yanks.

One day Dad and I were talking about the various celebrities he'd met and flown with over the course of his career. In addition to Prince Philip and Henry Fonda, he mentioned Arthur Godfrey (Dash 80), Arnold Palmer, Neil Armstrong, Danny Kaye, Charles Lindbergh (Dash 80), Howard Hughes (Dash 80), the king of Jordan (727), and the president of Peru (727). Dad also flew a *lot* of airline presidents and CEOs in various airplanes.

Dad said Neil Armstrong, a fellow pilot and astronaut, was one of his favorites. Dad took Armstrong flying in a 737 in the early 1970s. I remember Dad brought home NASA Apollo 11 moon-landing publicity photos, signed by Neil Armstrong, Buzz Aldrin, and Michael Collins, one each for my brothers and me. Dad was clear that this was a unique memento from that historic feat in 1969—the one Dad whistled for me to come home and watch on TV—and valuable, so we should take very good care of them. We now had a little piece of that epic NASA moment with their autographs.

"You know," Dad said, "that's the kind of job I had. I'm just a pilot, sitting there. Somebody else in the company made arrangements for me to take these guys for a demonstration flight. Most of them are pilots, so you put them in the seat and let them fly the airplane. Just a very brief introduction, say howdy to a whole bunch of interesting people. I never really got to know them." But he did have some enjoyable interactions, and if Prince Philip's letter is any indication, so did they.

Patience Is a Virtue

A successful test pilot needs to have quick reactions. Yet *patience* is another key characteristic—waiting for the proper test conditions; going carefully and precisely through each step of a test series; building upon what's learned in earlier tests before moving on to later tests.

Patience was a concept my brothers and I grew up with. If Dad was going to fly us somewhere, we knew that our itinerary was simply a goal, because weather or mechanical issues could easily cause a delay. If so, a few extra hours or even an overnight stay somewhere was fine. That's what kept us safe and alive.

We learned to pay attention to weather, and weather reports. Dad joked about "sucker holes"—those bits of blue sky peeking between the clouds that convince the inexperienced to believe the weather is changing for the better. My father drummed into us that patience is *very* important. Only fools rush in.

Dad insisted that the lesson of patience can apply to all aspects of life. Driving, for instance. Sure, you can pass that logging truck or motor home and save a couple of minutes in your trip from point A to B, but is the risk of passing worth that miniscule time savings? Pass with care. Do you really have to go out in that blizzard? Is getting to your job on time truly that critical?

Take a deep breath, slow down, and stay alive.

I do remember one time when Dad, reluctantly, didn't follow his own advice. It was a flight in a small airplane I shall never forget.

I was in college. My brother Tim—the brother nearest in age to me—had recently graduated from college and was working for Boeing. The three of us flew from Washington to Kansas one summer to attend a gathering of Wallicks in Independence, the small town near where Dad grew up on the family farm.

Tim had his pilot's license and was always eager for more flight time. He spent much of the trip in the pilot's seat, Dad in the right seat, and me in the back. While having my brother at the controls made me a bit nervous, knowing Dad could instantly take over helped ease that anxiety.

Any trip between Washington and Kansas in a small airplane is *long*. We were in a rented Cessna 210, which seats four and is pressurized for high-altitude flying. At 20,000 feet it cruises at just over 200 mph; it can go as high as 27,000 feet. It's also cramped, especially when carrying luggage for three. Depending on cloud cover along the way, the views could be terrific, but usually I read or tried to sleep. Carrying on a conversation was almost impossible because of engine noise; Tim and Dad wore headsets so that they could hear the radio and each other, but if I wanted to converse, I had to tap one or both on the shoulder, get them to lift one side of their headsets up, then yell into their ears.

The flight to Kansas was uneventful. At least, it must have been because I have no distinct memories of it. The return flight, however, was anything but dull.

We made it from Kansas to Boise, where we landed to refuel and update our flight plan for the rest of the trip to Seattle. We checked the weather, which wasn't good. Looking west from the Boise airport, there were huge thunderheads looming ominously. I was impressed and not a little frightened, looking at those enormous, billowing columns of white clouds. In western Washington, you rarely see such formations; our clouds hang low and drop their rain with mind-numbing regularity. All you see is the relentless gray of their underbellies. But east of the Cascade Mountains—in Idaho, Wyoming, Kansas—where the skies are typically blue, one often sees these thunderheads off in the distance, towering 20,000-plus feet over the landscape.

Commercial airliners simply fly over them.

Dad chatted with the guy at the counter of the small building that housed the private aviation section of the Boise airport, getting updated weather forecasts. I sat in an uncomfortable plastic chair, one of those molded types without armrests, attached to several others in a row and bolted to the floor, that were common in the waiting areas of many airports of that era. For a couple of hours, we waited out the weather, Dad explaining that these storms can move across a landscape with speed. Finally, Dad and Tim decided we would try to fly *over* the weather, given we had a pressurized Cessna that could fly as high as 27,000 feet if necessary.

We left Boise and climbed high, then higher, being tossed like a toy in the fist of a child throwing a tantrum. The same atmospheric conditions that create the thunderheads create *very* bumpy air. An unseasoned traveler would have lost her cookies within the first ten minutes. I felt a little green around the gills, but managed to keep my lunch down. Anything not fastened down was tossed inside the small cabin. The suitcases stowed behind me would suspend in the air at the level of my head every time the airplane suddenly dropped in a downdraft, then slam back onto the floor along with my stomach when we bottomed out onto firm air again. My neck crunched with every lurching bottoming out. It got worse and more dramatic the closer we got to the thunderheads. I was afraid I'd throw up, something I'd never done in all my flying in small airplanes. And although I trusted my father implicitly, I couldn't help fearing the worst.

Finally, after my head hit the ceiling during one especially dramatic drop through the air—because of my only-loosely fastened seat belt—Dad decided we should return to Boise. I was never so thankful to turn back in my life. Shaking from nerves, I nearly kissed the tarmac after we landed and deplaned.

We resumed a watchful wait in the lobby of the airport, checking weather forecasts and possible alternate routes home. Tim, for reasons forgotten now and not clear to me at the time anyway, really wanted to get home that day.

What surprised me then, and now, is that Dad succumbed to that pressure. We did briefly discuss getting a motel room for the night. But ultimately, we climbed back into the Cessna and took off again.

This time, the plan was to fly *under* the weather.

We followed a highway threading from Boise through northeastern Oregon's Wallowa Forest and Mountains into southeastern Washington. There were instances when the hillsides and trees on either side of us would briefly disappear in clouds shrouding the higher peaks. The air was smoother, but the lack of visibility was almost as frightening as the thunderheads.

I don't think I've ever been so nervous in my life. All I could do was sit in the back of that tiny airplane and… trust my father with my life.

We made it home. I wasn't eager to fly again anytime soon. And for that, my father was profoundly sorry. He worried for years that I was soured on flying because of that experience. I reassured him that wasn't the case, although many times over the ensuing years, all I had to say was, "Dad, remember that flight out of Boise…?" and he immediately knew which flight I meant and why it held such a prominent place in my memory.[74]

An Absence of Fear

I never heard my father say he was afraid of anything. Well, late in his life he often said "Getting old isn't for sissies," so perhaps he feared the infirmities of old age. When describing some of the more dangerous situations he found himself in during his career as a test pilot, he never said he was afraid at any moment.

I've thought about that a lot over the years. Was he truly never afraid, or did he just not want to admit that he was?

I've concluded it's the former. Test pilots could not climb into those cockpits day after day and fly the required tests if they were afraid.

Humans are designed to have a fight or flight reaction to extreme danger or stress. Those who gravitate toward dangerous professions, like test piloting, have personalities and physiologies that lean toward the fight end of that response spectrum. Adrenaline, when it kicks in, allows one to focus solely on what's important to save one's life. When those dangerous situations arose in my father's career, his adrenaline kicked in and his response was to "fight" to save himself and those onboard the airplane with him. His focus and instincts allowed the best correct response to be made to the challenge he faced.

Several times over the years, I tried to get my father to talk to

---

[74] Near the end of my father's life, he fell gravely ill. He was hospitalized and put on a respirator. I was told that the effect of the respirator-required sedatives meant he couldn't understand or respond to anyone. Well, I've never believed that to be true; people in induced comas surely still hear those around them. I talked to Dad as I normally would. The second day, as I drove to be with him again, I saw the same sort of thunderheads that had surrounded Boise all those years ago. When I got to Dad's room, I sat beside his bed and stroked the thin skin on his motionless hand, tethered to the bed rail. "Dad!" I said excitedly, "I wish you could look out the window right now. There are enormous thunderheads out there, just like that flight out of Boise. Do you remember?" Right on cue, he nodded his head slightly, the first voluntary movement I'd seen him make. He heard me, and he certainly remembered.

me about this characteristic, this trait that all good test pilots share—an ability to remain calm and react instinctively and quickly, without fear, when faced with unexpected and life-threatening situations. During one conversation in 2004, he said, "One learns through experience. You approach a test with caution if you've never done it before. You hone your senses with experience—listen for, feel for, change in the airplane. Your senses are so focused and sharp, there's no room for fear or anxiety; they're just not there. Over time, various surprises teach you what to look for. Most test pilots don't need to think. They rely on their instincts and react *instantly* if a surprise arises. One has a feel for it. Not every test pilot has it."

Sometimes I would come at this topic by asking Dad to define an aviator, as opposed to a pilot. In the world of flying, there is a distinction, and I think it helps one understand how they're different than the average pilot. "An aviator has a feel, as opposed to the mechanical approach of a pilot," Dad said. "A pilot is an airplane driver, for example an airline pilot. An aviator *flies* the airplane and does it well. It's an insider distinction, but an important one to true pilots." E. B. Jeppesen, an American aviation pioneer, put it this way: "There's a big difference between a pilot and an aviator. One is a technician; the other is an artist in love with flight." Or as Brien Wygle might say, an aviator has good hands.

When I was twelve or so, my parents, my brother Tim, and I flew to San Juan Island one weekend day. The San Juan Islands are a group of islands in the northwest corner of the contiguous United States. At mean high tide, there are over 400 islands and rocks in the archipelago, 128 of which are named. They're part of Washington State—together they make up San Juan County, with San Juan Island the county seat—yet they're very close to Vancouver Island, British Columbia. The San Juans, as we locals refer to them, are reached by boat, ferry, or small airplane, and are a beautiful tourist destination, hosting the largest concentration of bald eagles outside of Alaska. As a child, I took many boat trips to the San Juans with my uncle Jesse and aunt Annette.

My father said we were going to visit a friend of his, a pilot named Ernie Gann, who with his wife, Dodie, lived on an 800-acre ranch on San Juan Island. We spent some time at the Ganns' home. My most vivid memory is of Mr. Gann's studio—a converted chicken coop—where he wrote and worked on his paintings. It wasn't until many years later that I realized who the man, the author, was: Ernest K. Gann, the writer and pilot who authored such bestsellers as *The High and the Mighty*, *Soldier of Fortune*, *Fate Is the Hunter*, and one of my favorite books, *The Antagonists,* which was made into the movie, *Masada*. Many of Gann's books had aviation themes, and were made into movies. Dad met him because both belonged to QB's—Quiet Birdmen, an exclusive and secretive club for male aviators founded in 1921 by World War I pilots. Dad admired Ernie's ability to put into words what aviators felt about flying.

Mr. Gann's prose helps me understand why flying so absorbed my father, and why he and I couldn't quite speak the same language about it.

> Before takeoff, a professional pilot is keen, anxious, but lest someone read his true feelings he is elaborately casual. The reason for this is that he is about to enter a new though familiar world. The process of entrance begins a short time before he leaves the ground and is completed the instant he is in the air. From that moment on, not only his body but his spirit and personality exist in a separate world known only to himself and his comrades.
>
> As the years go by, he returns to this invisible world rather than to earth for peace and solace. There also he finds a profound enchantment, although he can seldom describe it. He can discuss it with others of his kind, and because they too know and feel its power they understand. But his attempts to communicate his feeling to his wife or other earthly confidants invariably end in failure.

I always tried to understand what it was about flying that so captivated my father. I failed on the deepest, truest level, because I didn't share his passion, but I always remained sympathetic to his need to fly, and a little jealous that he had such a joyful force in his life. Reading authors like Ernest Gann, Richard Bach (author of *Jonathan Livingston Seagull*, another writer my father enjoyed) and Beryl Markham (*West With the Night)* brings me a little closer to understanding that passion.

In 1999, my father was inducted into the Museum of Flight's Pathfinders Hall of Fame. Several hundred people attended a ceremony held at the museum's auditorium. One other person was also inducted that evening. Each honoree would make a brief speech after a slideshow presentation of his career. The other gentleman went first. I was sitting next to my father as we watched his slideshow and listened to his speech. I noticed my father getting quietly agitated as the other man spoke. Dad was really working the coins in his pants pocket. I didn't understand why. Later, Dad told me that he was upset that the man, who had also worked for a time as a test pilot, said he was *afraid* much of the time he was flying and credited God for his survival. I, too, had been surprised at the man's comments, but I received them as honest confession. Dad's reaction was much more severe. Dad felt that if the man had been afraid, he had no business flying, that his fear put others, as well as himself, in danger. I sensed that my father felt as if his own accomplishments and induction to the Hall of Fame were somehow tarnished by sharing the evening and stage with someone who was not only afraid when he flew, but publicly admitted it; who didn't have the right stuff, who lacked the true affinity and passion. A man who wasn't a true aviator.

That was a very puzzling evening for me. The strength of my father's negative reaction surprised me, especially since he so rarely said anything negative about anyone. I didn't understand why he should care if someone else admitted being afraid. Asking one of my father's colleagues about that night, he said he agreed with my father's assessment.

Now, I think my father was right: there's no room for fear in the test piloting business, and anyone who is afraid should find another line of work. Fear muddles judgment and makes for poor decisions, and can even lead to panic, which is never good. Everyone on the test airplane needs to trust that their pilots are focused and brave enough to handle whatever may be thrown their way.

Mark Twain wrote, "Courage is resistance to fear, mastery of fear, not absence of fear." If a pilot has any fear, it shouldn't be of flying, but of dying. That distinction is what will keep the pilot alive. Chuck Yeager wrote in *Yeager, An Autobiography* (1985), "I was always afraid of dying. Always. It was my fear that made me learn everything I could about my airplane and my emergency equipment, and kept me flying respectful of my machine and always alert in the cockpit." I was simply asking my father the wrong question. Had I asked, *Are you afraid of dying?* I'm sure I would have gotten a different answer.

I do believe, when it comes to fear when flying, that there's a huge difference between being the pilot in command and a flight test engineer or a commercial passenger who's along for the ride. The latter two simply have to harness their fear, maybe prepare for a crash, while trusting the pilot to choose the best possible reaction if an emergency occurs. Luckily, such situations are rare.

When I interviewed flight test engineers, I often brought up this topic. How did they handle the fact that they had no control to try to fix things when something went wrong, that they had to rely completely on the pilots? All of them said simply that they trusted them. In the rare case that they didn't, they found ways to avoid flying with that pilot or took their concerns to my father or whoever was director of Flight Test. Nevil Shute, British novelist and aeronautical engineer, wrote in *Slide Rule: The Autobiography of an Engineer* (1954), "The happily married man with a large family is the test pilot for me." The test pilot with much to lose is the one to trust.

Dennis Mahan, who flew as a flight test engineer with so many test pilots over a long career at Boeing, shared these thoughts with me. "These guys who say they were never scared are fooling somebody. Perhaps only themselves. But that's still okay with me. I will agree, based on my own meager experience, that during some of these events things happen so fast and people are so busy reacting that fear doesn't enter into it. It is, perhaps, only later with some time to reflect that they become a little concerned about what might have been were it not for their superhuman skills. As for us guys and drama, speaking only for myself, we just did what we did on a daily basis. It was interesting and usually fun. Once in awhile, but rarely, it got a little tense but I don't remember thinking about that much, and the concept of drama certainly never crossed my mind."

Those who didn't feel as Dennis did surely found other places to work. As my father said, "Flight Test was the ultimate place to work within Boeing. Once people got in, they stayed, from pilots and engineers on down to the mechanics." Those with the right mentality and constitution were drawn to jobs in Flight Test, drawn to the challenge, excitement, and risk. Anyone afraid would have sought work elsewhere.

Dad once summed up his experience as a test pilot this way. "I learned early that airplanes can bite. But they can also tell you things if you listen." Then, with that twinkle in his eye and a grin, he added, "I also had a back problem: a yellow streak." No, he wasn't suggesting he was a coward. What he meant was that he didn't want to die when he was flying and testing airplanes, so he let his "back problem" ensure he remained cautious and never did anything stupid. Good way to approach pretty much anything in life. I certainly apply those lessons learned from my father in my own life. How fortunate I am to have had such a smart yet adventurous role model and mentor.

Checklists

One way test pilots—all pilots—try to minimize the risks of flying is with checklists. I became aware of checklists from the time I was old enough to pay attention while flying in small private airplanes with my father. Every flight we took included going through checklists before starting engines, before taxiing, and then before takeoff. If I was in the copilot's seat, I read the checklist to my father. Watching him as I read each item, I noticed Dad knew what was coming before I had a chance to read it, because he'd already be touching a certain dial or knob, or moving the control wheel to check flaps; he'd memorized the list. That didn't mean we skipped any of it. We *always* read through the checklist. Same thing when approaching an airport for landing—pull out the checklist and read through all the items before final approach. Once on the ground, we went through a final checklist for shutting down and parking.

Every. Single. Flight. Always, without fail.

For private airplanes and commercial jets, the manufacturer provides checklists for routine parts of every flight—preflight, taxi, takeoff, approach, and landing—as well as abnormal and emergency situations. These latter may seem counterintuitive: a checklist for an emergency? Don't the pilots just react and deal with an emergency, no time to find a checklist? Yet it's in those high stress, chaotic times when checklists prove most valuable, honing the pilots' focus on those critical items that are most likely going to save the airplane *so that he or she doesn't have to rely upon memory.*

You'd be surprised how many accidents on commercial flights have occurred just after takeoff or on approach because checklists weren't followed and flaps or some other control surface weren't set appropriately.

Humans are the weak link in the performance of complicated machinery, so the redundancy of having a checklist to verify what's often done from memory eliminates many potential errors. In a cockpit with a crew of two or more, each crewmember listens and watches the other to make sure the checklist is covered, another layer of redundancy.

The use of computers in the cockpit to verify certain items and alert the crew if something hasn't been done adds another layer of redundancy and safety. Ultimately, responsibility for ensuring proper use of checklists at the proper times rests with the captain, who is in charge of the aircraft and responsible for the safety of all onboard.

I know from flying with my father that there are certain cues that alert pilots when to use certain checklists. For instance, after doing a visual ground check of his Cessna 185, making sure it's fueled, has oil, the tires have air, that the emergency locator beacon is onboard and works, and so on, Dad and I would climb into the four-person cabin. First thing Dad would usually do after we were in our seats is open the window on his side, which popped out a few inches from the bottom, then tune the radio to the tower channel if we were at an airport with air traffic control, or the general aviation frequency if there was no tower. He'd then hand me the preflight checklist, and I'd start reading through the items. The only item that applied directly to me was "Fasten seat belts." When he was ready to start the engine, he'd look around the airplane to make sure no one was walking in the area, then yell "Clear!" very loudly through his open window. Certain no one was near, he'd start the engine. Next we'd go through the taxi checklist. I'd read an item and watch his hand move to a certain instrument or in some other way physically verify checking the item, something psychologists refer to as "muscle memory," which enhances the visual verification. When the tower cleared us to taxi, we'd head onto the ramp to the spot where he'd do the engine run-ups with brakes on, a cue to run through the takeoff checklist, checking flaps one last time and whatever else the checklist required. With the tower's approval, we'd move into final position and take off. After takeoff, my job was to enjoy the flight and the scenery while helping keep an eye out for other aircraft in the vicinity. I was never able to spot other airplanes as well as my father—his keen vision always amazed me. He knew what to look for. Finally, when we were approaching an airport for landing, I'd once again read from a checklist as Dad verified each item. In some cases, we added items to the approach checklist based on where we were. For example, if landing at Roche Harbor Airport on San Juan Island, you buzz the landing strip to make sure there aren't any deer in the way.

Growing up as I did around pilots and airplanes, I took checklists for granted, thinking everyone must use them for important tasks. As a family we used them frequently, like when we went snow skiing so we wouldn't forget a key piece of equipment. (A family with four kids means a *lot* of equipment, clothing, and food for a full day of skiing.) As an adult, I use checklists when packing for a vacation or for any outdoor activity that involves a lot of clothing and equipment, and for important work tasks. So I admit being a little shocked to learn that surgeons just recently considered the benefit of using checklists in the operating room, and that some are still resistant to instituting their use.

Dr. Atul Gawande, an associate professor at the Harvard Medical School and surgeon at the Brigham and Women's Hospital, wrote *The Checklist Manifesto* (Metropolitan Books, December 2009) to address the benefits of checklists in high-pressure, complex occupations, such as medicine. Dr. Gawande's research included visiting Boeing, talking with experts in what he calls Boeing's "checklist factory," where all of the company's checklists are created. There, he learned that when things unexpectedly go wrong—in the cockpit, in the operating room, in any high-stress situation—a checklist that focuses on the critical items that can't be missed, a checklist that a team of people is trained to utilize, is what saves the day. By emulating what Boeing had done, Dr. Gawande and his research colleagues created a two-minute checklist for the operating room. Used in eight study hospitals, there was a thirty-six-percent reduction in complications and a nearly fifty-percent reduction in deaths.

My Father's Last Official Boeing Test Flight

Boeing adopted the same upper age limit for its pilots that the FAA applied to airline pilots: no flying after age sixty.[75] As you can imagine, this didn't sit well with the pilots themselves. Most, like my father, grudgingly accepted it; others tried—unsuccessfully—to fight it with lawsuits.

My father turned sixty in May 1984. He had no immediate plans to retire from Boeing, and he would keep flying private aircraft, but he made sure he flew Boeing jets right up to that last day of his fifty-ninth year.

To commemorate Dad's sixtieth birthday and his forced retirement from flying Boeing jets, one of my father's long-time colleagues, George Stutsman, wrote the following poem:

[75] In 2007, the FAA changed the age limit to sixty-five.

GENTLEMAN PILOT

Here's to a guy who is at home in the sky,
Many want to be like him, it's sure worth the try.
He started in Kansas, with the wind and wheat stubble.
To challenge the sky to him was no trouble.

He's flown for the Navy, Corsairs in the fleet,
To land on a carrier, my friend, is trick neat.
With the war years behind him and a degree in his hand,
Started flying for Boeing in his style always grand.

He's flown all the models he could strap to his butt,
He's handled the hardest with no fear in his gut,
He's stalled them and cruised them in the rain and the heat,
With a talent perfected and a cool hand hard to beat.
He's flown them on takeoff with the tail skid on fire,
And landed hard and short without blowing a tire.
But the rules now have caught him, alas and alack.
His years number sixty, he can't call them back.

So for company pilots it's sad to relate,
The flying has ended, a grim twist of fate.
All this is history, recording time that has gone by.
It all comes out clear, this boy can fly.

And above all the flying comes this vote from the clan,
Sam Lewis Wallick is one gentle man.
So look up in the sky for one hell of a view,
As clattering by goes the P-12 and Lew!

My father loved that poem. So do I.

Dad's last official Boeing test flight was on a 737-300. Wearing his light-blue nylon Boeing Flight Test jacket with a big 757 patch on the left shoulder, his name over the left breast, an Experimental Flight Test patch over the right breast (and probably a 767 patch on the right shoulder but I can't see that in the photos), he smiled broadly as he shook hands with various colleagues—including Brien Wygle—and ground-crew members. His hair, thick as always and worn in the same style as when he started at Boeing, but slightly longer on the sides and now a shock of white, contrasted handsomely with his tanned face.

49 Lew Wallick preparing for his last official test flight with Boeing in 1984, the day before he turned sixty. Photo: Boeing Archives.

In honor of his last flight, the ground crew placed a sign against the nose wheel of the 737: KICK HERE. This was in recognition of my father's long-standing faith in Boeing's ground crews. "I used to get upset at the length of the preflight check," Dad explained to me. "Military guys did their own walk-around, a visual from the outside. It took thirty minutes. I concluded it was a waste of time because we had as many as fifteen maintenance and quality-control guys; if they told me the airplane was ready, I said okay, kicked the tire, and got on. But I also said, 'If something goes wrong with the airplane and I crash it, I'm going to come back and haunt you!'" Dad started this practice with the first flight of the 727. Thereafter, the ground crews would paint KICK HERE on the nose wheel of many of the airplanes my father flew, teasingly reminding him which tire to kick. On the first flight of the 757, the ground crew put a bumper sticker with KICK HERE on the nose wheel. With a grin, Dad removed it, pasting it to the side of his flight bag. His practice of kicking the gear to show his trust of the ground crews was one of the things that made him a favorite on the flight line.

I don't know what the test plan was for that last official flight my father made in the 737. I do know that he made one deviation: he rolled it.

Shhh. Don't tell anyone.

I recently learned that flight actually wasn't my father's last time flying a Boeing jet. Retired Boeing test pilot John Cashman informed me that my father not only flew the first 727 out of Renton Field in 1963, but also the first flight of the last 727 from that same airport twenty-one years later.

On August 14, 1984, there was a rollout ceremony for the final 727. The original flight crew—my father, copilot Dix Loesch, and flight test engineer M. K. "Shuly" Shulenberger—participated in the festivities.

50 Rollout ceremony for last 727 with original flight crew (from left) Dix Loesch, M. K. "Shuly" Shulenberger, and Lew Wallick.

Two weeks later—three months *after* my father's sixtieth birthday—John was captain of the first flight of that last 727, built for Federal Express. Paul Leckman was copilot. Dad went along, aware of the historic significance of this last first flight and making a memorable bookend to his career association with the airplane. "I offered Lew my seat at the end of the runway," John said. "He flew the first and last parts of the flight, with a landing at Boeing Field. He never lost his smile."

Dad eventually admitted to me that he rolled all of the airplanes through the 737; he never rolled the 747, 757, or 767. And as far as Dad, my uncle Jesse, Brien, Don Archer, and anyone else I've talked to about this knows, no one has, at least just for fun. I was puzzled by this until Jesse made a comment about the 747. He said it was the first model in which the crew couldn't manually disconnect the flight recorder. I think that explains why the rolls stopped with the 737; they could no longer be done secretly. No one wanted to get fired.

"In the 727, I did 'flutter tests,'" Dad told me one day, that twinkle in his eye. "You know, rolling the plane from one side to the other. I'd roll to the left, then I had to roll to the right to twist out of it! I only did this with trusted personnel onboard. I never tried to do two consecutive rolls, although the plane could easily do it."

In 2003, I invited Don Cumming, Don Archer, Dennis Mahan, and Jesse to sit down with my father in front of a video camera and share some memories about their time in Flight Test. Many wonderful stories unfolded. During this session, Dad finally admitted to rolling all of the early jets. The guys laughed with approval, getting confirmation of what they had assumed happened but had never heard my father verify. When Dad still played coy with regard to actual airplanes rolled and the number of times he rolled them, Don Cumming asked, "Does a T-tail [727] roll differently than a..." to which Dad smiled and cut him off, replying, "Not if I can help it!"

Don Archer jumped in. "I remember, years later, when Tex [Johnston] didn't work for Boeing anymore, an airline pilot rolled a 727 on a training flight and the airline fired him. There was going to be a lawsuit and the pilots' union was going to try to help him get his job back. The union hired Tex to be an expert witness, to say it's nothing to roll one of these big airplanes. The airline had Don Knutson [a Boeing test pilot]."

Dad nodded with the memory. "They were looking for somebody to say it was dangerous. So they contacted the Boeing Flight Test people."

"Don [Knutson] testified that Tex had said, 'If you do that, we'll fire you.'" Don Archer continued. My father added, "The thing that was interesting is, we ran a survey, and we decided that Don Knutson was the only guy in the whole darned organization who had never done a roll!"[76]

Some people are incredibly lucky. Their work is their passion. My father and his colleagues in Flight Test count themselves among those lucky few. Throughout his career, Dad never lost his sense of fun, as demonstrated by rolling the 737-300 on his last official test flight. He always remained passionate about flying. Rolling jets was a minor part of his career and life story. My father was an exceptional test pilot, intelligent and skilled, and highly respected within the aviation community. Yet what endeared him to me, and to so many others, was his *joie de vivre*; the rolls were just one way he expressed it.

My father was a warm, happy, positive guy—affirming, supportive, enthusiastic, encouraging, and polite. A true gentleman. Those of us lucky enough to have known him are better people because of his influence on our lives. Everyone else… well, next time you fly on a Boeing aircraft, I hope you'll think of my father and his colleagues and thank them for helping make the entire planet accessible to you.

---

[76] Jim Knutson, Don's son and an airline pilot, remembers his father testifying on behalf of the airline, Continental. Don spent many years as an instructor pilot, teaching key airline pilots how to fly new models, and later investigating accidents involving Boeing aircraft. He knew firsthand the tragic result when a roll wasn't done correctly. Jim doesn't know if his father ever rolled a Boeing jet. Don certainly had the requisite skill. Describing his father as "tight-lipped" about such things, Jim said, "Whether he did or not, he would never have said."

EPILOGUE

Ah hell. We had more fun in a week than those weenies had in a lifetime.
—Pancho Barnes

My father enjoyed retirement. He especially liked taking family and friends fishing on remote lakes in British Columbia, flying there in his amphibious Cessna 185. I went with him three times and will cherish those father-daughter trips for the rest of my life. Dennis Mahan and his son, David, joined Dad on a trip in 2003. Dennis was thrilled that his son's first flying experience included sitting in the copilot's seat next to Boeing's former chief test pilot, and occasionally handling the controls. Landing at the Nanaimo, British Columbia, airport to clear customs, Dad made an uncharacteristically hard landing. "There was complete silence in the airplane for several seconds after we landed," Dennis said. "Then your dad said, 'Take *that*, Earth!'"

Dad passed away in 2009. I miss him every day. I especially miss having someone who always listened, offered good advice, and supported me, no matter what. I am so lucky; I had my father in my life for fifty-two years and felt his love for me each and every one of them.

Not long after my father passed, I had an unusually vivid dream, one that convinced me I *had* to complete this book, the project Dad and I started together in 2002.

I'm standing alone on a precipice high above the ocean. It's dark, yet a full moon brightens the ground, the water's surface, and the star-filled sky all around me. The sea murmurs far below. A slight breeze caresses my face, tossing my hair back.

It's beautiful. I feel at peace.

Far away, among the billions of glittering stars, a small light catches my eye. I focus in and follow it, something I often did as a child with my father, watching shooting stars and the lights of airplanes cross the night sky.

Approaching steadily, the object brightens.

An airplane, I wonder? It moves horizontally across my field of vision, still in the distance but gaining in size, getting closer.

Then, abruptly—as if noticing me—it stops and hovers. I'm surprised. Airplanes don't hover. Like a spaceship in a sci-fi movie, it turns 180 degrees, facing me head-on. After a brief moment of stillness, the giant airplane—a 747, I suddenly realize—sets a slow and sure course straight for me. I have no sense of fear. I feel calm and full of wonder. I watch, transfixed, as the aircraft silently draws near.

Maintaining an altitude mere feet above me, the 747 comes so close that its vast size fills my field of vision. Everything else—moon, stars, ocean—is obliterated. I peer inside the cockpit, dimly illuminated by the instrument displays. I see a pilot and copilot in their seats. Standing right behind them, one hand on each seat back, looking directly at me and smiling, is my father.

I smile back. A sense of warmth washes over me, like the enveloping love of one of his big squeezing hugs.

Then, with my father's guidance, the enormous airplane slowly, silently, and ever-so-gently passes just above me. I reach out with my right hand, palm up, and lovingly stroke its belly as it glides by, like petting the soft underside of a horse.

"Thanks, Dad," I whisper as the airplane slips past me, disappearing into the night.

Now I understood: my father's life and career were the legacy he'd given me. All I had to do was write it down.

Completing this book would allow me to honor him while preserving his legacy as an aviator and as a parent. The unexpected benefit? The void left by my father's passing has been filling with the genuine friendships I have forged with his colleagues and friends, who have generously shared their stories and expertise with me. They've helped me create a much fuller picture of my father, a mosaic of our collective memories. My new friends are the best. No wonder my father liked them so much.

51 Father's Day, 2000. Photo: Author's collection.

CAST OF CHARACTERS

Samuel Lewis "Lew" Wallick, Jr. (May 25, 1924–August 16, 2009) Lew was born in Independence, Kansas, the second of five children raised on the family farm. At age eighteen, he became a Navy aviation cadet and earned his commission in January 1945, becoming a Navy Aviator and fighter pilot. After World War II, he finished college, earning a mechanical engineering degree at Kansas State University. After a brief time at Beech Aircraft, he joined Boeing as a flight test engineer in 1951, in Wichita, and was soon promoted to test pilot, flying B-47s. He attended Test Pilot School at Edwards AFB in 1953. Transferred to Seattle in 1955, Lew flew all of Boeing's jets during his thirty-five-year career: the B-47, B-52, Dash 80, KC-135, 707, 727, 737, 747, 757, and 767, as well as most of the derivatives. He was project pilot for the 727. Lew became Chief Test Pilot in 1970 and Director of Flight Test in 1974, positions he held until his retirement in 1986. Lew was honored with the American Institute of Aeronautics and Astronautics' Chanute Flight Award, and in 1999 was inducted into the Museum of Flight's Pathfinder Hall of Fame.

Brien Wygle was born in 1924 in Seattle, Washington. In 1927, his family moved to a farm near Calgary, Alberta, Canada, where Brien spent his childhood. Pursing his dream to

fly, Brien joined the Royal Canadian Air Force (RCAF) in 1942 and served as a pilot in Europe, India, and Burma. He graduated from the University of British Columbia with a degree in mechanical engineering in 1951. Brien joined the Boeing Airplane Company as an Engineering Test Pilot that same year. During his twenty-eight years as an active test pilot, Brien flew all Boeing airplanes from the B-47 through the 757 and 767. He performed the first flight on the 737 and served as copilot on the first flight of the 747. Brien worked for Boeing for thirty-nine years, becoming Director of Flight Test in 1970, VP of Customer Support in 1974, and VP of Flight Operations in 1979, before retiring in 1990. He is a Fellow of both the Society of Experimental Test Pilots and the American Institute of Aeronautics and Astronautics.

Brien has lived in Medina, Washington, for nearly sixty years. He and his wife, Norma, had four daughters, all of whom live in Sun Valley, Idaho. Norma passed away in 2003.

Don Archer was born in Omak, Washington, in 1931. His family moved to Yakima, Washington, where he graduated from high school. After attending Yakima Junior College for a year, in 1950 he became a cadet in the US Coast Guard Academy. After two years, Don resigned from the Academy to try to become a Navy fighter pilot during the Korean War, but astigmatism disqualified him. To avoid becoming a foot soldier, Don enrolled at the University of Washington as an aeronautics student, in the advanced Air Force ROTC program.

During his last year at the University of Washington, Don met and married Gloria; they celebrated their fifty-ninth anniversary in 2013.

After graduating from the University of Washington in 1955, Don fulfilled his Air Force duty by working for two years as a flight test engineer at Edwards AFB, where his son was born. Don was discharged from the Air Force in 1957 and started working at Boeing as a flight test analysis engineer in November of that year, one month before the first flight of the 707. By 1958, Don was lead engineer of the aeronautics test analysis group, and in 1963 became supervisor of the aeronautics and flight controls analysis group. In 1965, Don became unit chief of all analysis groups, and in 1970 was named manager of all flight test engineering operations and analysis groups. In 1980 Don became Assistant Director of Flight Test Engineering, and in 1984 he was promoted to Director of Flight Test Engineering. Don retired in 1991.

Don once told me his favorite airplane was the 707. "We were the first with the best. We determined how to test jet transports for certification, the methods which are still in use today."

Don and Gloria currently live in Lacey, Washington, and have two children, David and Loreen, and two grandchildren. Loreen worked at Boeing from 1979 to 2000, before moving to Albuquerque, New Mexico; her husband also worked at Boeing. David currently works at Boeing on the 787 program.

Don Cumming was born in 1933 and raised in Helena, Montana. He attended Stanford University, earning a degree in mechanical engineering. During his last year at Stanford, Don met a United Airlines stewardess named Nancy; he earned his best grades while they courted. They married in June 1958 and honeymooned on their way to Seattle. Don spent his entire thirty-six-year career at Boeing in the flight-testing field. He started as a test engineer on the B-52 and retired as Chief Engineer, Flight Test Engineering. Don was involved in the development and certification of all Boeing commercial and military models between 1957 and 1993.

Don and Nancy have two children, daughter Jill, and son Brian. A graduate of the Air Force Academy, Brian spent fourteen years as a fighter pilot, including during the first Gulf War, before retiring from the military to become a pilot for FedEx. Don and Nancy live in Issaquah, Washington.

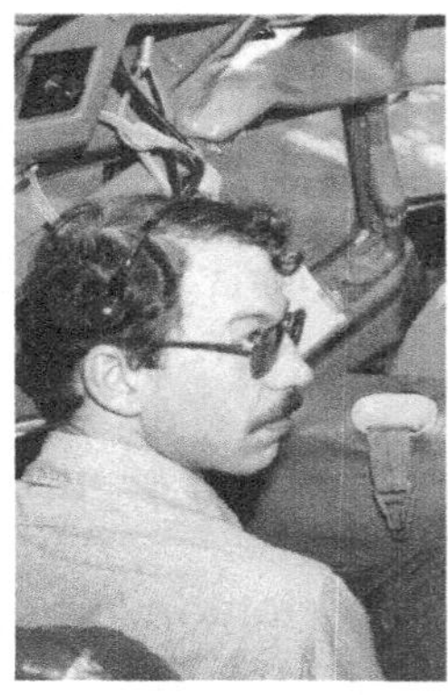

Dennis Mahan was born in Troy, Ohio, in 1942. He graduated from Ohio State University in 1965 with a Bachelor of Aeronautical and Astronautical Engineering. In 1963, he had a summer job at Edwards AFB. In July 1965, he hired on at Boeing Flight Test in the analysis unit, working for Don Cumming. During his thirty-two years at Boeing—all in Flight Test Engineering—Dennis was involved in test programs on the 707 through 777. He also got fifty flight hours in the Dash 80 during a NASA research program in 1967. Dennis was the Operations Supervisor on the number one and number five test airplanes during the original 777 certification program. During his last thirteen years at Boeing, he was a Flight Test Operations Supervisor.

Dennis resides in Seattle, just east of the south end of Boeing Field. His wife Cheryl is a current Boeing employee, and his son David is a park ranger in Whitman County, Washington.

Harley Beard (February 2, 1924–January 3, 2007) Harley was born in Detroit, Michigan. He attended Wayne State University from 1941–1942, then enlisted as an Air Corps pilot in 1942. (The Air Corps became the Air Force in 1947.) Harley's World War II flying included a tour in a B-24 Liberator stationed in Italy. On a December 1944 flight, all four of his bomber's engines ran out of fuel. Harley and the crew

bailed out over the Adriatic Sea; eight of the eleven crewmembers, including Harley, were rescued by Italian fishermen. After the war, Harley spent nine years at Wright Field as a test pilot, where he flew alongside Chuck Yeager, Guy Townsend, and Bud Anderson.

The Air Force sent Harley to test pilot's school at Edwards AFB in 1953, in the same class as Brien Wygle. Brien remembers during the end of their six months training, the two young pilots agreed to meet in their jets at 15,000 feet over the Mojave Desert for a mock battle. Hoping to get the drop on Harley, Brien climbed to 20,000 feet, but Harley was waiting at an even higher altitude and came swooping down on a surprised Brien. From that day on, Brien always accused Harley of being the bigger cheat.

Harley also met Lew Wallick at Edwards AFB when Lew's class started three months later; Harley and his wife sold the Wallicks some furniture when they left Edwards AFB.

After a stint flying in the Korean War in 1955, Harley was stationed in Peru, Indiana, where he didn't get along with his commanding officer. Hearing Tex Johnston was looking for test pilots, he sought a job at Boeing. After fifteen years in the Air Force, Harley hired on at Boeing in 1957 as an experimental test pilot. Harley started by flying the F-86 chase plane and as copilot before eventually being named project pilot on the Dash 80.

Harley had two sons and a daughter: Gary, Neal, and Gail. Both sons flew during the Vietnam War, one in the Air Force, the other in the Army, and oldest son Gary went on to work as an airline pilot.

William J. Allsopp (June 21, 1918–January 2, 2008) Bill was born in Scotland, moving with his family to British Columbia, Canada, when he was an infant, and eventually ending up in Detroit, Michigan. While attending junior college,

Bill took flight-training courses at Wayne University, where he met his wife, Geraldine. They married after Bill started training as a Navy pilot. Bill flew in the Pacific Theatre during World War II. After the war, Bill earned a degree in aeronautical engineering at the University of Michigan in 1949, and quickly moved to Seattle to start work at Boeing as a flight test engineer. He was briefly recalled by the military during the Korean War, then returned to Boeing where he worked for thirty-five years.

Bill and Geri had a son and two daughters and lived in Normandy Park, outside Seattle.

Photo Credit: Allsopp family collection.

Dix Loesch (May 26, 1918–August 8, 2007) Richards Llewellyn "Dix" Loesch, Jr., was born in Chicago, Illinois, and raised on a small farm in Colorado. He attended Massachusetts Institute of Technology, earning a Bachelor's of Science in Aeronautics. After graduation, Dix joined the Navy and completed flight training in 1942. Dix flew in several campaigns in the Pacific, including Guadalcanal, where he was wounded. He earned the Distinguished Flying Cross, the Purple Heart, and the Air Medal. In 1944, Dix met and married Peggy. They came to Seattle when Dix was hired by Boeing as a test pilot for the B-47 and B-52 flight test programs. Dix was copilot on the first flight of the Dash 80. After Tex Johnston transferred to Florida, Dix was named Director of Flight Test, a position he held during development of the 727, 737, and 747.

Dix and Peggy had two sons, James and Andrew. Jamie is a

retired Boeing test pilot.

Jesse Wallick was born in Independence, Kansas, in 1934, the youngest of five Wallick children raised on the family farm and nine and a half years younger than Lew. After two years in the Air Force, Jesse attended Kansas State College, earning a Bachelor's of Science in Mechanical Engineering in 1959. After working at Boeing as a summer student on the Dash 80 while still in college, Jesse hired on full time as a flight test engineer soon after obtaining his degree. Jesse was Flight Engineer on the first flight of the 747, and was eventually promoted to test pilot, where he often flew alongside his older brother.

Jesse was introduced to Lew's wife's niece, Annette, and soon after married her in 1962. They have two children, Todd and Brett, and currently reside in Arizona.

Paul Bennett (October 16, 1932–July 10, 2012) Paul "Pablo" Bennett was born in Alliance, Ohio, where he grew up on his family's farm. He graduated from Culver Military Academy (high school) in 1949. While attending Denison University, he decided to leave school to enlist in the Air Force Cadet Pilot Training Program. His training complete, he was sent to Korea where he flew the F-86 Sabre jet, completing fifty combat missions and eventually earning the rank of major. After leaving military service, Pablo obtained a degree in aeronautical engineering from the University of Colorado and came to Seattle to start a thirty-four-year career at Boeing. Career highlights included being chief test pilot for Air Force One, and delivering the Dash 80 to the Smithsonian in 2003 after it sat waiting, for seventeen years, in the desert before being restored to flying condition in Seattle.

Paul had three children, Robin, Kristin, and Paul.

Jim Gannett (February 4, 1923–June 17, 2006) Jim's dream to become a pilot started when his father purchased him a $1 ride in an airplane. Jim earned a Master's in Aeronautical Engineering from the University of Michigan. As an Air Force pilot from 1950 to 1954, Jim flew at Edwards AFB, testing experimental aircraft alongside pilots like Chuck Yeager; he also flew combat missions for nine months during the Korean War. In 1954, Jim accepted a job at Boeing and moved his family to Seattle, where he started working on the Dash 80 and 707 programs. Jim eventually also worked on the 727, 737, 747, and the military AWACs airplanes. Jim was named project pilot for the SST program, which the government decided it wouldn't fund in 1971. Jim's passion was developing better instruments for airplanes, a passion he pursued well into retirement, when he obtained a patent for a new navigational aid. He also pursued his passion for flying after retiring, piloting private airplanes until just days before he passed away.

Jim married Eleanor (Ellie), and they had three children, Craig, Laurie, and Julie. They lived in Redmond, Washington.

John Cashman, born in Illinois in 1945, earned a Bachelor of Science degree in Aerospace Engineering at the University of Michigan in 1966. While in college, John began flying and earned his pilot's license in 1965. He hired on at Boeing as an engineer in 1966, where he worked in 727 structures and 707 aerodynamics engineering before becoming a flight crew member in 1974. From 1989 to 1990, John served as chief pilot for the 767 and the 767-X (developmental name for the 777). In October 1990, he became 777 program chief pilot, and

commanded the first flight of the 777 on June 12, 1994. In October 1997, John became Director, Flight Crew Operations and Chief Test Pilot. He worked for Boeing for over forty-two years before retiring. He now works as an industry consultant.

Photo Credits: Boeing Archives, except for Bill Allsopp.

ACKNOWLEDGMENTS

So many of my father's Boeing colleagues have given me their time, their stories, their technical editing, and their encouragement over many years, making this book first a possibility, then a reality: Dennis Mahan, Don Cumming, Don Archer, Brien Wygle, Dix Loesch, Jesse Wallick, Harley Beard, Bill Allsopp, Tom Edmonds, Steve Taylor, Scott Linn, Peter Morton, and John Cashman. Thank you. I can't say that often enough or with sufficient sincerity.

To the folks at the Museum of Flight, for taking this book under your wing and helping promote it; to Bob Bogash and T. C. Howard at the Museum of Flight Restoration Center, for sharing photos and stories, showing me some great old airplanes, and letting me sit in my father's favorite seat (the pilot's seat in the original 727), thank you.

Thank you to Michael Lombardi and staff at the Boeing Archives for your willingness to help track down photos and generously share them with me.

To those friends who believed in me and made sure I never gave up on myself or this book—Mike Britt, Dawn Rasmussen, Miki Robinson, Katie Cook, Lance Young, and so many others—having you all in my corner means the world to me. Chris Scott, you went the extra mile and offered to read, comment, and proofread; Laura Mueser and Sheri Croft, you jumped in to proofread last minute; I owe you all a huge debt of gratitude.

Kickstarter and crowd funding—what a concept! Kickstarter supporters truly made this project fly. Peter Morton, you championed my project and were instrumental in reaching the funding goal. To all who supported *Growing Up Boeing* via Kickstarter (over one hundred of you), my gratitude. Your support convinced me the project was worth completing and gave me the freedom and resources to do it right. Many of you went above and beyond, becoming patrons of this book with your generous donations: Brien Wygle; Peter and Marie Morgan; Dick Taylor; James Raisbeck; Michael Britt; Don and

Nancy Cumming; Don and Gloria Archer; Dennis Mahan; George Stutsman; Scott E. Carson; Jesse and Annette Wallick; Fred and Mary Mitchell; Ken and Sandra Higgins; John and Mary Jo Cashman; Jon and Sherry Whitworth; Scott Linn; Terri Wallick Williams; Shelle Singer and Elizabeth Turner; Kate Oliver; Janet Miller; Brian Tate; Dawn Rasmussen; Bruce Zunser; James H. and Esther Bunt, Jr.; Dean and Charlotte Rasmussen; Steve, Kris, Isobel, and Finley Taylor; Chris Scott and Mid-70s AFPRO AWACS team; Chris Ralph; David Longridge; Laura and Ted Mueser; Cliff Moore; Scott A. and Lorna Wallick; Bob Davis; Jacqueline Blue; Cordell Bahn; Bob and Norma Rasmussen; Robert Sutton; Peter O'Toole; Stuart Lau; Chuck Kluenker; Sheri and Sam Croft; Delmar M. Fadden; Jim and Linda Hemminger; Ron King; Thomas Imrich; Lyle R. Eveland; Bill Blansett; John Hindmarch; Aaron MacMillin; Chris Chamberlain; Aly Gissing and the Gissing family; Mike Dobeck; Lauralynn Dixon; David A Conley; Don Kyte; Michael Pollowitz; Miki Robinson; Chris Sloan; Robert Bleeg; Lance Young; Katie Cook; Kelly Beckwith Verduin; Richard W. Olds; Charles Church; Donald Stickles; Patty Glynn and Stewart Tolnay; and The Grey Beards (K. Chester Chen; John Banbury; Jules Berger; Gary Clifford; Dayton Robinson; Paul Forseth; Sandy Graham; Steve Kuo; Roger Layman; Frank Rasmussen; Dick Peal; Ed Pottenger; Bob Simpson; Dick Spradlin; Dennis Wood).

To my long-time editor at *Bark* magazine, Susan Tasaki, thank you for your early editing and ongoing support and advice. Dana Delamar, a huge thank you for stepping in at the last minute, and not only making my words shine, but also walking me through the publishing process. You rock. Sherri Shaftic, your cover design exceeded all expectations; thank you. Karla Holman, thank you for the web site design and the Kickstarter video.

Last but not least, a heartfelt thank you to the greater aviation community—Boeing and beyond—for all of your encouragement and offers to assist in any way you could. What a great group of people!

ABOUT THE AUTHOR

Re-creation of photo 24, with Rebecca Wallick in the pilot's seat of the original 727, undergoing restoration.

Rebecca Wallick was born in Seattle (because Bellevue's hospital didn't have a maternity ward at the time) and raised in Bellevue, Washington. She describes herself as a recovering attorney, transitioning to a much happier career as an author. Rebecca resides with her Australian shepherd Finn MacCool, her favorite trail-running companion.

Made in the USA
Monee, IL
22 September 2020